Investigating Developmentalism

"The drama of development is in full swing – tragedy is seen as comedy, comedy collapses into chaos. But there are streams of creativity showing glimpses of a different future. The authors of this work make an audacious statement about much of that story."

—Manoranjan Mohanty, *Distinguished Professor and Editor, Social Change, Council for Social Development, New Delhi, India*

"This much-needed book sees developmentalism as a protracted social dream turned nightmare. Working through the real, unreal and hyper-real of developmentalism and the (il)legitimacy of its enchanting implications, the book develops what has remained largely underdeveloped in 'development studies' and the 'anthropology of development': the cultural studies perspective to developmentalism."

—Anup Dhar, *Professor of Philosophy, Ambedkar University Delhi, India*

Dev Nath Pathak · Amiya Kumar Das
Editors

Investigating Developmentalism

Notions of Development in the Social Sphere

palgrave
macmillan

Editors
Dev Nath Pathak
South Asian University
New Delhi, India

Amiya Kumar Das
Tezpur University
Tezpur, India

ISBN 978-3-030-17442-2 ISBN 978-3-030-17443-9 (eBook)
https://doi.org/10.1007/978-3-030-17443-9

Cover illustration: Cover Painting 'Spill 2' (detail) by Anoli Perera (2017; Spill 2 Acrylic, charcoal, ink and pencil on archival 40 x 40 inches)

This Palgrave Macmillan imprint is published by the registered company Springer Nature Switzerland AG
The registered company address is: Gewerbestrasse 11, 6330 Cham, Switzerland

In Memory of Dr. Rabindra Ray-

Intellectual iconoclasm that fired our imagination

In celebration of the art of polemics!

Preface: An Appetizer for the Raw Meat

In Kalahandi, Odisha in India, there is a folk proverb, ***na gai na goru, sukhe nid karu*** (No possession, and yet one is happy in contentment). Kalahandi is however a place with notoriety in the history of post-independent India. It has been often deemed as Ethiopia of India. Famine, draught, and epidemic malnourishment characterized Kalahandi. Irredeemable sense of deprivation was coupled with the transformation of Kalahandi into a theatre of development programmes steered by innumerable agencies including the state. But, one always wondered as to what kept the proverbial contentment alive in the land of deprivation. Despite the abject poverty, the natives of Kalahandi held that one worries more if one possesses wealth; there is little tension in poverty and hence one sleeps peacefully. Perhaps such lore made the folk, what is locally termed, *sukhbasi* (who lives happily).

Living in the milieu of non-development as well as development has been accompanied with people's worldview, a phenomenological domain fraught with enchantment, charm, beliefs, subjective orientation, and many such things usually taken for granted, and expressed occasionally through nuggets of wisdom. This is writ large in the face of this book that follows this preface. But it is not only such seemingly innocuous charm. The domain of folk is also rife with many sarcastic notes, which too constitute the mainstay of this book. For a brief comprehension of this, we shall turn to two more instances, adding to the appetizing starter for this book.

This was a late 1980s India. Like any other historical milieu, this was one with its own set of politico-developmental folklore too. An eminent anthropologist Kirin Narayan encountered a fragment of this in a nugget of folksy idea coming from one of her respondents. And the nugget suggested, India is a 'banana republic'. And why so? Because in the speeches during the public meetings for the upcoming elections, Mr. Rajiv Gandhi harped on a refrain, almost reverberating like a sweet song in the popular conscience. The refrain was '*humein yah banana hai, humein wah banana hai*', meaning 'we have got to make (*banana*) this, we have got to make that'[1]. One can traverse back and forth in time and stumble upon such folk riddles capable of enabling a critical discourse on developmentalism, a collective fantasy with associated verbal and visual expressions. The various manifestations of 'banana-logic', with enchanting sarcasm and suggestion, could be put together to write a social history of developmentalism in India, and stretching it to the larger regional framework of South Asia on some other occasion.

And another folk logic appears straight in the scheme of cultural politics. With the manifold developmentalist schemes and fiscal-taxation policies executed from 2014 to 2019, by the Government of India, many of the Maithili-speaking folks in north-east of Bihar in north India resorted to a folk proverb, *Puri-Jilebi Tel Mei, PM, CM Jail Mei* (throw the sweet-tempting dishes into the boiling oil, likewise chuck the prime minister, chief minister into the prison). The proverb has been used to critically target political leadership in past as well, and these days it is used to express popular-folk subversion of the regime of the incumbent Prime Minister of India, Chief Minister of the state. The expression evokes people's ability to resist the charming hogwash of development and a somewhat economic anarchy which resulted from the erroneous developmentalist imagination of the Government of India.

It is seemingly a worldwide phenomenon, and hence not exclusive of India alone, as the book may remind in significant bits and pieces throughout. Development is thereby not a mere clinically calculative, systematically schematic, terribly teleological, lazily linear aspect of human society. It is far more than what may be 'seen' by the pundits of development, soothsayers and analysts, statisticians and sociologists. It is also a little more than the 'unseen' of development that is usually central

[1]See Narayan (1993: 179).

in the discussions of helplessly anxious seekers of alternative models. In between the seen and unseen, this book, a compendium of essays, posits the intrigue of a performative developmentalism, as it were. The charm, magic, mythology, and pantheons of divinity succumb to this intrigue. And so does the word development as it entails mystical enchantment in the midst of disenchantment, discontent underneath the content, frenzy integral to dreams, and destructive impulses in the aspirational pursuits.

The book presents manifold provocative occasions, in order to summon for a qualitatively different journey, without vending a conclusive solution to the intrigue with the hope that we return to the intrigue even after going through this book in the mode of an Alice-in-Wonderland. We avoid answering the intrigue in finitude since no single volume can exhaust the devil in the details on the terrain of empirical evidences. The book, in short, tends to operate with the immortal divinity of the devil, of developmentalism, while mirroring an eclectic composition.

As students and teachers of sociology and social anthropology of development, we have been fairly familiar with various strands of development discourse. We have also encountered the stalemate in the language-game of the experts, who have covertly constructed a simpler matrix of pro-against-reconciliatory mode of understanding development. Sociology and anthropology have travelled a long way in their focus of inquiries with manifold critical realization, to the dismay of a large number of regressive-conventional scholars. The invasion of the disciplinary boundaries is beginning to show. The cracks in the fort allow more playful research imagination, moot questions, and venturing into unsafe territories of enquiry. This is despite the predominance of a large tribe of sociologists and anthropologists who subscribe to the strategy of playing it intellectually safe in order to avoid rejection and ridicule. Or perhaps, they are too lazy and also decapitated by their academic training to look at the developmentalist world like a wondering Alice. This book joins the daredevils and plays it entirely unsafe, so as to propose a novel way of dealing with a seemingly familiar area of curiosity.

The book hinges on the realization that the intellectual puritanism in approaching development does not help in putting the devil of developmentalism on the anvil. To the dismay of the experts, it ought to be said at the onset of the book, in this preface, that the predecessors do not offer enough to grasp the meanings people adhere to while being in the process of development. This book thus puts together some of those aspects, such as enchantment, illusion, aspiration, mysticism, and performance, without turning blind to the discontent of development. It seeks to divulge a quasi-belief system constructed and supported by politico-cultural industry, our love and hatred (socio-emotional matrix), human actions and subjectivity, which determine the phenomenon of developmentalism.

This was a fascinating journey for the two of us, the editors, who operated with a mode of learner-exclaiming, gasping, biting nails, and wondering throughout. We steered through our agreements and disagreements in discussing the various aspects of developmentalism, and the essays that could be put together to chisel out a modicum of fullness. We imagined that we had put the raw meat of the intrigue on simmer; we however decided to not put too much of salt. And the rawness of the meat remained, so as everyone could bite in and feel the character of the meat better. Thus, we are bad cooks, if so, by choice and thought-out decision. We admit that we are in for trouble, so be it. Academic preoccupation with the cooked may annoy many who would notice the rawness of the meat, if they read this book. Besides, it is capable to cause disease if the meat is of bad quality and that too semi-cooked. What does it all mean in real sense? Our approach is seemingly a misfit in the prevalent framework of development discourse which is practised by both academics and activists. We tend to vend well-arranged raw meat in the time when everyone is habitual of eating the cooked variety. We are humbly expecting our readers to join in the act of intellectual cannibalism of some sort, killing the fellow human and eating their meat. But we want to mention here that it may be taken as a prelude to the various anticipated ventures, exploring the panacea for the disease caused by the raw meat. After all, every act of killing and eating the meat of the dead can cause utmost disgust, strong reactions, and soul searching. We have taken the risk self-consciously, in order to provoke our potential readers for further enquiry, and prevent any contentment with the scheme of thinking underpinning this book.

We are grateful to the many of our contributors who trusted our cooking-skills at their own risk. They were kind and quick, in revising the drafts more than twice in the period of one year. Many of these essays were also discussed in an international seminar at Tezpur University in March 2016. And many more were commissioned later in tune with the conceptualization of the book. As it happens more often than not, the seminars related to the thematic area of development turn out to be a premise to recycle the familiar. Unfortunately, the seminars are no longer that ideal space where scholars would try out new ideas, unfamiliar aspects of an issue, with due adventurism and youthfulness. And hence, they turn redundant in the last analysis despite the fact that it was in a seminar that one made new friends, one fell in love, or one came through a disastrous disillusionment about academics. This book is an optimistic repartee to the boredom and hopelessness with the seminars and conferences. However, we place on record our gratitude to the colleagues in the department of sociology at Tezpur University who extended their generous help in organizing the seminar. We are also thankful to the Tezpur university administration for providing us all necessary support.

We reiterate our thanks to the contributors who supported this endeavour sincerely. They have patiently received and utilized, the peer review comments, in the rounds. Twice, the revision was done in the light of the reviews conducted and organized by the editors, and the last one was arranged by the publisher. We express our special appreciation for the commissioning editor of Palgrave Macmillan Ms. Mary Al Sayed for a professionally upright manner of handling this project and providing us necessary feedback to improve the contents. The critical and sufficiently encouraging reviews by the two anonymous reviewers, commissioned by the publisher, must be acknowledged. We extend our gratitude to the anonymous reviewers for reading the draft chapters with patience and delivering the sanguine feedback in time. They were concise, lucid, and helpful comments. We are thankful to Prof. Jan Nederveen Pieterse for his inspirational works and motivation which guided us in the fine-tuning of the book. And we also acknowledge a large number of our predecessors who have walked extra-miles in rummaging through the idea of development. To name a few of them, they were Profs. Prabhat Patnaik, Manoranjan Mohanty, Shiv Visvanathan, Rabindra Ray, among others. Our critical engagement with them has been fairly enabling. We are also thankful to Profs. Anup Dhar, Ashok Acharya who graciously endorsed the book. We thank our colleagues Profs. Virginius Xaxa, Chandan Kumar Sharma, and Kedilezo Kikhi for their encouragement in bringing out this volume. We express our thankfulness and appreciation for Dr. Bodhisatva Kar who participated in the deliberation but could not contribute to the volume due to some unavoidable circumstances.

New Delhi, India — Dev Nath Pathak
Tezpur, India — Amiya Kumar Das

Reference

Narayan, K. (1993). Banana Republics and V. I. Degrees: Rethinking Indian Folklore in a Postcolonial World. *Asian Folklore Studies*, *52*(1), 177–204.

Contents

Notes on Contributors

Amiya Kumar Das teaches Sociology at Tezpur University, Assam, and is Assistant Editor of *Explorations: E-Journal of Indian Sociological Society*, India. His main research and course curriculum are broadly in the areas of sociology of governance, development sociology, and sociology of health and illness. He is involved in evaluation and monitoring studies on the government-run welfare programmes in Northeast India as well. Apart from teaching and research, he is also involved in natural and organic farming.

Nivedita Ghosh is an Assistant Professor in the Department of Sociology, Jesus and Mary College, University of Delhi. She is pursuing her Ph.D. from the Department of Sociology, Delhi School of Economics. Her areas of specialization are Visual Anthropology and Ethnographic Filmmaking. She has acquired training in Ethnographic Filmmaking from the Granada School of Visual Anthropology, University of Manchester.

Yugank Goyal received his Ph.D. in Economics and Law from University of Hamburg, Erasmus University Rotterdam, and University of Bologna as Erasmus Mundus Fellow. He has an LL.M. from University of Manchester and Bachelor of Technology from NIT Surat, India. He is a founding faculty member of OP Jindal Global University. Having studied engineering, economics, and law, his work swiftly assumes interdisciplinarity. He has published on matters related to legal institutions, development economics, higher education, and intellectual property.

Ektaa Jain has recently submitted her doctoral thesis with the Centre for the Study of Social Systems (CSSS) at Jawaharlal Nehru University (JNU), New Delhi (India). Her research interests are sociology of fashion and communication, study of handicrafts and artisanal communities, performative culture, Gandhian philosophy among others. Her more recent publications include: Performing the Printed: In the Robe with the Meanings of Block Printing, in ed., *Culture and Politics in South Asia: Performative Communication*; 'Khadi: A Cloth and Beyond'. *Gandhi Marg Quarterly*.

Lakshita Malik is currently a graduate student in the Department of Anthropology at University of Illinois at Chicago. She completed her M.Phil. in Sociology from Jawaharlal Nehru University and submitted her dissertation entitled 'Urban Domestic Spaces in the Indian Context' in 2018. Her ongoing work focuses on the nature of public participation and the performance of masculinity in urban India.

Dev Nath Pathak teaches Sociology at South Asian University, New Delhi, and is editor of *Society and Culture in South Asia*, co-published bi-annually by Sage India and South Asian University. Among his recent publications are *Living and Dying: Meanings in Maithili Folklore* (Primus, New Delhi, 2018), *Culture and Politics in South Asia: Performative Communication* (co-edited with Sasanka Perera, Routledge, 2017), *Another South Asia!* (Primus, 2018), and *Sociology and Social Anthropology in South Asia: Histories and Practices* (co-edited with Ravi Kumar and Sasanka Perera, Orient BlackSwan, 2018).

Pranta Pratik Patnaik teaches in Department of Culture and Media Studies, Central University of Rajasthan. His major publication includes one book on *Media Representations and Gendered Subjectivities* (2012) and three chapters in edited books—'One on Media, Cultural Rights and Third World' (2012, New York); second on 'Fat Gay Masculinities' (2013); and third on 'Bodies of Pleasure: Rethinking Gender, Space and Identity' (2015). He has presented several papers in national and international conferences on topics ranging from politics of representation in television and cinema to issues of developmental imbalances.

Salah Punathil teaches at Centre for Regional Studies, University of Hyderabad. Currently, he is a Postdoctoral Research Fellow at Max Planck Institute for the Study of Religious and Ethnic Diversity, Gottingen, Germany. His research interest includes ethnic conflicts and violence, borderlands and migration, and Muslims in South Asia.

Tathagatan Ravindran is an Assistant Professor in the Departamento de Estudios Sociales of Universidad Icesi, Colombia. His Ph.D. is in Anthropology from the University of Texas at Austin. His doctoral research deals with indigenous identities in Bolivia in the context of resistance to neoliberal economic policies. His broader interests center around political anthropology, collective identities, social movements, race and ethnicity, and South–South comparisons. His articles have been published in *AlterNative*, *Critical Sociology*, *Development and Change*, *Antipode*, and *Latin American and Caribbean Ethnic Studies.*

Rabindra Ray obtained his doctorate degree from Oxford University. He taught sociology at Delhi School of Economics, University of Delhi. His research interests include the study of Europe, Europeanization and issues connected with the concepts of modernity and post-modernity, violence, and terrorism. He is the author of *The Naxalites and Their Ideology* (1988, OUP), *Living with Difference: Essays in a Philosophical Anthropology* (2005, Yash Publisher), and *Western Atheism* (2006, SSR).

Anna Romanowicz is an Assistant Professor at the Department of Ethnology and Cultural Anthropology, Jagiellonian University in Krakow, Poland. Her research interests include the role of the middle class in development and recently the intersections between practices of romantic love and social class. She is an author of *Unintended Revolution: Middle Class, Development and Non-Governmental Organization*, published in 2017 by Jagiellonian University Press.

A. S. Shimreiwung teaches Sociology at Tezpur University, Assam. He has research interest in Northeast India studies, development and identity politics, and holds a Ph.D. from Jawaharlal Nehru University. Among his recent publications, he has co-authored *Migration, Identity and Conflict: Lived Experiences of Northeasterners in Delhi* (Co-authored with Tiplut Nongbri, Rawat, 2017) and co-edited the book *Encountering Modernity: Situating the Tangkhul Nagas in Perspective* (Bibliophile Asia, 2014).

List of Tables

CHAPTER 1

Introduction: Developmentalism—On a Trope of (Dis)Enchantment

Dev Nath Pathak and Amiya Kumar Das

Though an introductory outline of a book solicits a disciplined presentation of a framework, location of the book in the larger discursive ambit, and justifications of the objectives of the book, this introductory chapter seeks to take liberty while doing most of the expected. It plays with polemic, an ancient intellectual art, in support of the framework of the book. It is essential to do so since the matter at hand is sporty, issues under discussion entail theatrics, and details of the ideas appear dramatic. The contextualization of the book solicits more than a clinical recounting of the predecessors, a neat-systematic deliberation on the moot points. A creative usage of such an art of polemic is thereby reflective of the contents and discontents, what we shall deem adequately dramatic, integral to the idea of development. As the book aims at bringing about a realization that both, verbal and visual, heard and seen, are prominent sites of experiences of developmentalist con-

D. N. Pathak (✉)
South Asian University, New Delhi, India
e-mail: dev@soc.sau.ac.in

A. K. Das
Department of Sociology, Tezpur University, Tezpur, India

D. N. Pathak and A. K. Das (eds.), *Investigating Developmentalism*,
https://doi.org/10.1007/978-3-030-17443-9_1

structions, seeing and showing entails a denial of the repressed sound and sight in the larger terrain of developmentalism. Likewise, hearing and saying could not be absolved of the potential repression, if not total erasure, of fine nuances and countercurrents of the phenomenon. The complexity of the formulation gets simpler as this introductory outline advances toward the key motifs underlying the book. To keep the curiosity on, this can be said that the book unfolds a drama named development in which unseen is as crucial as seen, unheard is as significant as heard, unsaid is as pivotal as said. Critical evaluations, unmasking, and debunking are great sources of enchantment about the idea of development. So are uncritical submissions of agency and will to the politico-cultural constructs, the artifacts of development. We make a modest attempt in the following to make sense of the dramatics of development, which we invariably refer to as developmentalism.

This introductory note solicits a musical-lyrical commencement for a quick glance at the popular cultural engagement with the apprehensions of development prevalent across the hemispheres. A popular contemporary musician and singer from Malta, and a fascinating teacher of music, Julia Zahra's song titled *Just an Illusion* speaks volumes about imagination, aspirations and everything that belongs to a vocabulary of innocence, so to say.

She reveals the aspirations and imaginations of innocence, through this wonderful song which captures the essence of the disenchantment and disillusion of a person, who wants to be famous. This goes as 'I've been told about living like a star; Hotel Rich, champagne and caviar; But no one ever showed me the reverse; And that really hurts, babe, it really hurts…'.

The song makes sense if one puts it in a larger scheme of imagining. It was concluded long ago that it is humane to dream, or one could mischievously play with the Cartesian formulation, while reading Freudian thesis on dreaming, and propose in a drawing-room banter over steaming cup of coffee or cheesy glass of wine, *I dream, therefore I am.* This improvization on the Cartesian Cogito, which emphasized the verb 'thinking,' is not entirely whimsical. Many classical anthropologists persuaded us to believe: the collective dreams, therefore, it is. The dreams of collective, mythology of a community, religion in a society are indeed a well-established area of enquiry. And hence, a foray in the thick mythological corpus ensued, from (archaic) James Frazer to (banal) Rolland Barthes. We navigate from mythology of collective with pivotal archetypes to mythologies at the intersection of market, industry, and society. We traversed from a Durkheim's totem in primitive society to new Left scholars' fetish in the post-industrial societies in human socio-cultural history. They all entailed dreaming, though with changing springboards, from collective to individual, from manufacturers to consumers, and so on. The windmill of dreaming, individually and collectively, is eternally working toward perpetual mythologizing of past as well as present. This was aptly summed up by a few folklorists and anthropologists of folklore too. They brought to our attention, the national necessity to folklorize-mythicize everything from reinvented tradition to renegotiated modernity. It was owing to the national folklorization that the postcolonial societies derived legitimacy for the nation-building endeavors.[1] And the perpetuity of folklorization engulfs even the dot-com age. Internet is as efficient an arena to accomplish foklorization as was conventional community in real time, life, and space, even to our dismay.[2] This amounts to, among various other things, a cultural politics redefining our aspirations, imaginations, politics, and development that constitute the mainstay of this book.

Therefore, returning to Julia Zahra's verse, there is an allusion to the complexity behind dreaming. The lyric emphasizes the other side, dark one, of being a star. An artist is treated as merely a product rather than as a being. Stardom, thus, is merely an illusion. The singer persuades people not to get hypnotized with the illusion of stardom and run after it blindly. This was also a message strongly delivered in a critically acclaimed film, a psychological drama, *Requiem for a Dream* (Aronofsky 2000), based on a novel by the same title. The protagonist's travail from ordinary to extraordinary, aspiration and endeavor, wrecks the possibility of redemption. The dark side that Julia Zahra alluded to becomes a pervasive determinant. And we can go further back in time to find more in support of the macabre affects of the dreaming, imagining, and aspiring that led humans to various intended as well as unintended destinations. A Faustian drama or a Dr. Frankestien's ambitious experiments is within this scheme. The corpus of popular literature, cinema, music, and poetry comes to aid in problematizing something that was deemed humane. The vocabulary of innocence thus stands for critical scrutiny. And in that spirit, it seems that everyone gets awed with the glaze of the individual ambition and collective dreams of development. Seldom does anybody see the darkness behind it, or if we do, we tend to stay blissfully ignorant, akin to the proverbial Nero who played on the lute while the city of Rome was ablaze.

If we look around ourselves carefully, we would come to know that our ideas and imagination of the world, knowledge, and values are shaped by an on-going and dominant discourse of development. The trope of developmentalist imagination is fraught with artifices, activities, creating a collective inclination to the notion of development. Dear to various stakeholders of this discourse, from leadership, manufacturers, consumers, and electorate, it has by now turned out to be a well-tested axiom that we live in a 'developmental' society. Or, even more appropriate is a suggestion: we live in the age of developmentalism, with a mind-set inclined to a nearly sacred notion of development. The developmental society is akin to the society of spectacles, wherein, following Guy Debord (2014: 2), 'The spectacle is not a collection of images; it is a social relation between people that is mediated by images.' And Debord goes on saying what spectacles are: 'Not the lived thing but representation, not technological creations, they are worldview. And in between, spectacles' being representation rather than real, and being a worldview rather than merely techno-mediated creation, there is a gulf of meaning that the aphorismic-polemic-hermeneutics of Debord creates. In this deep pool of insights, one gets to see not only a critical polemic, but most importantly an anxious reasoning with the cultural-political adversity in the wake of progress. The anxiety, to recast in the scheme of this book, is that the illusion of development overpowers development; spectacles become relations; dreams turn pathological; aspirations become dreadful. And yet, to add to the complexity, no one dares to say anything against it, since every heart throbs with the desire to develop. Indeed, there is a vocabulary of innocence, truly innocuous, that comes to the service of the society of spectacles.

This stream of sense constitutes the spine of the book in which a situationist seeking, such as Debord's, unravel situations that have devoured 'ordinariness' for the benefit of 'extra-ordinary,'[3] where 'small is no longer beautiful'; the society of spectacles subverts the sweet-humane aspiration of an off-beat economist such as E. F. Schumacher[4] who had delivered a persuasive dream for many of the victims of large assembly line productions with a phrase, *small is beautiful.* In the regime of various ranks and files of spectacles, ranging from grand narratives of nations to the micro-narratives of communities and individuals, gods are primarily those who can appear towering enough and hence rulers of human conscience. In this regime, small is not beautiful, banal is.

The polemical stance that emerges in this wake, solicits more creative response rather than a cynical rejection or skeptical debunking of development. That we leave for better-equipped scholars of development studies or anthropologists of development who have performed this wonderful task of critically evaluating developmental schemes, its interface with market, state, and people inter alia. For us, the more important part is to make sense of the mediums and messages that are pivotal in the sustenance of the mind-set inclined to the idea of development. This informs us, as we unravel the issues of developmental society, in the situationist framework of Debord's society of spectacle, in this introductory outline of the book.

Developmentalism Is More Than Development

The broader framework underpinning this book posits 'developmentalism' as an ideology that weds economism and modernism. It means to promote the legitimacy and stability of development through capital market followed by the social welfare of the public. This stance is mostly to target a 'developing country,' the erstwhile 'third world.' As Easterly notes, 'like all ideologies, development promises a comprehensive final answer to all of society's problems, from poverty and illiteracy to violence and despotic rulers. It shares the common ideological characteristic of suggesting there is only one correct answer, and it tolerates little dissent. It deduces this unique answer for everyone from a general theory that purports to apply to everyone, everywhere' (Easterly 2009). This all-pervasive appearance of the notion of development and collective frenzy about it, the mind-set, is what assumes significance in this book. It is indeed more than a few of the schemes and plans of actions promoted and adopted by state, agencies, and civil society. Developmentalism thus assumes to be a trope of enchanting ideological-political and cultural idioms, value-orientation and recipe for actions. As the wholesome import of this book highlights, developmentalism is more than an economic phenomenon that critical development discourses show us.

As per the Oxford dictionary, the word developmentalism has two broad meanings. One hints at the philosophical or theological doctrines or schools of thought concerned with development, and two, a more popular one is, 'an economic policy concerned with improving the economy, and thus national autonomy, of an underdeveloped country by fostering the development of dynamic internal markets through such means as imposing high tariffs on imported goods.'[5] As evident, most of the discussion in social sciences on the category of developmentalism centralizes the second meaning. A historical trajectory surfaces for attention. It spans from the twentieth-century stress on developmentalism qua economic prosperity of the underdeveloped societies to a latest buzzing of neo-developmentalism in the decade of 2000. Ever since the Brazilian economist and former policy maker Luiz Carlos Bresser-Pereira gave a currency to the idea of neo-developmentalism in 2003,[6] suggesting the renewed life of state activism toward the economic goals, there has been almost no return to the first meaning inscribed in the dictionaries. The first one tactfully, though tangentially, brought in theology and philosophy. Unlike the economic deterministic ways of seeing, the tropes of theology and philosophy offer a chance to play with possibility. It is in the realm of the second meaning that one can smuggle in some of the neglected aspects of developmentalism such as mind-set, collective inclination, notions of sacred and profane, commodity, and fetishes, inter alia. Needless to say, economics does not disappear for a beholder looking at the artifice of development, commerce is not divorced from culture, and power is not detached from performances. And hence, this book consists of essays that bring about a sense of the unison of various factors. This resonates with a creative anxiety Worsley (1984) expressed elsewhere, as he underlined an interplay of economic, cultural, social, and political aspects of developmental process departing from economic determinism. In an innovative way, Worsley examines the theoretical and methodological problems of the existing mainstream developmental paradigms. He hits the nail on the problem of dividing the world in terms of development parameters. And, in yet another context, Smith (2008) delivered a bewitching thesis on the resurrection of witchcraft in the service of neoliberal logic of development among a Kenyan ethnic group Taita. Metaphors and performances incite people to reflect on taken-for-granted relation of schooling with development among other things. Theatricality of developmentalism, however, is fraught with tension of local and outsider, indigenous and modern.

Some of these exceptional works are in the backdrop of this book that joins in the wedding of economic and cultural interest while suspending both economic and cultural determinism. Within such a framework of developmentalism, we get to perceive the subservience of the old pantheon of gods and goddesses, ideologies and utopias, imagination and realization. They are refashioned so as they could suit the socio-cultural framework of developmentalism. It may inspire awe for lay beholders, criticism among the informed intelligentsia, and ambition for the ever fictitious middle class. The nuanced academic may revile it with sophisticated theoretical and statistical figures and perhaps dub it as an appendage of neoliberal dream merchants. This leads to an understanding, elsewhere Anjan Chakrabarty and Anup Dhar (2010) posited, that development and dislocation are intrinsic.

The connection is perceived across the political and economic history of India, colonial as well as postcolonial, queering the familiar idea of development. Most importantly, this approach aids in understanding that the cognitive enslavement in the former colonies did not pertain to the ennobled goals of modernity alone; instead, it was associated with development discourse. Developmentalism thereby acquires epistemological spin when perceived through the prism of a capital-centric orientalism, which the third world is transformed into 'the world of the third' (ibid.). And in this continuity, it is important to see the contemporary stress on developmentalism as a part of Hindutva (majoritarian) politics.[7] It is held that this neoliberal developmentalism perpetuates the agenda of exclusion and inclusion, vilifying the marginal while benefiting the religious-communal majority. In short, the contemporary manifestations of developmentalism are with dramatic accompaniment of what Appadurai elsewhere called, 'fear of small numbers,'[8] suspicion of smaller fragments of communities.

Development discourse filtered through election campaigns, reality shows of news media, contemporary myths of popular tales, platforms for micro-communications such as WhatsApp and Facebook, and folklore of our times engenders an intrigue. This is the trickery of enchantment, colored with the alter ego of modernity, sustained by the misfit strangers of the enlightenment project qua modernity, and groomed into indigenous notions of progress. Zygmunt Bauman (1991) persuaded us to see as to how everything grotesque, swept under the grand carpet named modernity, forcefully surfaces to determine the micro-narratives. People's faith, collective frenzy about identities, manifestations of pride and prejudices, among other things come to determine everything, including, as this book persuades to believe, developmentalism. Variety of sources, mediums with messages, engenders enchantment about the notion of development. Needless to say, this intrigue is cloaked by the closely related ideas of governance, progress, and populist politics.[9] And very closely following the intrigue of enchantment is a perpetual sense of disenchantment, as many critical readers of Max Weber, including Gananth Obeyesekere (2012), suggest. To fathom the individual pursuits of psychoanalytical awakening, Obeyesekere had to start his discussion on a critical premise. The self in South Asia grooms up on a complex trope, of double notions of enlightenment; one pertains to Rene Descartes' Cogito, and the other is a Buddhist sense of awakening. There is a dialectic of modern-rational disenchantment and intellectually enchanting sources of socialization, guiding the seekers of awakening. No wonder, dreaming of development brings about a chance of collapsing binaries of enchantment and disenchantment. Thus, the content and discontent of development assume more complexity in implication. It can enchant and disenchant at once. The dreaming Cogito lands in a messy situation dealing with the Janus-faced developmentalism.

The political philosophers and sociologists have underlined the relation of modernity, democracy, and identity in South Asia, looking at their affects of enchantment.[10] It aids in understanding the persuasive strategies of the values and notions, contestations and redefinitions, and eventually the becoming of people in India. In the same vein, it ought to be stated that development, though the nature and scope may vary, is rooted in a sense of enchantment, essentially coupled with skeptical arrival of disenchantment, or vice versa. The premise of this reasoning entails the assumption that development discourse will fall flat without taking into account these strands of enchantment. For example, there is no development if a youth of Banaras does not see the possibility of the bullet trains[11] running across the city of mythological significance; the idea of development is faint if there is no availability of free Wi-Fi[12]; there is a question mark to development if the prosperity is not quantifiably higher in comparison with that of the neighboring, specially, arch-rival nation-states in South Asia. And likewise, there is development if the Non-Resident Indians begin to tell their resident counterparts that India has same system of goods-delivery as they have seen in the USA. After all, this is the clarion call by the Indians overseas, parroted by the political leadership, on the occasion of the grand meeting on an officially designated day named *Pravasi Bhartiya Diwas.*[13] Development in India would mean, in the popular imagination attuned to the diasporic aspirations, becoming like one of those locations seas across. The empirical example of the enchantment of development is galore once we begin to factor in the popular cinematic, tales afloat social media, and various news channels dishing out (hyper-)real news. The umpteen sources of enchantment in our times are reminding us of the diverse fragments of the most important mythology. This is mythology, in anthropological sense and not something necessarily (and literally) opposed to reality. To understand its strand, it is imperative to have a discussion on the notion of developmentalism.

An Impatient Synopsis of Predecessors' Propositions

To reiterate a point made earlier, developmentalism promotes legitimacy and stability through the development of capital market accompanied by the vision of social welfare of the public. It includes the famous Rostow's stages growth model. The high age of developmentalism considered to have flourished after the Second World War. Bretten Woods institutions were promoting this ideology. It was prescribing a generic panacea for all kinds of developmental diseases, qua underdevelopment, in the developing countries. This ideology also persuades the state to adhere to the capitalist-models of development which had architects holding a new mirror to the developing countries wherein they can see their future in the advanced Western world. The third world countries were made to realize that once the developed countries were also like the underdeveloped one.[14] Innumerable critics, including Eric J. Hobsbawm (1995), Noam Chomsky (1999), Naomi Klein (2014), David Harvey (2010), and Eric Wolf (2010), have shown the agenda of the capitalist world which tries to create a linear history of the development. Following this, capitalism creates a situation for the nation-states to surrender to the 'free market.' The economic globalization has brought mixed feelings and reaction in various parts of world. Some of the marginal groups have moved upward whereas many disadvantageous groups are pushed to the margins. Hyper-globalization, as suggested by Rodrik (2011) and Inoue (2018), along with the process of high modernity, has compelled many social scientists to vehemently criticize developmentalism as a form of social engineering. Jean-Pierre Olivier de Sardan (2005) explains that development exists because there are institutions, agency, and imaginations. 'who take development as an object or an end to which they devote time, money and professional competence. It is the existence of this 'developmentalist configuration' that defines the very existence of development' (ibid.: 25–31). Differing from the idea and discourse of development studies and anthropology of development, Olivier de Sardan argues that 'development is neither an ideal nor a catastrophe, it is above all an object of study' (ibid.: 25). By quoting (Bastide 1971), he says that anthropology must take the preliminary pains of studying development as a social phenomenon like any other, just as kinship or religion. This adds to the scheme of this book that inquires into the practice and interaction of the people in everyday life. Even after critics have shown the façade of development, it has not been erased from people's imagination. Like magic and religion, the sense of development empowers people in different phase of life. In the conventional field of development studies, there have been endless debates on the failure and success of development plans, the end result of the development process. This book on the other hand centralizes the idea and mentality of development looking at how people give meaning to their action, behavior, thinking, and practice, revealing both enchantment and disenchantment of development.

Broadly in agreement with Olivier de Sardan (2005), people's perception, practice, and imagination of the world have meanings which need to be discovered. As he states, 'The social sphere is very complex .... the everyday life of development comprises compromise, interactions, syncretism, and (mostly informal and indirect) bargaining. These are the kinds of notions – which, obviously, do not exclude power struggles – that must be explored in order to explain "real" effects of development actions on the milieus they intend to transform. That implies breaking away from dualist explanatory "patterns", structuralist frameworks and culturalist references alike' (ibid.: 31).

In this regard, this is pertinent to recall that there has been skepticism, if not total decline, in the economic determinism of discourse of developmentalism after the 1970s. Meanwhile, the discourse on development as developmentality or developmentalism gained prominence across the world. Like the mysticism of the enlightenment modernity of the nineteenth century, the mystic of development's promise came under critical scrutiny. The mystical charmed persuaded to believe that development can provide with the right answer to all the questions and problem. Thus, we began to note that the design of development was also powered with the scientific ideology and support of technology (Pieterse 2010).

The idea of development and developmentalism has taken various forms. Its meaning is drawn from evolutionism, modernization theory, and development thinking paradigms. Two important discourses can help in correlating development and these paradigms. Firstly, there are a group of scholars who focus on the belief in, and enchantment by, development and second underline the disenchantment by development. These two discourses are the most sought after perspectives that give meaning to the idea of development. The first perspective focuses on the affirmative and innovative steps of development that posits development as a categorical whole. In this regard, according to Pieterse, development refers to 'the organised intervention in collective affairs according to a standard of improvement' (ibid.: 3). The idea of improvement revolves around the bargaining capacities in a historical context, intersected by class, culture, and power relations existing in particular time and space. Developmentalism on the other hand refers to the ideology guided by the principles of development. It criticizes the hegemonic dimension of developmentalism that focuses on the ideas of universalism and ethnocentrism. An overview by Cowen and Shenton

(1996) shows that the true meaning of development was given shape by the chaos created by progress in light of enlightenment. Everyone seemed to admit that scientific modernity qua spread of capitalism created underdevelopment, and the way out of it was the ideology of development. The pathways were already there in the classical works of Adam Smith, David Ricardo, among others. Cowen and Shenton also regard the Saint Simonians and Marx in the same league of theorists. Though each framed it differently, with distinct variables and goalposts, development appeared as an agency that could transform the society. Furthermore, Keynesians called for state regulation and social welfare management while seeking to strengthen capitalism. With this conception of state intervention for development of a society, this idea became an authoritarian one. Arthur Lewis (1954) in his 'dualist theory' puts the central focus on industrial growth rather than investing in 'traditional' sector. He argues that it is the surplus labor gained from the 'traditional' sector that can help the industrial sector to flourish. W. W. Rostow did not lag behind in showing stages of development as a linear path of progress. For him, development takes place through five stages—traditional society, pre-take-off society, take-off, the road to maturity, and mass consumption. Also, it is through the 'trickle down' effect that the traditional societies would taste the fruit of development laid down by the developed societies. The mainstream discourse on development was however criticized by alternative development theorists.[15] But the point of reference was similar for both the discourses, i.e., celebrating the redemptive power of development. However, alternative perspectives also aid in grappling with novel facets. Gandhian thinking in India, for example, follows the alternative path of development whereby self—reliance of the village economy is seen as bringing in development for the nation. In this wake, development is not only a thing-there (outside), it is also a thing-in (within). Furthermore, the theoretical alternatives began to show the anomalies. Dependency theory and world system theory came as alternative critical perspectives on development. These two perspectives were critical of Rostows 'magical' prescription of five stages of economic growth. They provided with revolutionary explanations about the 'core' causing underdevelopment of the 'periphery' in the structure of the world. This too suffered from an alleged mono-causal explanation and could not offer the epistemological shift in development thinking. It still played in the hands and clutches of development (Pieterse 2010). The alternative perspective however brings forth rejection of the primacy of economic development, while pivoting freedom (from coercion and censorship, from repressive sexual codes, etc.). Fulfillment of human potential was regarded as the main aim in achieving development for a society. Amartya Sen (2001) philosophized the essence of development through freedom, and Martha C. Nussbaum (2011) postulated on capabilities that influenced the perception of development and poverty of many multilateral organizations such as World Bank, ADB, and IMF. Informed by some of these advancements in the thinking on development, a cultural turn is visible in the program of various agencies, including UNDP. They enable to admit the developmental goals as more than economic gains. The Human Developmental Report of the United Nations Development Program emphasized on alternative development thinking by bringing in the concepts of life expectancy, educational attainment, and poverty. Despite the sophistication of theories and philosophy, efficacy of plans and policies, some of these innovative interventions fall short of telling us: How folks enchant themselves about development?

The above trajectory of thinking about development is not exhaustive enough; rather, it is an impatient recounting. But it suffices to get a sense of the changing approaches to the questions pertaining to development. It broadly ranges from capital-centric, to statist, to people-centric reasoning. One common thread running across them is a taken-for-granted validity of development. It is a foregone conclusion of sort that a society has to develop. Seldom do we see a devil asking: Why at all should a society develop? Or what persuades everyone to share the dreamof development? What is that collective mythology in which development tends to be as sacred as any other god? In short, what engenders the enchantment of development and also disenchantment in the same sense?

Enchantment–(Dis)Enchantment, A Dialectic of Development

Developmentalism assumes a contemporary charm as the trope of enchantment accommodating past and present, indigenous and reinvented tradition, cultural and political. This is the case even though the statement of present may promise to depart from the exotica of past. The Prime Minister of India was reported as exclaiming 'No Snake Charmers or Black Magic, We are Digital India.'[16] Most of the national dailies reported the first Independence Day speech of the Prime Minister after he assumed the office. The speech pushed for a 'digital India,' considering digitalization as one of the markers of modernity and, of course, development. The Prime

Minister asserted, 'the world used to think we are a land of snake charmers and black magic. But our youth has surprised the world with its IT skills...I dream of a digital India. It was once said railways connects India. Today I say IT connects India' (ibid.).

In this 'connected' India, cities and villages are imagined to be equally connected with broadband, expediting the availability of education and telemedicine facilities to every Indian. It envisages plans for service delivery through mobile phones. And most curiously, it anticipates the election campaigns through social media platforms like Twitter and Facebook. The dream has nearly come through the way it did for Franz Kafka's Gregor Samsa. The opening sentence of Kafka's novella, Metamorphosis reads, 'One morning, as Gregor Samsa was waking up from anxious dreams, he discovered that in bed he had been changed into a monstrous verminous bug.'[17] Such was the dream (nightmare?) coming true since it entailed, along with digital penetration of the far-flung hinterlands, the spread of fake news, photoshopped images, misinformation, and affective political polarization too. No longer was the national media (newspapers and television channels) the stakeholder. Folks switched on to various online portals, social networking web sites, and handles online, which could make messages fly, fast, and furious. A performative turn in politics all over the world attracted attentions of the social scientists (Alexander 2011; Butler 2015; Bharucha 2014). Through various means, old as well as new, power and performance, politics and culture, actors and audience, inched closer. In the context of South Asia, the interplay of culture and politics also underlined a collapse of distinction between social and political. It showed that performance was no longer restricted to a defined arena, a predetermined script, and trained set of actors. The performative turn brought about the possibility of everyone joining in the performance set by the industrial stakeholders. This was the realm of enchantment that came under a larger rubric of performative communication in contemporary South Asia (Pathak and Perera 2017). Among other things, this scenario was suitable for the politics of development. The idea of development gained in new lease of life, since it was not only in terms of the policy statements, manifesto of political parties, and analysts' meticulously dry mathematics. Development acquired a cultural life, dipped in tales, soaked in aspirations, wet with imagination, so to say. This also included return to an idealist dream of development through a transformative visions and creative practices that connects the outside development with inside spirituality. They called it as aesthetics of development,[18] emphasizing new visions and imaginations. However, this was an utter failure at recognizing that every bit of aesthetic is also political and any instance of idealism is a historical construct too. While romance with aesthetics is an idea that informs the need to look at developmentalism differently, surrender to the romance is not so much of interest, duly upheld in this book. Hence, we also need to be informed by Chakrabarty and Dhar (2008), in order to understand that a capital-centric development is invariably detrimental to the freedom, growth, and even human aspirations. With a curiously Marxian reading of Rabindranath Tagore, the scholar duo upheld the imperative of development as freedom from the variety of deterministic forces.

This complexity of hope and despair with development is more vivid on the trope of cultural artefacts. Singhal and Rogers (1989) showed that the television entertainment business played didactic role in driving the sanctity of development to the viewers qua citizens. A tele-serial 'Hum Log' (We, the People) and the Latin American rock and video song 'Cuando Estemos Juntos' are two cases in point. When Doordarshan was the only television channel, run and managed by the state in India, 'Hum Log' represented an extension of the hybrid combination of education and entertainment, nation-building, and fun, inspired by the Mexican experience with pre-development soap operas. It was a runaway hit, as people identified with the characters and their dreams of becoming better. The serial also featured socio-normative constraints and anomalies confronting Indian society, such as family disharmony, unequal status of women, lack of national integration, unsuccessful planning and health programs, problems of urban life, and the lack of national welfare programs. In the 'good old days' of the state-owned television channel in India, the medium was playing up the desire and aspirations, possibility and constraints, of the middle-class India. It was the television's construction of public which was in the perpetual process of embodying values, of family, kinship, nation, and state.[19]

The anomalies start taking different forms as we turn to the contemporary mediations, on the trope of performative politics. The continuum of development, the Hindu god Ram, and the Prime Minister of India Mr. Narendra Modi paradoxically implies a politico-cultural construction of divine 'sanctified by a formal democratic process' (Rajagopal 2016: 129). In such a wake, public sphere governed by images and spectacle, secrecy and surveillance, is coupled with spectacular bursts of violence.

Thus, through the television media, a critical engagement with a particular idea of development was promoted. In the age of multichannel broadcast system in India, today there is abundance of melodramatic tales on similar issues, each leading to the popular sacralization of development. The trope is indeed vast enough to skip the narrow space of discussion here. Suffice to say, melodrama of development in the popular televisual shows, including reality shows, is vivid in India. For, it is safe to assume that every middle-class parent dreams to send a child or two to one of those television talent hunt shows. There is a critical realization that the talent hunt shows are more about trade and commerce of the television channels than about showcasing of the young talents.[20] The melodrama attached with winning and loosing in the so-called reality shows reveals the mediated middle-class aspirations of contemporary India.

Another side of the mediated manifestation related to developmentalism is in favor of the politics of protest. In 2003, the Government of Odisha singed a Memorandum of Understanding with a multinational company, Vedanta Alumina, for the establishment of the mining plant in Lanjigarh, originally inhabited by an endangered tribal group called Dongria Kondh. Protests against the mining plant as well as the company, Vedanta, made news locally and internationally. In London, on 28 July 2010, many activists, including actors from the Hollywood blockbuster *Avatar* (2009), held a protest outside the venue of the annual general meeting of the mining company Vedanta against the mining project which is a threat to tribal worldview and ecosystem of Dongria Kondhs. The protesters disguised themselves like the characters from the endangered community called Navi in an imagined land called Pandora, in the film *Avatar*. The protest clearly signaled the shrinking of distance between the reel and the real, the cinematic and the socio-politico-cultural while underlining the problems of development.[21] After the release of the film, many plays have also been staged around the world along the theme of developmentalist exploitations of the lands and people. Yet another documentary film, *Mine: Story of a sacred Mountain* (2009) by an NGO named Survival International, depicts the life and struggle of the local communities. This film too draws a parallel between the imagined community, land, and war of people in the Niyamgiri hills in Orissa.[22] In the similar ways, a documentary film, *Development Flows from the Barrel of The Gun* (2003), presented resistance of the downtrodden (tribal and dalit) against the state agencies on various developmental projects. The film showcased a panorama of cases, including Utkal Alumina in Kashipur, Orissa, Koel Karo dam in Jharkhand, World Bank-funded forestry project in Dewas, Madhya Pradesh, steel plant at Nagarnar in Chhattisgarh, and the new port in Umbergaon inside Gujarat. The development drama transforms the ordinary actors into spectacular protesters, the dead into martyr, with clear theatrics surrounding pros and cons of development.[23] State agencies turn complicit in the criminal aspects of development project at the face of any protest in most of the cases covered in the film.

Quite in tandem, Narmada Diary (Patwardhan 1995) portrayed the protests around the development project, the Sardar Sarover dam on the River Narmada in Western India. Allegedly, the dam, if completed, is supposed to have drowned about 37,000 hectares of fertile land, displacing over 200,000 adivasis (the area's indigenous people) and cost up to 400 billion rupees. In addition to these figures, there is an apprehension of an enormous loss of ecological, cultural, and human nature.[24] The film sums up the paradoxes of the 'mega' projects in the name of development.[25]

Developmentalism is indeed an interesting tale on the trope of enchantment. If it tells the critical responses of the people, intelligentsia, and literati, it also conjures a ray of hope, so to say, pervasive about silver lining in the bleak horizon. Many of the popular cinemas in Hindi stand testimonial. They underline the anomalies, and yet they attempt to improvize on people's optimism and faith. It may appear in the way poverty-driven endeavors show an 'affective history' of human aspirations in the cinematic tales. Starting with cinema in post-independent Nehruvian India, depiction of poverty was coupled with urge for reform, nation-building, and modernity. The range of such cinematic tryst with destiny of India includes many popular films from Achhut Kannya (Untouchable Maiden, 1936, Franz Osten) to Mother India (Khan, 1957). The earthy characters (protagonists as well as antagonists) showed an inclination to the historically emerged entity called India. The goalposts changed in post-liberalized India, and the larger goals of socio-national ethos were replaced by sheer urge to develop for consumption. In short, post-liberalized India shows a replacement of the species who wanted to contribute to the making (nation) by those who want to contribute to consuming (development). This remains a motif despite the clarion calls for Make in India, given by the political leadership. Citizens remain largely consumers who dream of development for better consumptions. These dreams of development for better consumptions prevails upon all, poor and rich, including the urban poor.

Urban poverty, rather than poverty laced with social anomalies of caste and gender, occupied the center stage in some of the popular cinematic works lately. We were entertained by *Slumdog Millionaire* (2008) and *Peepli Live* (2010). And we were reminded of the quest of democracy in the register of development in *Welcome to Sajjanpur* (2009) and *Well done Abba*

(2009) and the likes. The post-liberalization cinema of development in India began to propose new set of enemies (villains) of a combine of protagonist, development, and democracy. These new villains were corruption in governance, electoral practices, and development programs. On the one hand, these popular cinemas maintained the melodramatic tales, mostly rag-to-riches stories, while underlining the anomalies of post-liberalized polity and economy of India.

Suffice to say, the trope of enchantment gets richer with the intervention of television channels participating in the public sphere with their own stake in the drama of development ever since the commencement. With the launch of the Satellite Instructional Television Experiment in 1975–1976, the television in India began to broadcast educational messages through satellite to 2400 villages in the six states of Andhra Pradesh, Karnataka, Bihar, Orissa, Rajasthan, and Madhya Pradesh. Some of the stated objectives were to improve rural primary education and provide teacher training, aid in improving health and hygiene and nutritional practices and contribute to family planning and national integration.[26] However, an apprehension of misleading television of development was in sight way back in the 1980s. More precisely, in 1982, a Working Group on Software for Doordarshan remarked, 'India embarked on television in the name of development but used it in practice to provide trivial entertainment and to churn out government-oriented rather than people oriented news.'[27]

With the age of multiple television channels, the private merchandize also joined in the league of spreading messages on the register of development. However, mostly, it has been about the job of a typical dream merchant that television channels perform for an aspiring to develop India. Promising to air news while showing views in the prime time, the television-driven Indian media found new partners online, news portals, social networking Web sites, and Twitter handles. Not only journalists but also lay viewers have begun to realize the problem with television content in contemporary India.[28] But then, television along with many other cognates online is the provider of the most consumed contents in the length and breadth of India. The dream of digital India thus has brought about a Kafkaesque Gregor Samsa waking up with a metamorphosis of body, with a restless soul.

Traversing the rich terrain of enchantment, it seems befitting to recall Rist (1997) proposing to consider development as a new religion[29] in which scientific rationality is excruciatingly powerful, giving rise to laboratory states (Nandy 1996; Visvanathan 1987). Truly, it alludes to a paradox of developmentalism, akin to the imageries of development on the terrain of enchantment. There is a larger faith in development, a necessity, and yet there is a recognition that things are not doing well. A critical stance may unearth a decline in the moral stature of development as an ideology. Such a critical reading of the pitfall of developmental ideology underlines the collective naïve trust in mega organizations and mega technology. Moreover, critical engagement with developmentalism also enables to see as to how it may induce various kinds of conflict by pitting traditional communities against each other with competitive relationship. And that the prevalent paradigms of development upset the checks and balances, spreads cultural homogenization and manifold environmental destructions.[30] However, this all does not dismiss people's faith in the charm and necessity of development. Unlike the critical-academic scholarship or a reflective chattering of socio-cultural elites, people operate with an idea that developmentalism may begin to work, any moment. Just like gods may be cruel at times in punishing humans for bad deeds, but they may turn benevolent, any moment. There was a 'sacred canopy,'[31] a larger ambit of faith that gave a sense of ontological security to the believers in a historical epoch that held religion as the most important socio-cultural system of meanings. In spite of the intervention of modern means, the folk inclination to faiths did not disappear, to the dismay of the votaries of the modernization thesis. There is a perpetuity in a tendency to folklorize new entities and thereby add value of divinity to them.[32] No wonder, new gods, as well as god-men, have been always in good supply. Faith in development joins in the list, as a way to provide the believers a sense of security. And hence, we witness continuous optimism and quest with the mind-set of developmentalism in spite of the recognition of failures mostly reminded by the critical readings of the scholars.

Likewise, feminists' critics, ever since the 1970s, have led a new way of engaging with development. [33] Boserup (2011) criticized development for being a system which excluded women and proposed a break with a series of dogmas established in the development discourse and policies. This led to emphasize the notion, 'women in development,' showing more active and dynamic role of women with due access to funds earmarked for development. Since the 1980s, another approach, namely gender and development, offered manifold criticism of the logic that economic benefits alone can empower women. The social policies of microcredit were deemed useless the masculinist domination was undermined. And, moving a few notches ahead, Vandana Shiva (1988) propounded 'Ecofeminsim' in India, as she departed from postcolonial agenda of development. In this agenda, she perceived continuity of colonization, exploitation for wealth creation in the modern-Western-patriarchal economic vision. The feminist interventions solicit a challenge to developmentalism in order to restore the significance of women and marginalized, peasants and tribals in postcolonial India.

The trope of enchantment with development is indeed informed by a curious dialectic. It elucidates people's hope and despair, associated with development. And this is what makes this book relevant as it embarks on divulging the Janus-faced characteristics of developmentalism. A brief note of what informs this dialectic, and the nature and scope of such a dialectic, is imperative. Historically, India's interaction with centers of capitalism began in a colonial setup. The attraction to capitalism-driven economic development seeped in the agenda of nation-building post-independence. The endeavor for a transition from semi-feudal agriculture to capitalist farming, accompanied by democratization and federalization of a largely fragmented society established under the Constitution of India, was crucial markers (Singh 1990). The first Prime Minister of independent India, Pandit Jawaharlal Nehru was inclined toward self-reliant economic growth involving not only infrastructure building, advances in science and technology, education, and research, but also community-development. However, the romance with mixed economy only amounted to sluggish, if not absent, development. The dream to be independent-developing country met with many historical moments of embarrassment. However, this was not entirely a story of failure. The basic institution building, in terms of trade and commerce, planning and development, governance and welfare state, took foundation. The dreams were innocent, the implementations were in good faith, and possibility seemed larger than life. This was only halted by the tumultuous political moment, in the Emergency,[34] which paradoxically centralized the issue of poverty without offering any way out. There were moments of celebration, even though brief and partial, such as the Green Revolution that propelled agricultural output, experimental initiative toward tapping other resources such as dairy, and development schemes that involved rural workforce. More radical shift seems to appear since the early 1990s, as development planning sought for the enhancement of human well-being rather than mere economic growth.[35] The drama of development has been integral to the statecraft in India ever since the independence from the colonial power. However, the temperament of the drama began to change with post-liberalization of the economy. The thickness of the plots, enrichment of the props, and intrigue of the performances began to show. Many of the development schemes and plans thereby exhibited inclination to the idea of human development. The popular demand and need of livelihood, education, and health featured as crucial for development.[36] Some other explorations also emphasize the grassroots activities of tribal communities, such as Adi, Monpa, and Khasi tribes of North East India, in the larger purview of sustainable development and conservation.[37] Often the traditional-local-indigenous cultural practice either get rejected by developmental planners or co-opted as rhetoric. For the sustainability of development, there were different kinds of questions being raised, such as 'how 'local' is the local participation in the programs of development? What are the characteristics of the local in the local-in-participation?' (Pathak 2014: 436). These questions were largely based on the recognition that development fails due to the limit of cultural imagination in it, and hence, development amounts to be a butt of ridicule too, in popular imagination of the folk.[38] If there was a paucity of cultural imagination in many of the schemes executed by the state across India, with support of the international agencies, there were other instances which registered jubilation. In a largely patriarchal society with secondary status in the normative-juridical order for women, Sri Mahila Udyog Lijjat Papad sets up a different example by turning women into units of production. A case study of the Lijjat Papad[39] emphasized women's empowerment in the social entrepreneurial ventures that produced one of the most popular snacks that triumphed Indian market ever since its advent. Governed by, as stated by the venture, the Gandhian ideal of *Sarvodaya*, Sri Mahila Udyog Lijjat Papad, has been a trendsetter of sort.

But the success story of women empowerment, be economic or political, ought to be taken with a pinch of salt. In India, women's reservation in electoral politics is well known as a lip service. It is there in principle, and it is questionable in practice. Women's responsibilities and power are performed by their husband, brothers, or fathers. In Hindi-speaking northern India, the menfolk representing their elected womenfolk are popularly known as *Sarpanch Pati* (husband of a woman head of a Gram Panchayat, a local body of governance). Dohmwirth and Hanisch (2018) scrutinized women's empowerment through cooperative membership in the women-only dairy cooperative societies in Karnataka, in South of India. It was established with the objectives of economically and socially empowering women. Their empirically rich study revealed that the empowering effects of women are limited only to better leadership abilities. Membership in the cooperative does not enhance women's control over income or make them a decision maker in the household. On the contrary, members of women-only cooperatives opined that they had even less control over their income when they compare themselves with unorganized woman dairy producers. At the same time, these women face severe entry barriers to participate in the mixed-gender cooperatives.

The dialectic of enchantment and disenchantment with development unfolds with dramatics of details. This book is pitched in the backdrop of this drama of development.

The Raw and Cooked: The Book and Booked

Resonating with the broader contextual backdrop, various strands of the potential dialectic of enchantment–disenchantment with development unfolds in the essays across the book. The cases from various parts of India solicit discussions from economists, sociologists, anthropologists, and historians to refresh our understanding of development. And most importantly, in the ultimate analysis, the book equips us to approach what we have enthusiastically discussed in this introduction as developmentalism. By so doing, the book envisages an emergence of much-needed discursive trope, somewhat underdeveloped in the larger areas of development studies or anthropology of development in India. Presumably, this discursive trope that can allow to fathom the real and unreal, qua hyper-real of development, and the (il)legitimacy of its enchanting implications. However, more importantly, this book is inclined to unearthing the reasons why developmentalism sways despite the limits of development manifest in various realms of living. The interplay of enchantment and disenchantment also demands a provisional, if not permanent, suspension of judgement usually associated with the approaches in development studies. The chapters in this book therefore vend narratives, stories, imageries, motifs, idioms, metaphors accompanied with facts and rigor of analysis. Adopting various means and thereof messages, the book emphasizes that the notion of developmentalist enchantment is integral to 'here and now,' emphasizing the spectacles out of mundane, while also concealing a host of issues. This is not a transcendental sense of enchantment, hence vulnerable to the moments of crisis and discontents.

The first section of the book, titled Discontentment and Disenchantment, is a typical act of a Doubting Thomas. This is perhaps likely due to our training in social sciences, which make us, among other things, a diehard skeptic. The book begins with a bad news; rather a recycling of the bad news, we have already heard on several occasions in past. And the news is that things are not fine with development. The moot question is, how bad it was, is, and could get in contemporary India? The essays in this section complement each other in laying out the critical discursive turf to flag the aspects of discontentment and thereby disenchantment with the notions of developmentalism. And one begins to wonder in this section whether the litany of lament about development is any less a source of enchantment for the skeptics. Rabindra Ray and Amiya Kumar Das in Chapter 2 titled The Danger of Development Today: An Inevitable Polemic present a polemic on the pitfalls of development. The chapter locates the historicity of the idea of development and its hegemony as a system of knowledge. Provoking in a persuasive manner, it underlines the ability of development as a monstrous entity, which can devour other forms of knowledge. And once devoured, there is no coming back, even as excreta, and hence, other variety of knowledge is often erased from the epistemological plane of popular conscience. The author duo put forward questions, with more questions, in order to unmask and debunk what they show as a Western import. Joining in the league, performing the act of incessant doubting, is Chapter 3 by Yugank Goyal titled The Enchantment of Urbanization: Closer Look at Market's Narrative in Indian Cities. It locates a curious blind spot, in the governance of development. Premised on a reading of polyphonic enchantment, from the realm of modernity to that of development, the chapter exposes fissures between haves and have-nots visible in the structure of urbanization in non-Western countries. Goyal asserts in the essay, 'Enchantment then, has simply shifted sides. While nature was an enchanting source for us for millennia, it is the notion of development today. Development, as it sits on the other side of nature. On the side of bullet trains and Wi-Fi. This shift took place through economics, as a philosophical science. The subject led to a resurgence of all things material, and in doing so, the market.' Instead of being confined to the conventional economists' preoccupation with market and various strands of capitalism, the chapter unspools a terrain of enchantment associated with developmentalism. With a mix of scepticism, polemic, and engagement with critical aspects of development, this section sets the stage for the larger discussion in the subsequent sections of the book.

If the first section of the book reincarnates the old questions, anxiety, and polemic, in order to jolt us awake from the complacence of having exhausted critical comprehension, the second section undertakes a fascinating inroad into the details. The chapters in this section bring forth the devil of the details with nuanced engagement with a few representative terrains. However, this is not exhaustive, as this terrain has many more mediums working round the clock to yield manifold messages. Suffice to say, some of the crucial details, conducive for the discussion that this book aims at, surface in the selective terrain in this section. Aptly titled Dramatics and Enchantment, the section vends essays to demonstrate a few instances that can create a tangible body of dramatics. Pranta Pratik Patnaik in Chapter 4 titled The Art of Showing: Imagining Development in Indian Mediascape invites us to see an enchanting realm of reconciliation and rebellion in the wake of mediated development. It probes into television as one of the influential mediums in contemporary India. Patnaik affirms in this essay, 'The audience is brought under a magic spell of development and the media does not leave any stone unturned to sustain their version of development'. With empirical study in support, the chapter demonstrates the politics of representation in televisual texts related to developmental projects undertaken by the government. If television is a site of enchanting contestation, so is the real world. Ektaa Jain in Chapter 5 titled Crafting Development and Developing Craft: An On-Going Dialogue explores a rather humanistic drama of development. Traversing backward in history of India, engaging with the freedom struggle along with the spinning of *khadi* and hand-made production, the chapter conjures an epic-theater situation. In such a grandeur of narrative, the chapter locates the issue of artisans' empowerment, nation-building, and imagination of development through symbols.

Furthermore, Nivedita Ghosh in Chapter 6 titled Documentaries and the Development Project: Filmmaking as a Discursive Practice joins in the debate with a medium, documentary film, most frequently associated with the realm of development. She underlines it as a favorite tool of agencies that strive to take forward the development project to far-flung corners of what is known to be the third world. Using Foucauldian perspective, the chapter posits that the practice of making documentaries does not merely involve arriving at a location, filming, and moving on to post-production. Rather, it allows us to address the disenchantment with the making of development documentaries that thrives on rampant discursive constructions around the field and the filmmaking practice. Taking the debate to a more intimate realm of personal, in Chapter 7, titled 'Tayyari Jeet Ki': The Production of Childhood as a Cultural Trope of Developmentalism, Lakshita Malik explores the cultural investment in the notions of development, making of a grand political narrative imposed on the everyday life.

Delving into a range of materials including films, popular magazines, and advertisements, she delineates childhood as a site of performing caste/class-based differences in the history of the natural development of man. Visual representation emphasizes the recent trend of grooming the middle-class children as the repository of natural talent, with parental investment and guidance. The chapter brings in the disillusionment with the Nehruvian models of development, but at the same time demonstrates the growing charm of developmentalism.

The second section of the book thereby accomplishes to show the dialectic of enchantment and disenchantment vis-à-vis developmentalism performed on TV, practices of artisan, documentary filmmaking, and popular visual representations in magazines, cinema, and advertisements. A more headlong engagement with the cases of disenchantment manifests in the unfolding of the discontents of development, in the third and the last section of the book, titled Details of Discontents.

The class and mass, reflective and unreflective, and grand narratives and micro-narratives come together in the essays in this section. Salah Punathil in Chapter 8 titled Development, Marginality, and 'Contested Space' in South India, shows the disenchantment of development in the social life of the fishers in the coastal areas of Kerala state in South India. Foregrounding the role of development process and taking a political ecology perspective, he analyzes the historical and structural conditions of a 'contested space' of disenchantment and demonstrates how the disenchantment of development lead to various forms of routine conflicts and everyday crisis in the life of coastal communities. He suggests that the persistent violence between diverse communities in Indian context could be read better if we take disenchantment of development as a critical point of enquiry. On the other hand, A. S. Shimreiwung in Chapter 9 titled Resurgence of Community in the Midst of Despair: Development's Changing Course in Northeast India argues that the contested process of development in Northeast of India, involving numerous actors and issues that has besieged the region since India's independence from colonial rule, has been intrinsic of state-making project of India. Building on disenchantment with statist approach to development, this chapter explores community's responses in Northeast India to the failure of developmental processes in the region, and how citizens struggle to become co-partners of development. With an ethnographic study at disposal, Anna Romanowicz in Chapter 10 titled (Re)Producing Middle Class: On Development as Middle Classes Mission argues that development is an important tool for the mobility of middle class. It furthermore complicates the issue by showing the complicity of development in the maintenance of the middle-class dominance of over lower classes. She presents shifting meanings of development that occurred with the advent of economic neo-liberalization. In a nuanced manner, the chapter demonstrates the ineffectiveness of development activities, which lies in deep interest of this class. Discontents thus meet with human aspirations. Lastly, in this section, in Chapter 11 titled Frictions in Resistance: Imagining Post-neoliberal Developmental Possibilities, Tathagatan Ravindran presents a comparative (also complementary) experience from India and Latin America. He maintains that even after the global economic crisis, Indian elites and professional middle classes continue to be enthralled by the hopes of high modernity qua developmentalism. There have also been occasions when conflicts surfaced among the traditional (political) Left and the social movements that mounted resistance to development projects. Bringing examples from the Latin American resistance to neoliberal hegemony, this chapter reads post-neoliberal possibilities in India in light of experiences from the Global South, especially Latin America.

Like any other edited book, this one too is a package of some raw and some cooked food-for-thinking. The panorama of developmentalism is indeed too wide to be exhausted in one embodied entity such as this book. So there are selective issues covered in this book, with an attention to the objective of enhancing the discursive trope. At the cost of repetition, this must be said that it is not a typical development studies volume, in the sense that it seeks to understand a mind-set prone to the popular means and pervasive messages of development. It is a dramatic departure from what we are habituated into doing in development studies. The habituated practice of development studies, broadly confined to evaluative studies of programs and schemes, was justifiable in a socio-political situation that allowed critical thinking on development programs, along the lines of progressive politics. This is not the mainstay in this book; the book is not geared to merely to do a critical appraisal of welfare schemes or developmental programs as such. If such evaluative statements appear in chapters, which they do, it is only aimed at the larger discourse. The book as such is inclined to disclose the socio-political-cultural manufacturing of developmentalist mind-set perpetuated and sustained by a whole gamut of signs and symbols under the behemoth of developmentalism.

This volume also does not wish to present an exhaustive review the disembodied trajectory of theories, about which many of us have been critical. This is how development NGOs and funding agency driven scholarship has damaged the relation of theories and research. The usage of developmentalism is suggestive to unravel the mythology and mind-set pertaining to development. More than development programs run by state or NGOs, which ought to be evaluated for success of failure elsewhere, this book attempts to understand the collective minds, dreams and aspirations, hysteria and pathologies, by engaging with the politico-cultural artifacts of development. The raw and cooked, in this book, propose to understand developmentalism as a politico-cultural entity that enchants and disenchants the consumers/clients/beneficiaries/myth-makers etc.

Toward the Future of the Past

In the scheme of this book, development discourse has come of age, whereby invocation of new ways, approaches, material manifestations, research questions, and analytical framework is imperative. This is so in the wake of a regime that is mostly about seeing, seen, and being shown. Nothing is beyond 'exhibitionism,' as per the picture theory of Mitchel (1994), and everything visible (with a shadow of invisible) shall show the relation embedded in power. There is a pictorial turn in the world of experiences in general, and this turn suggests that, 'modern thought has re-oriented itself around visual paradigms that seem to threaten and overwhelm any possibility of discursive mastery' (ibid.: 9). Unlike Mitchel, we are not trying to understand the theoretical import of the verbal and visual representation. The book is however seeing single-mindedly to understand the discursive location of development, the various means which plays up the idea of development, in the regime of seeing and showing. This is done without aiming at the discursive mastery that Mitchel was apprehensive of.

Anthropology of development too exhibits an interest in the diverse regimes of exhibitionism. And hence, perhaps, scholars world over are willingly employing methods and tools, to unearth new domains of enquiries pertaining to developmentalism. Rather than strictly confined to understanding economic implications or success and failure, they are curious about visual tropes of development. Visual anthropology of development is showing novel methodological pathways, opening of new domains, and showing us the future of applied visual analyses.[40] In the field of interpretative visual analysis, there have emerged hermeneutical interpretations of audiovisual data. Instead of the closed field of conventional anthropologists, the new species of anthropologists of development stress on methodological advances in qualitative research based on visual data. The field of visual analyses of development has started to posit new understanding. It has shown various possibilities, including the mixing of diverse theoretical perspectives, such as Marxist and feminist, to sharpen visual methods, in order to fathom international development programs. Such an approach enables for a critical analysis of communicative and affective labor performed by visual and discursive representations of subjects of aid, donors, and the brand.[41] Indeed, this is relevant in a time when exhibitionism is a foregone conclusion.

Likewise, there is a significant trend of reading development through various performative means, including traditional performances and modern theater. While performance study is a well-established area of enquiry in India, one does not come across many works spotting development in association with performance. This has been, however, the case elsewhere in Global South, say for example in Africa. Theater is used as a way of increasing popular participation in the development process, in theater-for-development program. Development theater in Africa enables audience participation while also integrating indigenous and popular systems of communication.[42] In India, some of the works have closely observed the association of performative forms with emotions, history, and identity-politics.[43] The narratives exploring performances at the cusp of history and anthropology divulge the embodiment of experiences, very well capable of spanning the encounters with development. Drawing a continuum of tradition of performance and modern theater in India, the analyses have elicited an understanding of the all-pervasive nature of these cultural expressions.[44] They hold the key, indeed, to the future of past, the possibilities in understanding the phenomenon of developmentalism. And in the same breath, it ought to be suggested that social sciences in India need to take the visual route to see the unseen of development. The importance of visuals in anthropological studies was broached in the decade of the 1990s in India.[45] And the region of South Asia is known to have a thick history of visuals, aptly narrativized elsewhere.[46] However, the engagement with visual artefacts remained a fugitive at large in sociology and social anthropology in India, for a long time, despite some of the trailblazing contributions.[47] Likewise, even though performance is integral to classical anthropological works (if one dare make a sweeping matrix) from Malinowski to Victor Turner, it could seldom be seen beyond the conventional domains of rite of the passage. In this wake, this book makes a modest contribution, wedding visuals, performances, cultural articulations, polemic, and many other sources that can lead to an understanding of enchantment and (dis)enchantment. The route of the book is fraught with intellectual risks. But it is a risk worth undertaking toward making a chink in the armor of the prevalent development discourse in India.

Notes

1. There is a vast array of scholarship along this line; suffice to see Chatterji (2003).
2. See Blank (2009) and Bronner (2011).
3. This has been discussed elsewhere with regard to performing spectacles in the realm of education, see Pathak (2015).
4. See Schumacher (1973).
5. https://en.oxforddictionaries.com/definition/developmentalism, accessed on December 15, 2018.
6. For more along this line, see https://devl1980.wordpress.com/2012/04/24/what-is-neo-developmentalism/, accessed on December 15, 2018.
7. An editorial in a national daily captured elucidating the situation in contemporary India, https://indianexpress.com/article/opinion/columns/uttar-pradesh-bjp-hindutva-narendra-modi-yogi-adityanath-chief-minister-4578008/, accessed on December 16, 2018.
8. Appadurai (2006), however, does not offer any insight on the emotions beyond fear between the people in large and small numbers.
9. This is not only in the context of contemporary India. We are informed by deliberation on the developmental-populist politics in the context of Latin America, see Wolfe (2011).
10. See Pathak (2010), Kaviraj (2010), and Bilgrami (2014).
11. There was a promise during the general election in 2014 in India made by the then would-be https://indianexpress.com/article/india/delhi-varanasi-distance-to-be-covered-in-157-minutes-via-bullet-trains-report-4752685/, accessed on December 16, 2018, Prime Minister, Mr. Narendra Modi. This caught the imagination of electorate in India.
12. Aam Admi Party won assembly election in 2015 on a long list of promises including free Wi-Fi in Delhi, the capital city of India, see https://timesofindia.indiatimes.com/city/delhi/aap-targets-free-wifi-launch-by-march-2019/articleshow/64376066.cms, accessed on December 14, 2018.
13. For more information, see https://www.mea.gov.in/pravasi-bharatiya-divas.htm, accessed on December 16, 2018.
14. For a succinct summary, see Chakrabarty and Dhar (2017).
15. See, for example, Herath (2009) and Hettne (1976, 1983, 1990).
16. See the report on 15 August 2014, by NDTV portal, https://www.ndtv.com/india-news/no-snake-charmers-or-black-magic-we-are-digital-india-says-pm-modi-649191, accessed on November 20, 2018.

17. http://www.kafka-online.info/the-metamorphosis.html, accessed on November 20, 2018.
18. See an unusual volume by Clammer and Giri (2017).
19. See Mankekar (1999).
20. See https://www.scoopwhoop.com/Indian-Reality-Shows-All-About-The-Drama-TRPs/#.ctuprcswb, accessed on December 16, 2018.
21. https://www.thehindu.com/news/national/ldquoAvatarrdquo-actors-join-protest-in-support-of-Orissa-tribals/article16213335.ece, accessed on December 16, 2018.
22. http://travel.cnn.com/mumbai/none/video-indian-tribals-appeal-james-avatar-cameron-943069/, accessed on December 16, 2018.
23. For more, see http://www.indiawaterportal.org/articles/development-flows-barrel-gun-documentary-akhra, accessed on December 16, 2018.
24. See http://patwardhan.com/?page_id=159, accessed on December 16, 2018.
25. On similar theme, Sanjay Kak's 'Words on Water' and Franny Armstrong's 'Drowned Out' merit a mention.
26. See Singhal and Rogers (2001).
27. See Joshi (1985: 35).
28. https://www.thehindu.com/opinion/open-page/open-page-the-rise-and-fall-of-television-in-india/article10559957.ece, accessed on December 16, 2018.
29. Elsewhere, Rist (1997) considered a new religion of west.
30. Kothari (1996), Constantino (1985), and Pieterse (2000, 2002).
31. This is straight away from Berger (1990).
32. It is elsewhere discussed at length with primary focus on the ethnographic field of the Maithili speaking folk. See Pathak (2018).
33. See a representative example in Aguinaga et al. (2013).
34. The emergency, clamped during the regime of the Prime Minister Indira Gandhi, is considered a turning point in the history of Indian Politics. See the account by the eminent historian Ramchandra Guha at, http://ramachandraguha.in/archives/indira-gandhi-and-the-indian-emergency-the-hindu.html, accessed on December 10, 2018.
35. See Ghosh (2006) among many others who have delved into the trajectory of post-liberalization developmentalism in India.
36. See Tilak (2007).
37. See Singh et al. (2010).
38. This resonates with Escobar (1992) criticizing the teleological scheme that undermines endogenous ways of developing. The hallmarks of the first wave of post-development theory: (1) an interest not in development alternatives, but in alternatives to development, and thus a rejection of the entire paradigm, (2) an interest in local and indigenous knowledge, (3) a critical stance toward established scientific discourses, and (4) the defense and promotion of localized, pluralistic grassroots movements.

39. See Datta and Gailey (2012).
40. See Pink (2007) and Schnettler and Raab (2008).
41. See Tschirhart (2015).
42. See Mda (1993), for example.
43. See, for example, Hansen (1992), Singh (2017), and Parameswaran (2017).
44. See, for example, Sengupta (2014) and Pathak and Chhatre (2018).
45. See Sahay (1993).
46. See Motrescu-Mayes and Banks (2018).
47. Christopher Pinney and Roma Chatterji are among the exceptional few engaging with visuals of socio-political and aesthetic significance within anthropological ambit; among others in the larger ambit of social sciences are Tapati Guha Thakurta, Sumathi Ramaswamy, Geeta Kapoor, Jagath Weerasinghe, Iftikhar Dadi, and Salima Hashmi. Interestingly, very early on in the history of sociology and social anthropology in India, a doyen sociologist Radhakamal Mukherjee wrote, *The Culture and Art of India* (Mushiram Manoharlal Publisher) in the broader South Asian context.

References

Aguinaga, Margarita et al. (2013). Development Critiques and Alternatives: A Feminist Perspective. In M. Lang & D. Mokrani (Eds.), *Beyond Development Alternative Visions from Latin America* (pp. 41–58). Quito: Rosa Luxemburg Foundation.

Alexander, J. (2011). *Performance and Power*. London: Polity.

Appadurai, A. (2006). *Fear of Small Numbers: An Essay on the Geography of Angers*. Durham and London: Duke University Press.

Bastide, R. (1971). *Anthropologie appliquée*. Paris: Payot.

Bauman, Z. (1991). *Modernity and Ambivalence*. London: Polity.

Berger, P. (1990). *Sacred Canopy: Elements of a Sociological Theory of Religion*. London: Penguin Random House.

Bharucha, R. (2014). *Terror and Performance*. London and Delhi: Routledge.

Bilgrami, A. (2014). *Secularism, Identity and Enchantment*. Ranikhet: Permanent Black.

Blank, T. J. (2009). *Folklore and the Internet: Vernacular Expression in a Digital World*. Logan: Utah State University Press.

Boserup, E. (2011). *Woman's Role in Economic Development*. London and New York: Earthscan.

Bronner, S. J. (2011). *Explaining Traditions: Folk Behavior in Modern Culture*. Kentucky: University Press of Kentucky.

Butler, J. (2015). *Notes Toward a Performative Theory of Assembly*. Harvard: Harvard University Press.

Chakrabarty, A., & Dhar, A. (2008). Development, Capitalism and Socialism: A Marxian Encounter with Rabindranath Tagore's Ideas on the Cooperative Principles. *Rethinking Marxism: A Journal of Economics, Culture and Society, 20*(3), 487–499.

Chakrabarty, A., & Dhar, A. (2010). *Dislocation and Resettlement in Development: From Third World to the World of the Third.* London: Routledge.

Chakrabarty, A., & Dhar, A. (2017). Economic Development. In D. M. Brennan, et al. (Eds.), *Routledge Handbook of Marxian Economics* (pp. 310–323). London: Routledge.

Chatterji, R. (2003). The Category of the Folk. In V. Das (Ed.), *The Oxford Indian Companion to Sociology and Social Anthropology* (pp. 567–597). Delhi: Oxford University Press.

Chomsky, N. (1999). *Profit Over People: Neoliberalism and Global Order.* New York: Seven Stories Press.

Clammer, J., & Giri, A. K. (2017). *The Aesthetics of Development.* New York: Palgrave Macmillan.

Colson, Christian (Producer) & Boyle, Danny (Director). (2008). *Slumdog Millionaire*, UK, Warner Bros Pictures.

Cowen, M. P., & Shenton, R. W. (1996). *Doctrines of Development.* London and New York: Routledge.

Datta, P. B., & Gailey, R. (2012). Empowering Women Through Social Entrepreneurship: Case Study of a Women's Cooperative in India. *Entrepreneurship: Theory and Practice, 36*(3): 569–587.

Debord, G. (2014). *The Society of the Spectacle.* Berkley: Bureau of Public Secrets.

Dohmwirth, C., & Hanisch, M. (2018). Women and Collective Action: Lessons from the Indian Dairy Cooperative Sector. *Community Development Journal, 53*(4), 675–693.

Easterly, W. (2009, October 13). *The Ideology of Development.* Retrieved from https://foreignpolicy.com/2009/10/13/the-ideology-of-development/. Accessed on December 12, 2018 at 6:30 PM.

Ghosh, M. (2006). Economic Growth and Human Development in Indian States. *Economic and Political Weekly, 41*(30), 3321–3327.

Hansen, K. (1992). *Grounds for Play: The Nautanki Theater of North India.* Berkley: University of California Press.

Harvey, D. (2010). *The Enigma of Capital: And the Crises of Capitalism.* New York: Oxford University Press.

Herath, D. (2009). The Discourse of Development: Has It Reached Maturity? *Third World Quarterly, 30*(8), 1449–1464.

Hettne, B. (1976). The Vitality of Gandhian Tradition. *Journal of Peace Research, 13*(3), 227–245.

Hettne, B. (1983). Peace and Development: Contradictions and Compatibilities. *Journal of Peace Research, 20*(4), 329–342.

Hettne, B. (1990). *Development Theory and the Three Worlds*. Harlow: Longman.
Hobsbawm E. J. (1995). *The Age of Extremes: A History of the World: 1914–1991*. London: Abacus.
Inoue, T. (2018). *Public Relations in Hyper-Globalization: Essential Relationship Management—A Japan Perspective*. London: Routledge.
Joshi, P. C. (1985). *An Indian Personality for Television: Report of the Working Group on Software on Doordarshan*. New Delhi: Ministry of Information and Broadcasting, Government of India.
Kaviraj, S. (2010). *The Enchantment of Democracy and India*. Ranikhet: Permanent Black.
Khan, M. (Producer & Director). (1957). *Mother India*, India, Mehboob Production.
Khan, A., and Rao, K. (Producer) & Rizvi, A. (Director). (2010). *Peepli Live*, India, UTV Motion Pictures.
Klein, N. (2014). *This Changes Everything: Capitalism vs. the Climate*. New York: Simon & Schuster.
Kothari, S. (1996). Whose Nation: The Displaced as Victims of Development. *Economic and Political Weekly, 31*(24), 1476–1485.
Landau, J. (Producer) & Cameron, J. (Director). (2009). *Avatar*, United States, 20th Century Fox.
Lewis, W. A. (1954). Economic Development with Unlimited Supplies of Labor. *Manchester School of Economic and Social Studies, 22*, 139–191.
Mankekar, P. (1999). *Screening Culture, Viewing Politics: An Ethnography of Television, Womanhood and Nation in Postcolonial India*. Durham and London: Duke University Press.
Margarita, A., Miriam, L., Dunia, M., & Alejandra, S. (2013). Critiques and Alternatives to Development: A Feminist Perspective. In *Beyond Development Alternative Visions from Latin America*. Amsterdam: Rosa Luxemburg Foundation.
Mda, Z. (1993). *When People Play People: Development Communication Through Theater*. Johannesburg: Witwatersrand University Press.
Mitchel, W. J. T. (1994). *Picture Theory: Essays on Verbal and Visual Representation*. Chicago: University of Chicago Press.
Motrescu-Mayes, A., & Banks, M. (Eds.). (2018). *Visual Histories of South Asia*. Delhi: Primus.
Nandy, A. (1996). *The Romance of the State and the Fate of Dissent in the Tropics*. New Delhi: Oxford University Press.
Nicholas, T. (Director). (2009). *Mine: Story of a Sacred Mountain*. Survival International.
Nussbaum, M. (2011). *Creating Capabilities: The Human Development Approach*. Cambridge, MA: Harvard University Press.
Obeyesekere, G. (2012). *The Awakened Ones: Phenomenology of Visionary Experience*. New York: Columbia University Press.

Olivier de Sardan, J.-P. (2005). *Anthropology and Development: Understanding Contemporary Social Change*. New York: Zed Books.
Parameswaran, A. (2017). *Performance and the Political: Power and Pleasure in Contemporary Kerala*. Delhi: Orient Blackswan.
Pathak, A. (2010). *Modernity, Globalization and Identity: Towards a Reflexive Quest*. Delhi: Aakar Books.
Pathak, D. (2014). Cultural Imagination of Human Development? Framing Questions in a Preliminary Quest. *International Critical Thought, 4*(4), 433–447.
Pathak, D. N. (2015). In Pursuit of the Spectacles of Success: Implications of the Dominant Rationality in the Domain of Education. *History and Sociology of South Asia, 9*(2), 126–145.
Pathak, D. N. (2018). *Living and Dying: Meanings in Maithili Folklore*. Delhi: Primus.
Pathak, D. N., & Chhatre, A. (2018). Melodramatic South Asia: In a Performative Scape. In D. N. Pathak (Ed.), *Another South Asia* (pp. 163–185). Delhi: Primus.
Pathak, D. N., & Perera, S. (Eds.). (2017). *Culture and Politics in South Asia: Performative Communication*. London: Routledge.
Patwardhan, A. (Director). (1995). *Narmada Diary*, India.
Pieterse, J. N. (2000). After Post-development. *Third World Quarterly, 21*(2), 175–191.
Pieterse, J. N. (2002). My Paradigm or Yours? Alternative Development, Post Development, Reflexive Development. *Development and Change, 29*(2), 343–373.
Pieterse, J. N. (2010). *Development Theory: Deconstructions/Reconstructions*. London: Sage.
Pink, S. (Ed.). (2007). *Visual Interventions: Applied Visual Anthropology*. New York and London: Berghahn Books.
Rai, H. (Producer) & Osten, F. (Director). (1936). *Achhut Kannya*, India.
Rajagopal, A. (2016). The Rise of Hindu Populism in India's Public Sphere. *Current History, 115*(780), 123–129.
Rist, G. (1997). *The History of Development: From Western Origins to Global Faith*. London: Zed Books.
Rodrik, D. (2011). The Globalization Paradox: Democracy and the Future of the World Economy. New York: W. W. Norton.
Sahay, K. N. (1993). *Visual Anthropology in India and Its Development*. Delhi: Gyan Books.
Schnettler, B., & Raab, J. (2008). Interpretative Visual Analysis. Developments, State of the Art and Pending Problems. *Forum: Qualitative Research, 9*(3). http://www.qualitative-research.net/index.php/fqs/article/view/1149.
Schumacher, E. F. (1973). *Small Is Beautiful: A Study of Economics as If People Mattered*. London: Vintage.
Sen, A. (2001). *Development as Freedom*. Oxford: Oxford University Press.

Sengupta, A. (Ed.). (2014). *Mapping South Asia Through Contemporary Theatre: Essays on the Theatres of India, Pakistan, Bangladesh, Nepal and Sri Lanka*. London: Palgrave Macmillan.
Shiva, V. (1988). *Staying Alive: Women, Ecology, and Development*. London: Zed Books.
Singh, L. (2017). *Raising the Curtain: Recasting Women Performers in India*. Delhi: Orient Blackswan.
Singh, M. P. (1990). The Crises of the Indian State: From Quiet Developmentalism to Noisy Democracy. *Asian Survey, 30*(8), 809–819.
Singh, R. K, Pretty, J., & Pilgrim, S. (2010). Traditional Knowledge and Biocultural Diversity: Learning from Tribal Communities for Sustainable Development in Northeast India. *Journal of Environmental Planning and Management, 53*(4), 511–533.
Singhal, A., & Rogers, E. M. (1989). Prosocial Television for Development in India. In R. E. Rice & C. Atkin (Eds.), *Public Communication Campaigns* (pp. 331–350). Newbury Park, CA: Sage.
Singhal, A., & Rogers, E. M. (2001). *India's Communication Revolution: From Bullock Carts to Cyber Marts*. New Delhi: Sage.
Smith, J. H. (2008). *Bewitching Development: Witchcraft and the Reinvention of Development in Neoliberal Kenya*. Chicago and London: University of Chicago Press.
Tilak, J. B. G. (2007). Post Elementary Education, Poverty and Development in India. *International Journal of Educational Development, 27*(4), 435–445.
Toppo, B., & Meghnath (Director). (2003). *Development Flows from the Barrel of the Gun*, India, Akhra.
Tschirhart, P. (2015). Re-imagining Poverty: A Critical Visual Analysis of the Communicative and Affective Labour of Gendered International Development Discourses. *Critical Studies in Media Communication, 32*(4), 240–255.
Visvanathan, S. (1987). From the Annals of the Laboratory State. *Alternatives, 12*(1), 37–59.
Watson, E., and West, P. (Producer) & Aronofsky, D. (Director). (2000). *Requiem for a Dream*, United States, Protozoa Pictures.
Wolf, E. R. (2010). *Europe and the People Without History*. Los Angeles: University of California Press.
Wolfe, J. (2011). Populism and Developmentalism. In T. H. Holloway (Ed.), *A Companion to Latin American History* (pp. 347–364). Oxford: Blackwell.
Worsley, P. (1984). *The Three Worlds: Culture and World Development*. Chicago: University of Chicago Press.

PART I

Discontentment and Disenchantment

CHAPTER 2

The Danger of Development Today: An Inevitable Polemic

Rabindra Ray and Amiya Kumar Das

Introduction

European civilization has always had its own internal critics, both practical and vocal. The spread of its influence, both earlier by conquest and later by imperatives of competition has bred a whole host of critics, more vocal and practical than the earlier. The chorus of voices arguing for alternatives and the realization that non-European peoples adapt to European circumstances in their own several ways is a staple of the academic consideration of the state of affairs. Meanwhile, the onward thrust of European civilizational perspectives seems to be swelling into an unstoppable tide, particularly as the affluence and comforts it affords have ignited all the hungers for a better life of those not fortunate enough to be born to such circumstances. Commercial elites and governments can do little but organize and direct

R. Ray
Department of Sociology, Delhi School of Economics,
University of Delhi, Delhi, India

A. K. Das (✉)
Department of Sociology, Tezpur University, Tezpur, India

D. N. Pathak and A. K. Das (eds.), *Investigating Developmentalism*,
https://doi.org/10.1007/978-3-030-17443-9_2

this tide in a direction that they hope will go some way towards satisfying these hungers. Most of them, of course, go about this business with a missionary zeal, tempered of late by environmental changes that most of them wish to believe are manageable. Meanwhile, the opposition to the European way of life, ferocious in its jihadi mood, turns against what it feels offended by, with a violent and utterly unreasoning passion, in the quest of an alternative Utopia, using the very European tools and exploiting all opportunities opened up by the European way of life. Critics there are, but singularly without practical and practicable alternatives.

The internal changes in the European way of life that have led to its worldwide influence are addressed under the rubric of modernity, modernism and modernization and lastly post-modernity. The vocabulary has been picked up by the Europeanized not only to describe and try to understand changes in their own way of life, influenced by the European, but also changes in their way of life which in their opinion bear kinship to what they consider its principles, and academia celebrates the variety of a plurality of modernisms spread all over the globe. Some believe, more earlier than now, that significant elements of modern Europe culture needed to be internalized by non-European people before they could be a party to the modern science and industry that has permitted the West its premier position, but the unfolding of events has shown in unequivocal terms that modern science and industry could be accommodated to the cultures of the non-Western people. Despite that, however, the material culture of the whole world has been transformed into a Western mould and even beyond the achievement of affluence, the everyday life of the non-Western people has been changed into the modern European model. Indigenizers and critics who owe allegiance to the internal critics of the European way of life chafe at the deep and widespread proliferation of European mores, but the tide seems to favour the ever deepening and widening Europeanization of the globe. If this whole process could be contained in the realm of merely discourse, it perhaps wouldn't matter too much, but the propagation of and the resistance to the European way of life involves some of the deepest human passions, and the whole is fraught with the threat and exercise of violence. In addition, the mode of production unleashed by European and Western science and technology threatens those very conditions of nature that foster human existence. At the same time, the development of the European way of life tends to threaten human spiritual, mental and even bodily well-being. But modern life access to its tryst with cataclysm charged by that most powerful of modern convictions, that of freedom wisely and sanely seems to require a superhuman and impossible collective effort, and, for the most part, preaches of restraint and continence tend to prescribe these for those other than themselves.

That so-called development should so have assumed the form of a humanity threatening disease, when the mass of humanity still labours in conditions of poverty is a paradox that only exacerbates the dilemma. To be sure, poverty and deprivation are relative phenomena, but the subsistence from nature of the relatively less civilized way of life—or what is so understood—has been rendered more and more impossible with the proliferation of the urge to civilized comforts, and within the ambit of the civilized way of life, poverty assumes dimensions that seen absolute. In addition, the burgeoning of goods and services and a sizeable section of the population who are capable of affording these renders the state of want and poverty more and more difficult to manage with a modicum of decency and dignity. The atmosphere is thick with the clamour of groups scrabbling for a place in the seam, and in alignment with the vocabulary of the civilized, the whole is cast in the rhetoric of "rights".

Development and Euro-Centrism

It was only a question of time that the colonies, with the ideas they had learned from their foreign masters, turned against the civilizing powers. But decolonization has not obviated European influence—indeed, it has only deepened it and made it more profound. The Europeanization of the globe did not end with the loss of European empire, but, in fact, only extended it. This Europeanization did not take place unhindered, but had to overcome the resistance(s) of those who preferred their own indigenous way of life. Nor did this Europeanization transfer the substance of European mores and ideas in total to the ex-colonies. Different parts of the world adapted to the European dispensation in each of their own several ways. The diversity of the world was reproduced in the diversity of Europeanization(s). In addition, people party to Europeanization interpreted their own cultures and histories in such a way as to claim modernity for their own indigenous developments which had little to do with Europe, but to the mind of those party to Europeanization encoded its principles or essence(s) (Bock 2009). A vocabulary of modernity developed, earlier as a euphemism for Europeanization, and latterly as a discourse of plural modernities, in keeping with those who saw Europeanist essences in their own independent and indigenous cultures and histories. But almost unanimously, machine industry and the trade practices that went with it were welcomed all over the globe. This came to be called development, though people enamoured of the Western way of life included in the term development, significant aspects of European mores and culture. True enough, machine industry and the science and technology that go with it can hardly be isolated from aspects of European culture in which they are imbedded, though there may be dispute as to what is essential to the transfer of the material culture of the West to the rest. There is a whole spectrum of degrees in the partisanship with the European way of life. The promise of affluence that goes with machine industry and the aspects of the European culture that go with it makes the formula of development almost near universally acceptable, but at a time when the culture of machine industry and the trade practices that go with it are threatening the very existence of humanity.

Development has developed into an unstoppable tide, letting loose all the appetites for an affluent and still more affluent life. Contentment and satisfaction are rare. The Occidental power and affluence dazzle, holding the promise of greater and greater wealth to the non-European peoples. The West is not only the most powerful and wealthy, but it promises a wealth of opportunity for those not as fortunately endowed. The non-European peoples see the secret of Occidental well-being, to be sure in science and technology, but also variably in (aspects of) European mores and values. This is entirely in keeping with the fact that the idiom of a global interchange is dictated by conformity to Western requirements.

The mention of privilege amongst those privileged enough to enjoy and contribute to the benefits of civilization is politically a taboo, and the upholders of the civilized benefits speak in an egalitarian tongue, supported by the very circumstances of such speech. In the outcry against hierarchies not native to the European mould of civilization, it has come to be considered that they are inhuman or dehumanizing. Where privilege does not strike a humanist pose, it is considered inimical to humanitarianism, and an unwarrantable usurpation of the rights of those excluded from the charmed circle of those deserving a sympathetic hearing. There is a yawning gap between the rhetoric of the discourse of the civilized and the practices to which such civilization is party. Like poverty, development is a relative phenomenon. There is no final point, no final goal of development, expect it to be decline, decay and death. With each step of development, the horizon of development recedes a step (Matthews 2004). Perpetually striving, always trying, that is the human lot, and always wanting and wanting more and more are the relentless pursuit of development. No one has enough, until they call a halt to appetite. But though related fundamentally to wealth, development in our times is not restricted to affluence. We have invented for ourselves a humanist twist to the affluence of development, a human development index that concerns culture, education, health, the relation between the sexes and (perhaps most of all) freedom. True enough, none of these is entirely reducible to wealth or of the same species as wealth. Learning, culture, the relation between the sexes, and the degree of freedom are hardly governed by the accumulation of wealth. Yet with wealth comes the desire to be included in the culturally superior. Affluence seeks the inclusion into the cultured, if only taste in articles of consumption. However, contemporary democracy in marks of taste reduces refinement to entertainment and learning to its efficacy in the market place. Still, the difference between the knowledgeable and the uncouth shows in the ways in which people conduct themselves and especially in human relations and aesthetic judgment (Bourdieu 1984).

There is much in the world that cannot be bought, and some of these are included in the current indices of development. But this also does not take away from the fact that development is the accumulation of wealth. And there is no gain saying the necessity and importance of a modicum of wealth in the acquisition of aspects of being cultured. But civilization and civil behaviour do not rest exclusively on wealth (Ferguson 2011). As civilized life makes greater and greater inroads into relations hitherto considered natural or personal, it does so either with a missionary proselytising proclamation of rights or an appeal to an emancipation rooted in a conviction of progress. As governance invades the private lives of individuals, it does so at the behest of the individuals themselves or in the name of the welfare and protection of these individuals. Almost as if by default, societies come to resemble more and more the totalitarian regimes that marked the Utopian thrust of the twentieth century. Of course, to be civilized in any significant sense of the term demands a degree of self-control and self-regulation that is close to being total. But the enforcement of such a regime by a regulatory authority that arrogates to itself the mission of civilizing those whom it considers not civilized enough cannot but be an imposition against which those who consider themselves its victims are bound to raise an outcry and struggle with the same missionary zeal and violence as the civilizing power. But, as societies grow more and more organized, the room for dissent shrinks except in the very organized forms against which they seem to be resisting. The intolerance of ruling powers is by now an established academic theme, but the intolerance of dissent is usually outside the purview of those who should know better.

Dissent occupies an ambivalent place in the logic of development. Originally, the dissent of Protestants in Europe has been carried into existing democracies without losing the favour and intensity it had in the original protestant sects. Likewise, the opposition to dissent, of which totalitarianism is the most extreme expression, borrows from the very dissent it contests, the original missionary favour and zeal. It needs to be mentioned here that the most totalitarian regimes subscribe to some dissenting ideology, found in their persecution of dissent with dissent. Yet, in the general run of affairs, dissent is considered as integral and necessary part of a healthy democracy, albeit democracy also includes outright opposition to and suppression of dissent, which the dissenting party attempts to exterminate. Dissent with development takes a whole variety of forms, from vocal agitation to violent confrontation. But, for the most part, dissent with development is a minority phenomenon and development itself an unstoppable tide, heavy with the threat of climate change, global warming and intensive conflict.

Modernity as understood by many like Jurgen Habermas and Charles Taylor is exclusively a European phenomenon. It is seen in affirmation as a fundamental source for emancipation. This gestation of medieval Europe being considered as the epicentre of modernity reflected in the carving of the periphery, devoid of creative activities and the focus on Europe in conquering and exploring the world that gave them the spitting image of modernity (Dussel 1995). In his central thesis, Dussel critically engages with this centrality of Europe as the origin of modernity and tries to establish modernity as an European phenomena but in a dialectical relation with a non-European alterity that is its ultimate content. This revelation of the myth of "origin" is constituted as the "myth of modernity" by Dussel.

The emancipatory nature of modernity is put under scrutiny by the post-modernists. The disenfranchisement of the relentless growth that the development process embodied in the process of modernity have led to a discourse beyond the emancipatory nature of modernity. There is a transcendence to engage with the consequences that the myth of modernity encompasses, the genocidal violence it endorses and reason of terror it augments (Dussel 1995). In doing so, the Euro-centrism of the modernity project is connected to the "fallacy of developmentalism". In simple words, it refers to the thinking that all other cultures need to follow unilaterally the European project of modernity. Thus, development is not seen as an economic or social category but rather as an ontological reality. Here occurs the subjugation of all cultures to the inevitable process of development. This entire process of movement of World History from the West to the East, leads to the creation of peripheries such as Latin America and Africa which alike Asia, is seen in a state of "immaturity". In understanding the dialectics and the subaltern discourse that decry the modernist project and development process per se needs to be seen in the light of the victims facing the genocidal wrath of the civilizing force. These victims might be embodied in slaves, the colonized, the women and the ecological destruction of the Earth. But what needs to be recognized is the singular global history that Euro-centrism seems to reflect, crushing and glossing over the non-European cultures and thriving for a quest of "newness" (Dussel 1995).

This exteriorization of newness was seen to be congruent to a blind faith in science, and science to be a sordid veneer of modernity (Quijano and Wallerstein 1992). Thus, this pattern of newness was applied with urgency and came to be seen as the new model of development for the world. The sole responsibility and mandate of power of this process of development were bestowed as the reigns of the Westerners. Thus, the experimental method central to science was not to be seen as a strategy of political control alone. The laboratory became a basis for the vision of society as well. Herein began the genocidal violence of modern science, that of vivisection. The scientific projects sought to endeavour expansion in areas of health, technology, medicine, etc. Progress and modernization legitimated violence, and the gaze of such violence was directed to the peripheral cultures dominant in the third world countries as objects of experimentation (Visvanathan 1997).

The attainment of the modernity project was twofold for the third world countries. It occurred not only through Westernization and science, but also at the hands of the elites who had a modernist approach, at the time of Independence. In other words, the newly independent nation-states viewed science as celebration to the threshold of modernity. Additionally, the nation-state cannot permit ethnicities that have a different world view which would otherwise serve as a contender for power. This manufactured a legitimacy for a society of equal and uniform individuals cementing the contract between the state and science (Visvanathan 1997). Following the Western model of development massive infrastructural projects as dams, railways were a commitment to the process of development. Intolerance of entities in this path was a sub-stratum. People like the peasants, tribal, the nomad who consisted of different traditions and cosmologies in the third world were seen as refractory to science. In accordance with the laboratory state, the rituals of tribalism and traditional farming need to be accultured or thwarted (Visvanathan 1997). This forceful separation of the marginal people from their means of subsistence marginalized them further.

The chapter does not attempt to provide a historical elaboration of the evolution of modern science and its repercussions in the peripheral countries. Rather, it tries to discuss the contemporary issues that the mismatch in the laboratory spills onto our society. In this vein, Ulrich Beck (1992) discusses the agonizing scepticism the rational modernist project entails. He maintains that in the classical industrial society, the logic and production of wealth dominates the logic of risk production. However, in a risk society, the relationship is reversed. The productive forces have lost their innocence in the reflexivity of the "modernization process". In the initial stages, the errors of science culminated into "latent side-effects". But as they become globalized, and it seems to be a regular pattern across the world, scientific investigation comes under the scrutiny of public criticism and achieves a central importance in political and social discourses. This emulsifies as the logic of risk production and distribution to the logic of the distribution of the wealth. Risk spills across the concrete borders of nation-states which are not class specific; and thus, these global hazards attain a new dynamic image of uncertainty (Beck 1992). This deterioration of society into an apprehensive society of risk does not, however, have a particular definition. But its outlines are clear in aetiologies like climate change, violence, terrorism, technology, and natural disasters.

Zygmunt Bauman talks of the consumer society responsible for risks that are beyond the control. In "Liquid modernity" (2011), Bauman delineates the classical industrial society and late modernity in terms of concrete structures in the former stage and inconsistent structures in the latter. According to him, risk embodies uncertainty, unexpectedness of outcomes, losses devoid of social security and safety. In this sense, Bauman remarks "Freedom is always linked to the necessity of compromise. Absolute freedom which at the same time reconciles both sides is impossible. Freedom is a paradox" (Bauman 2011). Without discrediting the liberating effects that the modernity project upholds, yet the idea of "freedom" that was the modus operandi of transforming the market has fizzled out as a guiding force. The consequences of modernity and its imprint on the environment are taking a toll on the masses in the margins. Henceforth, to reiterate in the wisdom of Ulrich Beck, the consequences are of "boomerang effects".

In simple words, this effect strikes back precisely those nations which had hoped to get rid of hazards by transferring them overseas, transforming the peripheral countries to be the breeding ground for international contamination (Beck 1992). In contemporary times, when the pursuit of science has failed, which is evident in the pattern of environmental disasters across the globe, the irony is that the endeavours of the state are still concentrated around science and its experimental method. The discourse of post-developmental studies has cried hoarse of the bankruptcy of the idea of development, but the debate comes to a halt in finding an alternative. Still the entire theory might not be rejected and need to be given credit for bringing onto the table, the violence that development and European modernizing project have entailed. The pursuit is of the alternative definition of development or alternative to development.

Development Paradox in India

Indian nationalism had, from the very beginning, ambivalent attitudes to Europeanism and modernism. While on the one hand they wished to enjoy the benefits of modern European civilization, of course, with the notable exception of M. K. Gandhi, on the other hand they wished to retain their Independence of it and to exercise discrimination in what they accepted and what they rejected. While on the one hand they were relatively open to science and its benefits, they were much more guarded in trying to preserve their own spiritual heritage and to develop it. In a summary, their attitude to modern and European thinking reflects that they wished to embrace its spiritual and artistic heritage. European sciences embedded in European culture and its spirit and the Indians, particularly Jawaharlal Nehru, hankered for a scientific temper, a spirit of science that could fire the scientific imagination. Of course, there are those who believe that Indian culture and its heritage already possess these and that ancient Indian culture is the mother of all the modern European arts and sciences, in addition to providing arts and science not available to European modernity and in some cases rejected by it. In almost all world cultures, including parts of Europe to which the Industrial Revolution and the accompanying culture of freedom of thought and expression are not native, there is a contest between indigenous nativizers and world-embracing modern Europeanizing civilizers. Nothing is or can be affected except as an outcome of this conflict of these cultures and the attempt of most of those party to this conflict to eat one's cake and have it too.

The basic adoption of this reductionist approach of knowledge as total social reality was divorced from the persistence of other forms of knowledge. This atomistic perspective of development confronted the other forms of cosmologies. The conflict that arises from the hegemony of Euro-centric notion of modernity emulsifies in aspects as elaborated in the following way: the liberation of social life tied from fixed identities that were sustained by suppression and violence, in pre-modern European society, sought emancipation through a different social and political power. This was embedded in social relations of capital and urban life. It emulsifies in the material context as well as in inter-subjective manner that was seen as a relation between the subject and its purpose for something (Quijano 2007).

In today's perspective, the muddle that emerges from this understanding, in terms of knowledge, is inadequate. Material life and property that were a consequence of colonialism were a relation between individuals for the purpose of something. The same mental mechanism was applied to "knowledge" as an inter-subjective manner and not as an inter-subjective relationship as was recognized in non-European cultures (Quijano 2007). It becomes more transparent in contemporary times when these domination practices are harbouring widening gaps of poverty, discrimination and exclusion for the subjects of this European rationality. Post-modern thinkers and post-development theory are a polemic to the totalizing and objectifying "subjects" outside the European context.

In provincializing Europe, Dipesh Chakraborty (2000) argues that the concepts introduced in relation to political modernity exemplified in contemporary understanding of democracy, state, the subject, individual and the public sphere. It is erroneous, he argues, to take these concepts in face value and employ the same to all cultures as the former centres their understanding in Europe as the sole subject. Such strands of perspectives ask us to debunk and decolonize the imported version of rationality and the cultural complex of "development" it bears. The economic change that ensued in Europe under capitalist growth reflected an "uneven and combined development" presumed expansion in linearity and uniformity. In simple words, the pursuit of developmental activities changed some areas more rapidly and created uneven inequality where none existed earlier. But it cannot be reduced to such linear simplicity. It paved the way to think critically about the idea of "regionality" and diversity in colonial and post-colonial India. Problematizing the colonial concept of "nation", Sudipta Kaviraj problematized the presumption of an unvaried identity across a spatial region like India. He highlights three processes viz. generalization, fragmentation and composition (Kaviraj 2017).

Regionality seems to encompass the political, cultural and economic forces and regions seems to be a consequence of the same. Establishing manufacturing industries, activities accruing to infrastructural expansion, dependence on agricultural lands for raw materials, demand for labour force created a novel inter-dependence and inequality in terms of income, opportunities and regional power (Kaviraj 2017). This unequal expansion of industrial development in particular regions, that catered to the needs of the colonial rulers, was arbitrary. The repercussion was an unequal development in different parts of colonial India. There was also an influx of migrants as labour to these industrial regions. This economic diversity and inequality shaped regionality which had deep political ramification. Sudipta Kaviraj (2017), historicizing this phenomenon, argued that these "modern" regions with the touch of modernity blessed by colonialism did not get eradicated after Independence. It rather got overwritten. In post-colonial context, as there was a change in overcoats from colonizers to the modern state, the relationship between the states and populations witnessed alteration that was not possible in earlier stages of history.

Post-Independence, the industrialization programmes enacted under the Nehruvian planning focused on installing heavy industries in backward areas. This was planned in agricultural areas that were hinterlands and source of livelihood in areas like Bihar, Madhya Pradesh and Orissa. Uncritical presumption was that massive industrialization would locate these regions on the plane of development. But it narrowed down to provide opportunities to people with professional degrees from different regions while the former mentioned regions had to be content with small structural benefits from the changing economy. The imagination of a singular and grand nation that would strive its path to rationality under the cultural complex of development processes was further punctuated when regions were broken down according to linguistic regionality. The breaking down of Bombay to Maharashtra and Gujarat is a prime example of the same. North-eastern states Mizoram and Arunachal Pradesh also followed the same logic (Kaviraj 2017). In a phase of liberalization, after the 1990s, the State government received a new lease to formulate policies that could attract FDIs by providing tax incentives. Some states like Gujarat and Andhra Pradesh fared well under their political leadership. These policies further accentuated regional diversities as private capital would flow to newer hubs with basic infrastructural capacities. Development driven by market, investment and growth necessitated a pre-requisite in terms of basic infrastructure rather than invest in the same (Kaviraj 2017).

Henceforth, it is not too early to reiterate that the singular and homogenous subjectivities that European modernity and rationality presumed across non-Western cultures are hollow. The kind of dispositions, regionalities in India, is a testimony to the same. The development strategies and initiatives that have been employed on the basis of regions in India is exemplary. As for instance in North-east India, development has been always security-centric. Chhattisgarh seems to have a "resource curse" as its government continues unabated mining, while the promises of social development have still not been delivered. In such contexts, development has been a dystopia that needs to be debunked and an alternative discourse needs to be mediated.

In any case, even the attitude of the European thinkers who welcome modernity and see the possibility of an unprecedented Utopia is usually also ambivalent. Most Westerners see modernity as inevitable and consider the mark of history, with a capital as inevitably progressive, and regard the contestation of its inevitable progress as retrogressive and reactionary. Modernity in Europe lives as a millennial doctrine of hope and progress. But a significant section of European thinkers who engage more deeply with the question is pessimistic and either feels that humankind cannot be improved or that in spite of whatever benefits modernity may bring, things are not getting better, but actively worse. Even those who welcome modernity sees deep and glaring ill-effects about the avoidance of which they remain divided. Post-modernity has added to the ill-effects of modernity, its imperialist intolerant trust, and though they still seem to regard modern views and the modern social configuration as an enlightenment, they tend to question its deployment in an anti-humanist and anti-humanitarian cause, privileging the West.

Modernity and development institute their own traditions at odds with the inherited culture. This makes for considerable friction, potent with the threat of violence, internal and international. As the edifice of sociality and normativity is dismantled and changed, society begins to dissolve into war of each against each, each against all and all against all. The fragmentation of society goes hand in hand with coerced ideological movements trying to build collectives based on inverted principles. This affects not only the outward behaviour of individuals but also distorts the very personality of those party to it. The force deployed against others has its personal complement in the leaching of aesthetic judgement to a morality of principle.

Whether *Satyagraha* is any defence against such intolerance remains to be seen when the suspect is, that the *satyagrahi* personality is itself party to such intolerance. The atmosphere is heavy with the threat of aggression and conflict.

Despite the Europeanization of the globe, it is not that the other civilizational tendencies have been obviated. But, contemporarily in scholarship, the highly influential argument of the hybridity of cultures, though hardly denying the presence of non-European civilizational tendencies, implies that the independent existence of these can only appear in an insightful analysis or when the defenders of non-European tendencies adopt an independent confrontationist attitude. And what the argument of hybridity is oriented to contesting the autonomous existence of a plurality of cultures and civilizational tendencies cannot be ruled out by mere argument of hybridity, for even if only hybrids appear, these hybrids are hybrids because they contain the mixture of civilizational tendencies other than the European, and the original European culture itself is threatened by the invasion of the non-European streams. In other words, hybrids are hybrids precisely because world consists of the intertwining of separate civilizational streams. What the argument of hybridity is assumed to argue—the non-existence of pure types and the relative homogenization of a unitary world culture cannot be sustained by the conviction of hybridity; rather, the reverse that the hybridity of cultures avows the intertwining of different, separate and distinct streams of making meaning of the world.

Conclusion

Indian civilization and its ideas and practices are perhaps one the oldest surviving, living cultures. Its Europeanization has been deep and far reaching and what is more, a deliberate intention of aspects of the republican ethos. But even if the European phenomenon in its singularity is not unavailable in India, it has only partly influenced much of the life in India and has even left sections of it untouched. Hybridity entails the co-existence of separate streams and that mutual influence of each upon the other. And though development is understood in its European and Europeanist provenance, the Indian tradition, too, is party to a development and not without influence on the European and Europeanist stream. While the educational programmes of the republic are highly Europeanized, hybridity and the autonomous and independent study of the Indian phenomenon can hardly be escaped. Outside the republican framework and its programmes, in popular culture and the educational effort of those committed to an Indianness, the traditional culture of the sub-continent flourishes and has swayed. There is always a divide between the educated and the not so educated, even in the West, but in India, the divide is a veritable chasm, and confrontationists can have a field day in counter-posing the two. True, the development of even the indigenous tendency is partly or even deeply influenced by European developments both in India and in Europe, but to the willing disciple, the civilizational thrust of the Indic heritage is not unavailable. European thinkers and Western scholars also have tried to study and understand this heritage, and indeed, some of them exceedingly insightfully and sympathetically, but, by and large, there remains a gap between Western and indigenous interpretations and practices. In addition, there is no paucity of Westerners who have viewed the Indic heritage unsympathetically and distorted and vilified its currency. These, too, have their Indian disciples, and for the most part, this is a significant section of the study of the tradition in America.

Political economy, which seeks to claim independent existence and to unlock the sectors of development and to guide it, is itself imbedded in culture and moulded by it. There are almost so many cultures as there are peoples, and development varies significantly over the range of peoples. Governments must cope with their own individual peoples and circumstances in trying to ride the mad scramble for wealth. In addition, inter-governmental relations, while each trying to gain as much from their exchanges as possible, are in a nexus of normativity which is hardly uniform. Though the occident occupies pride of place in dictating terms, its position is not unchallenged, and what the occident considers acceptable behaviour is not necessarily universally acknowledged. At the same time, the occident itself is hardly a non-partisan observer. Yet there is more to conflict and confrontation than merely naked self-interest. In any war, both wealth and normativity are at stake. As the cold war recedes, the pluralities are glossed over and concealed come more and more to the fore, when the institutions established to cope with international circumstances are still guided by the prejudice of a bi-polar world. As to whether institutions can effectively contain the diversity of voices in a moot point when the volume of information available has already outstripped manageable proportions. Where is the world heading?

References

Bauman, Z. (2011). *Liquid Modernity*. Cambridge: Polity Press.

Beck, U. (1992). *Risk Society: Towards a New Modernity*. London: Sage.

Bock, K. E. (2009). Comparisons of Histories: The Contribution of Henry Maine. *Comparative Studies in Society and History, 16*(2), 232–262.

Bourdieu, P. (1984). *Distinction: A Social Critique of the Judgement of Taste*. London: Routledge.

Chakrabarty, D. (2000). *Provincializing Europe: Postcolonial Thought and Historical Difference*. Princeton, NJ: Princeton University Press.

Dussel, E. (1995). Eurocentrism and Modernity (Introduction to the Frankfurt Lectures). In J. Beverley, J. Oviedo, & M. Aronn (Eds.), *The Postmodernism Debate in Latin America*. Durham, NC: Duke University Press.

Ferguson, N. (2011). *Civilization: The West and the Rest*. London: Allen Lane.

Kaviraj, S. (2017). Three Planes of Space. *Economic and Political Weekly, 52*(46), 56–63.

Matthews, S. (2004). Post-development Theory and the Question of Alternatives: A View from Africa. *Third World Quarterly., 25*(2), 373–384.

Quijano, A. (2007). Coloniality and Modernity/Rationality. *Cultural Studies, 21*(2), 168–178.

Quijano, A., & Wallerstein, I. (1992). Americanity as a Concept, or the Americas in the Modern World-System. *International Social Science Journal, 44*(4), 549–557.

Visvanathan, S. (1997). *A Carnival for Science: Essays on Science, Technology and Development*. New Delhi: Oxford University Press.

CHAPTER 3

The Enchantment of Urbanization: Closer Look at Market's Narrative in Indian Cities

Yugank Goyal

Introduction

Francis Fukuyama in his book, *Origins of Political Order* paints a picture of Melanesian society, inhabiting in the Pacific in several hundreds of tiny islands (Fukuyama 2011: i). The group is unbelievably diverse. There are more than 1300 languages—one language per 716 sq. km. For instance, the Solomon island group has a population of 523,000 and has distinct 74 languages! Even though English is the official language, hardly 2% of the population speaks it. These islands have been inhabited—by some estimates—for more than 30,000 years. The existing socio-political framework was relational and community driven. The tribes—for centuries—had hunted for their own tribespeople and had a community leader, called the 'Big Man,' responsible for gathering and sharing of the bounty for his tribe. Without redistribution in his tribe, the Big Man would lose his status.

Now, when British troops left the islands, they installed their Westminster style governments in these islands. The British-installed concept of electing a leader that would govern everyone in the group of islands

Y. Goyal (✉)
O.P. Jindal Global University, Sonipat, Haryana, India

D. N. Pathak and A. K. Das (eds.), *Investigating Developmentalism*,
https://doi.org/10.1007/978-3-030-17443-9_3

was totally unheard of. It led to a chaos. The democratic models of the West were an utter disaster in the islands, with enormous political turmoil and instances of rent seeking (Reilly 2002; May 2003; Nelson 2003). What Westerners view as rampant corruption is basically what the Big Men have always been doing there—'to redistribute resources to their kinsmen,' which now instead of pigs and shells are revenues of mining companies (Fukuyama 2011: iii).

If the example appears to be a bit too extreme, it reflects the pressure with which the immutability of modernity's development has occupied our minds. The vocabulary of development is phasing out words of and about nonhuman, while adding a number of technological terminologies in this expanding lexicon. Concerns of society get subsumed as a synonym of design and economy, while those of natural enchantment become buried in scientific thesaurus. Indeed, literature itself is a crucible in which modernity is getting crystallized, and this makes its advent, a real one. For where if not in fiction, should we expect magic and freaky to happen. Ghosh (2016) effortlessly puts us to think, how the exceptional, the unusual and the miraculous, which played such a central role in premodern literature, have been replaced in the modern novel by realist depictions of 'the routine.' For instance, even though climate change is one of the most ominous challenges humanity faces today, it has not been able to capture, in any profound way, the imaginations of fiction writers of our century. The modern era was marked by a process of 'normalization,' of knocking out anything (climactically) exceptional, whether from literature or from our minds. Natural events are freakish, not part of the 'regularity of bourgeois life,' which we have lodged comfortably outside the realm of our imagination (Goyal 2016).

Enchantment then, has simply shifted sides. While nature was an enchanting source for us for millennia, it is development today. Development, as it sits on the other side of nature. On the side of bullet trains and Wi-Fi. This shift took place through economics, as a philosophical science. The subject led to a resurgence of all things material, and in doing so, the market.

Development's link to enchantment is made through modernity. Modernity's emergence, in Latour's (1991) classic work, is the site of distinction between nature and culture. Saler's (2006) review builds this design of distinction in historiography. He says that since modernity is viewed as rise of disenchantment, we now witness that '*wonders and marvels have been demystified by science, spirituality has been supplanted by secular-*

***ism, spontaneity has been replaced by bureaucratization, and the imagination has been subordinated to instrumental reason.*'** No wonder then, that literature invokes the concept of enchantment when talking about nature, read environment. Agrawal and Gibson (1999) use the term of enchantment to title their research, which reminds the rising importance of communities in natural resource conservation, and also to revise it. Other types of examples abound as well. Poignantly visible is the idiom of development in a growing interest of tourists in Nepal to volunteer, which, Hindman (2014) finds embedded in the economic disparity between Nepal and the home countries of tourists.

Scholars contend that the age of enchantment is over with modernity. Everything is science, and therefore, there is nothing to be felt wondrous or magical about. Modernity gave us a particular trajectory of development, which is linear, Western and so-called scientific (Ghosh 2016). Very clearly, the idea of enchantment is the idea of wonder.

Let's flip this upside down. What do we consider wonderful, then? Or feel enchanted with? While nature enchanted us earlier, today, its science. Its progress. Its development. We fail to apply our own 'modern' disenchanted ways of seeing, to the existing linear narratives we are suspended within. Because science has enchanted us. And nowhere is this enchantment more visible than in development's most prominent poster-child, urbanization (UN Habitat 2016; Beall et al. 2010).

Pyyry's (2016) formulation of learning through the experience of enchantment is a useful metaphor here. It is, she says, adopted as a process of thinking, which, in turn, relies on 'multisensory engagements with one's surroundings'. Using an experience of photo-walks in the city of Helsinki, she portrays the importance of sensory encounters crucial in re-cognizing the world. This is exactly how development, through urbanization makes us learn about itself. We see, we hear and we feel. And we get enchanted with it. Bimal Roy's 1953 classic Bollywood movie, *Do Bigha Zamin*, illustrates this most vividly in a neo-realist setting. Pushed to repay his debt, Shambhu comes to Calcutta. The scene 'enchants' Shambhu and his son. The promise of earning money and returning to the village in three months becomes a much longer and punishing ordeal for the family. The city sucks them in, recalibrates their moral compass and performs its specter of grandness continuously. The hard and wretchedness of the city surfaces from time to time, but its enchantment never goes.

McKinnon's book (2011) displays the Western models of development in shaping and reshaping cities and urban spaces in Asia. UN Habitat's

(2016) Report reminds us of the unstoppable force of urbanization spreading in all of developing countries. These are manifestly the market-led development reforms and have become the triggers to view urbanization's unrestricted acceptance, a form of wonder, an enchantment for development and for market. The chapter uses the example of urbanization in India to excavate the silences buried in market-led design of development. The rest of the chapter is divided as follows. In part 2, we elaborate on the case of India and evaluate the type of growth taking place here, with a special emphasis on its influence on urban centers, and particularly the megacities which are sites of extreme depravation. Connecting urbanization with development and development with markets in part 3, we demonstrate the need to allay our excitement with existing focus on markets in the way understood in Walrasian lens. We show why markets may not work, and the extent to which this is now getting understood in the literature. Part 4 envisions the future and connects the arguments. Part 5 concludes.

Urbanization as the Idiom of Development

India, home to more than 1.2 billion people, in recent years has captured the attention of global media interested in emerging economies. More than anything, it definitely emerges as a bundle of contradictions. With world's third highest GDP by purchasing power parity, it houses 20% of the world's poorest. It has a strange distinction of being the country with one of the highest growth rates in last decade while being one of the only three countries in the world where the Global Hunger Index went up since independence (presently India is 15th most hungry nations). The emerging economic giant has more than 90% of its workforce in informal sector suffering from enormous vulnerability and justice system is crippled with 30 million cases pending in the courts. It has one of the highest growth rates in billionaires and continues to have more than 400 million living on less than $1.25 a day.

Last two decades have been monumental in Indian economic history. Post-colonial India has never seen the amount of wealth that it witnesses now. Average income has increased, and by some estimates, net poverty, and unemployment has declined. Yet, richest 1% of India held approximately half of India's wealth in 2010. In year 2000, this figure was 37%. Contrast this with richest 1% of the world. Their share in 2000 was 48%, which declined to 44% in ten years. Last two decades therefore were not only monumental, but also tumultuous.

We focus here on urban (crippling) infrastructure of India, where woes are not very different from the urban landscape of other emerging economies. One-third Indians today live in cities, producing two-thirds of GDP. The growth pattern in India reveals the concentration of wealth generation only in major cities of the country. At the same time, over 300 million live in metropolitan areas facing acute pressure in the process of constant negotiation they undertake for securing basic public utilities, services and safety. Cities therefore become the unique site to enter the discourse on what *kind* of growth is India witnessing. During the last century, share of population of cities with a million or more people has gone up from a quarter to three-quarters, while that of towns with less than 20,000 people dropped from half to 10%. But the growth in urbanization during last decade has been phenomenal. This was also a conscious effort of the State, evinced in the 12th Five Year Plan Report.

If one pries open the black box of urbanization, one finds acute pressures on unequal society, catapulting serious distributive concerns. At multiple levels, city life has become symptomatic of India's capitalism. But it is also indicative of how capitalism and liberalization has influenced cities more than anything else. A characteristic growth pattern is concentration of growth in major cities of the country. By 1995, India's GDP was shared evenly by rural and urban regions of the country. By 2008, urban centers were responsible for 58% of the GDP; and this is expected to rise to 70% in next fifteen years (Dobbs et al. 2012).

The spatial and temporal existence of a city in India remains afloat over an underlying misery of acute pressure of infrastructure and justice. If we look at average statistic of a typical city it is appalling. Recent data suggest that water supply is available for 2.9 hours a day in cities. About a third to half of households does not have sewerage connection, and the cities find it hard to treat more than just 20% of wastewater. Almost 60% had to share water at a public space. Waste generation in cities in India is rising at 13% per annum. A quarter defecates in the open. The cities are fertile ground for breeding severe forms of inequality, with access to basic services, rights and justice reserved for those who have larger bargaining power by virtue of their initial entitlements.

Consider the ten largest cities of India.[1] Indian GDP is $2.3 trillion. Of this, a staggering 40% (almost) comes from these cities. Mumbai alone accounts for close to 10%, and with Delhi, Kolkata, and Bangalore a quarter of the GDP is contributed by the four cities. Not surprisingly, these ten (and few more) GDP powerhouses are social experiments in their own right.

During last two decades, Mumbai's population has swelled to almost by 50% its size and Delhi's by 70%. These numbers conceal behind them, the horrors of everyday life for a migrant who comes in hopes of a better future, only to realize the city has little to offer. Daunted, but bereft of all savings, the migrant negotiates her space in the city and with growing demand gets absorbed. This process of absorption is the source of a growth that remains far from inclusive.

The large labor force is amalgamated in the city's everyday life. This takes place through livelihood impetus of migrant (and other) workers more than the state facilitated exercise of ensuring employment. State's ignorance to development imperatives leads to a situation where all the surplus labor force is absorbed in the informal sector. Entrepreneur of rising India as the man behind a tech-start-up is only a tiny fraction of the picture which constructs popular imagination. 'Rising' India is beset with millions of informal workers who are toiling hard to make their ends meet, as unglorified entrepreneurs, existing outside the regulatory net. While the informal economy functions as an important safeguard against low employment in the formal sector and against forces of impoverishment, this modicum of security comes at the price of pervading injustice, labor vulnerability and low-income trap. In addition, the existence of the informal economy also tends to undermine the respect citizens have for the government, thus contributing to weakening systems of law and governance.

Consider housing. The acute pressure on space conflicts with the desperate measures to secure livelihood. The result of the confrontation is settlements which the law of the land quickly labels as irregular and illegal. Mumbai by now, houses its 60% population in informal housings or slums, which cover only 6–8% of city's land area. Delhi's slum population is around 20%, and Ghertner (2008) suggests that virtually all of Delhi violates some form of planning or building law. No drive around these (and other) cities is complete without witnessing even pavement dwellers—hundreds and thousands of first-generation migrants living on the pavement and footpath by the roads. Poverty and deprivation are right on your face.

Informality (livelihood or housing) is a characteristic feature of Indian cities, and consequently, its growth pattern. The crucial link between high-rise buildings exhuming grandeur and the *chawls* and tiny squatters lined up behind a vegetable market is the informality. In some sense, therefore, there is no reason to believe that the problems of growth in India are a problem of legal performativity of informality. Roy (2009) captures these sentiments by declaring that India cannot plan its cities and focuses on planning failure owing to its informality (and insurgence). She helps us arrive at a point where it is easy to view the distinction between planning for growth and planning for resources, emphasizing why latter needs to be the focus—and which has hardly been. This management of resources needs to be done through '*dynamic processes of informality.*'

Ghertner (2008) delves deeper into slums as a concept in legal imagination and undertakes a discursive analysis to cull out what does slum and sum eviction stand for, for the judiciary, and consequently the State. A certain kind of anti-poor judicial orientation is better understood as a neoliberal bias within the judiciary. Illegality of slums is a recent juridical invention, inspired by laws of nuisance in India. Ghertner shows how the idea of nuisance is aesthetic in character, reflecting the preferences of the elite in a post-colonial city of Delhi. In the name of public interest and beautification, he shows how 'Indian cities' embourgeoisement is taking place not through a simple assertion of elite power, but rather through the more subtle production of a new aesthetic ordering of 'the public' and its 'proper' uses (Ghertner 2008).

It is important to observe the underlying pattern in this growth trajectory. The lines between legal and extra-legal are blurred. The schisms between haves and have-nots gaped wider. GDP kept on increasing. The hope, and perhaps sincere hope, was that opening the markets was a self-correcting mechanism and the good old trickling down will happen. Where will the wealth go? It has to—as science suggests—flow and spill over. But unfortunately, this didn't happen *at all.* A 100 kilometer (100 kilometer is a small distance in India) drive outside the border of these chaotic mega-cities will seem like a travel backwards in time. Even within cities, the gated communities and ghettoization is so normal that the acquired vocabulary for expressing the different regions of the city do not even come across as divisionary. The neoclassical imaginary helped us expect a better world, and when it has gone bad, now expects us to embrace the world so created.

Of special importance here is to appreciate whatever happened to the idea of markets and institutions. The growth of cities was expected to follow a framework defined by neoclassical variables. Institutional determinants being crucial, they were pushed through at massive rate. What was ignored, however, was the initial endowment in the regions and what kinds of institutions prevailed. They intensified their presence, exacerbated market failures and assured the rise of elites, at the expense of non-elites.

McKinsey Global Institute's Research (2012) shows the heaviness in the future of this growth pattern. There are 42 cities in India with a population of 1 million and above. This number is set to rise to 68 by 2030. During next fifteen years, 70% of new employment will be in cities. To meet the demand, India would need $1.2 trillion capital investment (this is almost half of the nominal GDP of India today). A new Chicago needs to be built every year to meet the demand for housing and commercial space. The country will need 20 times the capacity of metros and subways added in the last decade during next fifteen years. Numbers are massive.

Development and Market

This is the story of modernity's trajectory of development. In this trajectory, lie the tales of machines, markets and science. Market being the most dominant. The enchantment of machinations and luxury offered by the market and alienation from nature and the unscientific are strangest hallmarks of the times we live in. Strange because these hallmarks shine like fireflies, giving us an impression of an impending illumination, even when deep down we know, it will never be bright enough for us to see our path.

There is a certain ring to the terms development and urbanization, spoken collectively, to our ears! They seem to be so delightfully chiming with each other. But why?

Urbanization is an idiom of development. And the reliance of development on urbanization is a built on a promise of future. Urbanization is further explained by idioms of comfort, idioms of luxury and idioms of affluence. These idioms are refilled by imagination of televisions, air conditioning, refrigerators, cars, glitzy lights, geyser, dishwashers, glass buildings, lifts, shopping malls, fancy clothes, electronic goods and airports. Paan shops, chai wallas, barbers and second handbook shops along the pavement do not really come to mind. In fact, even if they do, we quickly brush them aside, lest it makes our idiom of urbanization, impure. Storytelling doesn't feature in boardrooms.

Boardrooms are enchanting. They promise a future. They bring crystallization to thought and digital action to the world. But without a story, the enchantment is short lived. We are still in the process of that short lived, moment of promise, definitely in India.

One might say that this is not a problem of this 'type' of development, but of its execution. It is a fair claim, but rather myopic. Execution cannot be a failure at such large-scale across the entire global South, unless there is something fundamentally wrong in the principle itself. In trying to find patterns of the failure, we locate one common sources. Its exclusion. That may not mean absence of inclusion. Mehta (2015) says, '*It's not that you'll get invited to every party on the beach. It's that somewhere on the beach, there's a party you can go to.*' Surely, exclusions abound. But why should development models exacerbate the existing iniquitous architecture we inherit? More importantly, why should exclusion become commonplace in development paradigms. Why is a particular kind of development, a prominent one? What is the source of this type of development trajectory?

Development designs of the previous and the last century have been built on the edifice of market-based mechanisms. Market is the fountainhead of innovation, enterprising and freedom, so they say. It outsources everything that is desirable in and for society, to individuals, who are expected to work for their own selves, selfishly. This selfishness carries within itself, the essence of production and growth. Predicated on this growth and centralized on Anthropocene, markets therefore, give birth to literal scenarios of development. Markets design and craft the narratives, aspirations and stories of development, and cast the spell of development on people. Microcosmic realities of successful cases become benchmark for large-scale extrapolation and in gaining unfettered access to pretty much everything, markets exacerbates the existing ways of looking at development. Development then becomes a goal to be fulfilled through market. The defense of development cannot take place therefore more than the defense of market itself and vice versa.

The Importance of the Social in the Economic

If there is anything as central in Development as the Forbidden Fruit in Genesis, it is the market. Market is the center of economic activity in neoclassical setting, which offers the language of development. Prominent economic frameworks bow to the supremacy of markets as the most efficient—and even neutral—way of ordering exchange in a society.

The problem in market mechanisms, despite creating a promising picture of the future, lies at its unreal imagination of the world. And therefore, development, which relies on market for its own purposes, fails in setting its own goals. Markets and economic transactions, as we now know, are embedded in a range of socio-political institutions which restrict markets to take insulated decisions. The underlying structures of power dynamics, informal norms, network infrastructure and social cleavages may exacerbate the existing iniquitous architecture of the market while it is evolving, instead of having market evolve as a tool even out the exclusionary institutional environment. These socio-political designs are initial endowments of the markets, and neoclassical economics has paid little heed to how it may impact emergence of an efficient and equitable market. As a result, development itself has assumed a similar value system to follow.

Perhaps one of the long-standing theories to absorb the critiques of neoclassical view of markets came from New Institutional Economics (NIE). Resting the scholarship's pivot on property rights, NIE showed the importance of markets, even while accepting the limits of information asymmetry (Akerlof 1970; Grossman and Stiglitz 1980; Spence 1973) and transaction costs (Coase 1960; Williamson 1979; North 1990). For NIE scholars, institutions matter and North's (1990) conception of institutions as 'rules of the games' became prominent framework to evaluate markets and offer reforms. The idea is that until a society doesn't have enabling institutions, markets won't work. NIE shows why institutions emerged the way they did and adds value by bringing in the theory of path dependence (David 1985; Arthur 1994). It explains why do inefficient institutions persist, and therefore, often markets may not be the best way to govern exchange. Here, history becomes important to understand economic development (Nunn 2009). So the focus is onsetting institutions right, and consequently, setting markets right.

While the idea is compelling, it fails to observe how institutions themselves could be a result of markets and distributional patterns existing. In fact, if we appreciate Williamson's (1985) view that '*in the beginning, there were markets*,' all the more reason to observe social environment which the market was embedded in. Bardhan (1989) dwells on this important distinction by showing that a desirable institutional change is severely hindered by asymmetry of bargaining power and distributive conflicts, thus cautioning the euphoria surrounding a non-interventionary state. This is clearly seen through examining the history of underdevelopment. Engerman and Sokoloff (1997) surveyed the diverging development paths of North and South America since colonization and neatly showed that societies with high inequality at the outset of colonization witnessed those institutions to develop which enabled a narrow elite to appropriate political power and economic opportunities. Indeed, Bardhan (1989) emphasizes the importance of the influence of differential capacity of social groups in coordination and mobilization, strength of vested interests and problems of collective action.

This is indeed the case in countries like India, and those which North et al. (2009) call as limited order societies, where the rents accumulate in the hands of minority elites who preserve the status quo. Entitlements matter. The question of what kind of institutions should be installed becomes eclipsed by the more important question of *who* will these institutions benefit. Existing distributive landscape of the society is crucial here, because the poor are often left out in the process of institutional reform, and rights accrue to those who were in more advantageous position to collect them in the first place. Barriers between classes are strengthened further, this time legitimized by legal frameworks. If not, the frameworks are redesigned by those groups with higher power which only give a deceptive impression of rule of law.

And the influence of these factors is pronounced in a developing/poor country, given the existing acutely hierarchical distribution of power and benefits. The locked-in effect of unequal distributional pattern is a result of elites to retain the status quo, and Bardhan (2006) shows this invoking the case of landlords blocking land reform institutions. Since a society plagued with deep iniquities and skewed bargaining power patterns will result in inefficient institutions, this society will also witness the kind of development which exacerbates the existing social cleavages, fossilizing unjust and inefficient institutions. Development, as a result, remains a pursuit in vain.

And yet, development, in its half-baked constructs, attracts. Development comes with a promise of better future, at a small cost of today. The future is made visible by those who have arrived there earlier. And everyone believes they can arrive there too. Advertisements, cultural narratives and movies tell the same story. The cost is then, the delay itself. And the delay comes with hardships. All of it, to achieve what one believes to be development. A nice flat in a multi storied building in Noida, with all of one's life's savings. Right in the middle of devastating pollution. But that doesn't matter. All that matters is whether development has been achieved or not. Market has given you that 'development.' I am an individual and I worked hard doing things that I hate, but market gave me what I wanted. I wanted a car, a home theater, a domestic servant. As an individual, I have developed.

The beauty of this is not how one feels 'developed' but the fact that everyone feels such. For everyone almost, the design of development looks the same. There is such consistent pattern of alienation, of straight jacketing answers and that of boring thrusts. Ostrom's (2005, 2015) idea brought forward the recognition to community-based organization who have successfully managed vast resources of common pool resources, devising innovative and customized solution to the problem of economic governance. The impetus on private ordering and appreciating the reflective and dynamic manner in which people find sustainable solutions without a third party authoritative rule is a celebration of diversity in the face of development universalization. Awarded with Nobel Memorial Prize in 2009, she breathed her last in June 2012. On her last day, she wrote a small piece, part of which said, '*We have never had to deal with problems of the scale facing today's globally interconnected society. No one knows for sure what will work, so it is important to build a system that can evolve and adapt rapidly. Decades of research demonstrate that a variety of overlapping policies at city, subnational, national, and international levels is more likely to succeed than are single, overarching binding agreements. Such an evolutionary approach to policy provides essential safety nets should one or more policies fail. The good news is that evolutionary policymaking is already happening organically* (Ostrom 2012).'[2] Here, she appeals for the evolutionary and sustainable approach to the development of city and urban spaces. Without falling prey into the world of consumerism, she urges us to think beyond the blind development which has an uncertain future in this difficult time.

The Idiomatic Enchantment

Charged with a developmental impulse, triggered by neoliberal hopes, India has now begun to embark on a journey which it claims leads to a destination called 'smart cities.' In a cover up of an urbanization gone horribly wrong, the idea of smart cities covered up in their digital clothing offers promise of building planned cities, focusing on transport, energy, health care, water, waste and catapulted with its promise of citizens' engagement actively. Though the vocabulary borrowed from information technology, efficiency and design become new recurrence of how the social will be mapped. A fertile ground for an innovation and urban ecosystem that stimulates economic growth and quality of life is underway. Massive investments and series of consultations are indeed State's call to a future run and governed smartly!

This we consider is a moment of institutional change. The growth moment in last two decades has concentrated itself in cities and built powerful elites who have secured most of the rents in the process of development, while non-elites lose their religion in everyday chaos of mega cities. The push for smart cities needs an alternative imagination. It is exactly now that we need to begin questioning our assumptions and restate our priorities rather than picking the ones that emanate from a crippling distributional landscape. We need to witness emergence of a New State, which governs capitalism through creation of entitlements. Further, the location of this governance has to be small towns rather than the already saturated big cities, which have exhibited exacerbated stress on resources and justice alike. In one way, an opportunity to develop an alternative paradigm of capitalism with a renewed understanding of the State is welcome.

Ministry of Urban Development of the government of India runs a web portal, www.indiansmartcities.in. The grammar of this discourse is visible in the portal. It says, '*The key features of a Smart City is in the intersect between competitiveness, Capital and Sustainability. The smart cities should be able to provide good infrastructure such as water, sanitation, reliable utility services, health care; attract investments; transparent processes that make it easy to run a commercial activities; simple and on line processes for obtaining approvals, and various citizen centric services to make citizens feel safe and happy.*' This brings to fore, the persistent priorities of the Indian state, where concerns on competitiveness and capital, inter alia. There is absolutely no mention of efforts toward creating alternative versions of entitlement which keep in mind redistributive concerns. Terms like 'commercial activities', 'investments' and 'obtaining approvals' are essential ingredient for any policy recipe which makes citizens 'happy'. A very myopic vision of a smart city is available in a concept paper, available online and exhibits similarities with the manner in which Planning Commission envisaged its role.[3] The goal is 'quality of life', and only one strand in one of the pillars uses the word inclusiveness (of scheduled castes and tribes). Nowhere, the document talks about creating entitlements. 'Equity' in the document means owned capital, while the word 'efficiency' dots the document all around. There is practically no mention of poverty, caste and gender. Except for appreciating the rise of the middle class, the word 'class' is used only to denote world-class. The document is elite in its size, font, size, figures and color. It is very colorful indeed.

Surely, this is a compelling document for development. It enchants us, intrigues us and makes us leapfrog into future as soon as possible. But there is a lurking fear that many will never be able to become part of this story. The society has decided to promulgate the values of certain kind and has reconciled to the fact that those who could not live up to the values will, if nothing, become aspirational. This is a development from the top. It engineers society creates its benchmarks and cultivates their aspirational institutions. Bardhan (1989) reminds us of Carl Menger's 1883 distinction between *organic* and *pragmatic* institutions, where the former are a result of individual pursuits, undersigned, while the latter emerge from conscious contractual design. He then, citing Elster (1989), claims that institutions may well begin organically, but be preserved pragmatically. The top-down development is pragmatic, or at least modernity calls for a pragmatic development.

So what have we got here now? An array of bewildering questions that were earlier eclipsed in mainstream thought process, now begin surfacing. Others, which prominently featured in the neoliberal motivation of growth pattern, have assumed a rather secondary position. This process has re-catapulted the State back into the picture. Indian state has moved from being a service provider at the time of independence to being a service facilitator. While the State transited across its roles, social inequity became dismal. The growth concentrated in cities produced an even more repulsive architecture of the social and the political in the cities. The third world chaotic mega-city which was expected to push its inspiration around it has ended up as a nightmarish example to follow. The growth story to be scripted in the coming decade will have to locate itself physically somewhere.

Tier II towns are then the next set of laboratory equipment indeed. Since we know where our faith in development models lead us to, we would like to express caution in adopting the same frameworks which made Mumbai and Delhi, what they are today—crumbling capabilities of distorted entitlements. State's role (and not intervention) assumes importance here, not only to avoid repeating mistakes of last two decades in Indian policy making, but also in engineering capitalism. In societies characterized by gross injustice and inequality, the institutions pave way for extractive markets, where one group rises at the expense of others and a general breakaway from poverty trap does not happen. In small towns in India, unless State actively engages with articulating its preference and adopts a framework built on central tenets of dignity, capability and access; story may continue, and this time, disastrous irreparably.

A relook at the Indian growth story binds these concepts. Faced with severe balance of payments crises in late 1980s, government of India decided to open the economy which had been lying rather closed since independence. The result was a massive wave of privatization, tailored to the needs to Indian industrial absorbing capacity. Industries went through the deregulating drive gradually. For twenty years, this process fundamentally altered the socio-political character of the country, unrecognizably. Popular imagination of growing super power, that India unmistakably with its one billion plus people is, fueled the perception that the growth trajectory is in the right place. After all, markets are handling it all right, and institutions have corrected themselves to yield most efficient solutions. Only when we begin scratching the surface, we learn of the enormous income gap, hunger and exasperated urban folks under a constant spatial and temporal negotiation. Our theoretical argument above shows that neither developmental efforts are always self-adjusting and correcting, nor is setting institutions right a panacea. With severe distributional distortions, institutions become tools in the hands of those with high initial endowments to ensure that the status quo is retained. This in turn makes development, sites of exploitative and divisive motivations. But because the story is neatly interwoven with the micro-images of 'things' and 'successful people,' it becomes more than just a gamble. It becomes a dream to be sold.

Conclusion

In the early 1990s, anthropologist Prakash Reddy spent some time in a Danish village called Hvilsager.[4] He was surprised to see that villagers hardly knew each other and were largely living in microcosmic world of their own with almost absent social network. At one point, Reddy notices, 'Coming as I do from India, and born and brought up in a village, I am used to seeing people... But here in this village, not a single soul was sighted...The doors of all the houses were closed and created a doubt in me, as to whether this village had any people at all.' In contrast, in India, in a similarly populous village, everyone would know everyone, commonly visiting each other, being interested in business and lives of others. Social relations would be common in India. If development's derivatives in India lead to an alienated, individualistic life as in Denmark, the question starkly posed is a heavy one, namely whether an Indian villager would want it to be like Hvilsager.

We don't have an answer to this question, and even if we do, there is little consistency the answer will carry. Taking this decision on behalf of people is disastrous, but in absence of needed clarity, development paths will be chosen. And in time to come, the value system imposed will be the value system accepted. This is identical to the idea of colonization that Nandy (1988) in his celebrated work, 'the Intimate Enemy', proposes—colonization does not happen by physical territorializing alone, rather when the colonized start thinking like the colonizer. Development is an attribute of what people think they should want, rather than what they really want. It's an enchantment.

Frankly, what ought to be the other 'type' of development, is itself an eluding query. Since we live in a world where colonization brought forward only one form of modernity, and thanks to the global governance institutions, we have only one form of development known to us, we are not sure of the forms the other types of developments could have taken place. We have conceptions of how they may look like (for instance, Gandhi's commune and local self-government paved such ways for us), but hardly practiced, they have never found a space to emerge. Development of modernity has crowded out development of anything else. And for as long as this continues, the design of development can be tinkered with, rather than changed entirely. And we do hope the tinkering helps us sustain. We will listen to its songs and keep getting attracted to it. Unlike Ulysses, who held himself tied to the ropes when he wanted to hear the sirens, we don't feel the need to. Or maybe, we don't have any ropes in the first place.

Notes

1. We consider following to be the ten largest towns in India, based on their contribution to the GDP: Mumbai, Delhi, Kolkata, Bangalore, Hyderabad, Chennai, Ahmedabad, Pune, Surat and Vishakhapatnam.
2. The full article is available at https://www.project-syndicate.org/commentary/green-from-the-grassroots?barrier=accessreg.
3. See http://indiansmartcities.in/downloads/CONCEPT_NOTE_-3.12.2014__REVISED_AND_LATEST_.pdf.
4. G. Prakash Reddy, *Danes Are Like That: Perspectives of an Indian Anthropologist on the Danish Society*, unpublished English manuscript. The original version is in Danish. Cited in Tanzi (1997).

References

Agrawal, A., & Gibson, C. C. (1999). Enchantment and Disenchantment: The Role of Community in Natural Resource Conservation. *World Development, 27*(4), 629–649.

Akerlof, G. A. (1970). The Market for "Lemons": Quality Uncertainty and the Market Mechanism. *The Quarterly Journal of Economics, 84*(3), 488–500.

Arthur, W. B. (1994). *Increasing Returns and Path Dependence in the Economy.* Ann Arbor: University of Michigan Press.

Bardhan, P. (1989). The New Institutional Economics and Development Theory: A Brief Critical Assessment. *World Development, 17*(9), 1389–1395.

Bardhan, P. (2006). *Institutional Economics of Development: Some General Reflections*. In Comunicação oral em CESifo/BREAD Conference, Institutional Economics, San Servolo, Itália.

Beall, J., Guha-Khasnobis, B., & Kanbur, R. (2010). *Urbanization and Development: Multidisciplinary Perspectives*. New York: Oxford University Press.

Coase, R. H. (1960). The Problem of Social Cost. *The Journal of Law and Economics, 56*(4), 837–877.

David, P. A. (1985). Clio and the Economics of QWERTY. *The American Economic Review, 75*(2), 332–337.

Dobbs, R. et al. (2012). *Urban World: Cities and the Rise of the Consuming Class*. McKinsey Global Institute.

Elster, J. (1989). *The Cement of Society: A Study of Social Order*. New York: Cambridge University Press.

Engerman, S. L., & Sokoloff, K. L. (1997). Factor Endowments, Institutions, and Differential Paths of Growth Among New World Economies. In S. Haber (Ed.), *How Latin America Fell Behind*. Stanford: Stanford University Press.

Fukuyama, F. (2011). *The Origins of Political Order: From Prehuman Times to the French Revolution*. London: Profile Books.

Ghertner, D. A. (2008). Analysis of New Legal Discourse Behind Delhi's Slum Demolitions. *Economic and Political Weekly, 43*(20), 57–66.

Ghosh, A. (2016). *The Great Derangement: Climate Change and the Unthinkable*. Chicago: University of Chicago Press.

Goyal, Y. (2016). Of Literature and Fossil Fuels. *Los Angeles Review of Books*.

Grossman, S. J., & Stiglitz, J. E. (1980). On the Impossibility of Informationally Efficient Markets. *The American Economic Review, 70*(3), 393–408.

Hindman, H. (2014). The Re-enchantment of Development: Creating Value for Volunteers in Nepal. In M. Mostafanezhad & K. Hannam (Eds.), *Moral Encounters in Tourism* (pp. 47–58). Surrey: Ashgate.

Latour, B. (1991). *We Have Never Been Modern*. Harvard: Harvard University Press.

May, R. J. (2003). *Disorderly Democracy: Political Turbulence and Institutional Reform in Papua New Guinea* (State Society and Governance in Melanesia Discussion Paper 2003/3). Canberra: Australian National University.

McKinnon, M. (2011). *Asian Cities: Globalization, Urbanization and Nation-Building*. Copenhagen: NIAS Press.

Mehta, S. (2015). Beyond the Maximum: Cities May Be Booming, but Who's Invited to the Party? *The Guardian*. Retrieved February 22, 2019, from https://www.theguardian.com/cities/2015/nov/30/beyond-maximum-cities-booming-party-ny-rio-mumbai.

Menger, C. (1883 [1963]). *Problems of Economics and Sociology* (F. J. Nock, Trans.). Urbana: University of Illinois Press.

Nandy, A. (1988). *The Intimate Enemy: Loss and Recovery of Self Under Colonialism.* Delhi: Oxford University Press.
Nelson, H. (2003). *Papua New Guinea: When the Extravagant Exception Is No Longer the Exception.* Canberra: Australian National University.
North, D. (1990). Institutions, Economic Theory and Economic Performance. *Institutions, Institutional Change and Economic Performance.* New York: Cambridge University Press.
North, D. C., Wallis, J. J., & Weingast, B. R. (2009). *Violence and Social Orders: A Conceptual Framework for Interpreting Recorded Human History.* Cambridge: Cambridge University Press.
Nunn, N. (2009). The Importance of History for Economic Development. *Annual Review of Economics, 1*(1), 65–92.
Ostrom, E. (2005). *Understanding Institutional Diversity.* Princeton, NJ: Princeton University Press.
Ostrom, E. (2012). *Green from the Grassroots.* Retrieved February 23, 2019, from https://www.project-syndicate.org/commentary/green-from-the-grassroots?barrier=accesspaylog.
Ostrom, E. (2015). *Governing the Commons.* Cambridge: Cambridge University Press.
Pyyry, N. (2016). Learning with the City Via Enchantment: Photo-Walks as Creative Encounters. *Discourse: Studies in the Cultural Politics of Education, 37*(1), 102–115.
Reilly, B. (2002). Political Engineering and Party Politics in Papua New Guinea. *Party Politics, 8*(6), 701–718.
Roy, A. (2009). Why India Cannot Plan Its Cities: Informality, Insurgence and the Idiom of Urbanization. *Planning Theory, 8*(1), 76–87.
Roy, B. (Producer), Roy, B. (Director). (1953). *Do Bigha Zameen* [Motion Picture]. India: Shemaroo Video Pvt. Ltd.
Saler, M. (2006). Modernity and Enchantment: A Historiographic Review Michael Saler Modernity and Enchantment. *The American Historical Review, 111*(3), 692–716.
Spence, M. (1973). Job Market Signaling. *The Quarterly Journal of Economics, 87*(3), 355–374.
Tanzi, V. (1997). Corruption: Arm's Length Relationships and Markets. In G. Firentini & S. Peltzman (Eds.), *The Economics of Organised Crime.* Cambridge University Press.
UN Habitat. (2016). Urbanization and Development Emerging Futures. *World Cities Report.*
Williamson, O. E. (1979). Transaction-Cost Economics: The Governance of Contractual Relations. *The Journal of Law and Economics, 22*(2), 233–261.
Williamson, O. E. (1985). *The Economic Institutions of Capitalism.* New York: The Free Press.

PART II

Dramatics and Enchantment

CHAPTER 4

The Art of Showing: Imagining Development in Indian Mediascape

Pranta Pratik Patnaik

The representation of development in Indian mediascape has witnessed an exciting trajectory where it becomes difficult to identify whether it is virtual or real. As a result, what constitutes as development has become one of the most pertinent questions in contemporary times. It is compelling to understand the meaning of development not through policy makers, academicians, media, and political leaders rather as a lived 'reality'. It is no longer understood solely in terms of economic and industrial growth rather includes good governance, gender equality, and environmental sustainability, reduction of disparities, poverty reduction and social capital within its ambit. The seductive discourse of development propelled by the media makes use of these aspects mentioned above, thereby legitimising a hierarchy of knowledge and a particular cultural standpoint. Despite the desperate attempts to re-define the process of development, the development experiment is considered to be a failure that cannot be accepted at face value. The key argument put forth to support this statement is the simul-

P. P. Patnaik (✉)
Department of Culture and Media Studies, Central University of Rajasthan, Ajmer, Rajasthan, India

D. N. Pathak and A. K. Das (eds.), *Investigating Developmentalism*,
https://doi.org/10.1007/978-3-030-17443-9_4

taneously steady increase in the level of poverty, inequality and corruption (Sachs 1992; Hanmer et al. 1997; Thomas and Allen 2000). However, the failure of development is attributed not only to its result of the coexistence of economic development in one area and social deprivation in the other (Rahnema 1997; Hanmer et al. 1997) but 'because of its intentions, its world-view and mindset' (Pieterse 2000: 175). Along these similar lines, Schuurman (1993, 2000) suggests that there is a crisis in development at two levels—Firstly, there is a crisis in the developing countries regarding increasing levels of poverty, exclusion and inequality. Secondly, there is a crisis because of a collapse of the dominant theories and paradigms of development that had captured our notion of development. From the perspective of the developed, Western countries, development is in effect a 'civilising mission', that is, saving the natives from themselves. It not only needs the articulation of a particular regime or discourse from the dominant group but also requires the subordinate group to be complicit in their subordination. This is how cultural hegemony works in creating a discourse of development. It, therefore, becomes essential to understand development from the viewpoint of culture as it is the closest expression of everyday lives of the people—both the propagators and (supposedly) benefactors of development.

If development is meant to improve the living standard of the people, then it can hardly ignore the cultural matters that are an integral part of peoples' lives. For example, it was Max Weber, who has rightly pointed out the relationship between culture and development through his work on Protestant ethics in the successful development of a capitalist industrial economy.[1] In this case, culture is a means of development. We also need to acknowledge the role of culture as part of ends of development. It implies, therefore, towards the protection of culture of the people in the wake of several industrial developmental projects. The crucial task is to share equally the fruits or benefits of development. The purpose of this chapter is not to highlight the inequality created through development but to identify the mechanism how development discourses get mediated through culture. The cultural aspects of development have to be seriously considered, no matter how we deal with the clear conflicts involved in it. As Amartya Sen (2001: 25) rightly points out, 'the reach of culture pervades every aspect of what we call development'.

It is against this backdrop that the chapter takes into consideration the use of culture in 'mainstream' television channels in support of the developmental projects. The mimetic model of development ignores human development in the country. There are large-scale industrial projects which have the support of the government despite its role in displacing a large number of populations. The government sells the idea of development through media, particularly television. The Indian media industry is worth examining as it is controlled either by some person having political inclinations or affiliation or are economically strong.

Televisual production of development discourse needs to be seen as a socio-cultural act, which involves lots of media personnel whose identities, subjectivities and statuses are played out in creating a media text. The chapter does not confine itself to the organisational constraints that set the limits on media content rather extends to consider the pleasures, competitions, conflicts and everyday meaning-making by social actors, engaged in media production. In other words, media producers are never only involved in the creation of media texts; they also participate in producing themselves as social persons in relation to others. In addition to this, producers of the televisual images and texts imagine audiences who will enjoy viewing their programmes. In the process of constructing the imagined audience, they reconstruct their identities. There is a continuous effort by the producer to invoke social institutions to attempt to fix meaning, control circulation and curtail appropriation of the media texts. Media production thus becomes a crucial domain where social structure, collective identities and selfhood intersect. It is within this understanding of televisual production, one needs to understand how it sells the idea of development, that is consumed and most importantly, reinforced and sustained.

Development on Indian Television: Tracing the Origins

Indian television was seen as one of the direct instruments for promoting the developmental tasks of the government. The concept of 'developmental television' (DT) was initiated in India to disseminate the development programme of the government. The rural population became the target audience who were informed about insecticides, fertilisers, hybrid seeds, new scientific discoveries and technologies related to agriculture that would yield high productivity. It was assumed that it would act as an incentive for the farming community to develop a modern outlook towards lifestyle/living pattern that would prevent their migration to urban areas (Dhawan 1972). The educational programming on DT was designed by educators and teachers of Central and State Institutes of Education. There was also the involvement of private players/advertisers in selling the idea of development. Ironically, the novel concept of DT did not deliver the required result. The reason attributed for its failure was the lack of research, coordination among different government departments involved in setting up DT system in India (Kale 1973).

However, the focus of the chapter is not to discuss the failure of the DT in early years but to demonstrate how despite the failure in several developmental propaganda of the government, media, television, in particular, has been able to sustain the interest of its audience in the word 'development'. The question arises how does the media works/sells through this idea of development? The answer lies in how the discourse of development gets wrapped in narratives of culture, identity, region, and ultimately extends to the nation. In the next section, in support of my argument, I would like to present a case study of a regional television network in Odisha—QTV (pseudonym)—an Eastern state in India. Simultaneously, I would also discuss the examples of other television channels and demonstrate how a parallel system works in both national and regional media when it comes to representation of development on television news. The case of QTV is put forth to underline the significance of regional television network to understand a pan-Indian character of televisual politics. Another reason to link the national and regional media network is due to the nature and pattern of media ownership that characterises the Indian television channels. There has been merger and acquisitions by larger media companies with the regional networks to capture the audience in both rural and urban areas.[2] The newly formed media conglomerates also target the small cities and towns where media penetration is relatively low, and there is a possibility of potential growth in advertising.

Furthermore, such mergers and acquisitions of media network companies exacerbate the situation by exercising power and influencing editorial policies of the TV channel. It ultimately results in commoditisation of news where accountability and transparency of media companies remain questionable. There arises a crisis in news reporting where incidents of development-induced violence are sidelined, and progressive stories of development appear on the screen and take centre stage. For example, police fired on a peaceful protest of Munda Adivasis in Jharkhand on February 2001, who were protesting against the Koel Karo hydroelectric project (Reddy 2001), which was reported by the newspaper but not covered by the electronic media. The mass media frames the entire issue in terms of those who are pro-development and anti-development putting the viewers into a position where they have to choose to commit to one side or the other. The poor farmers, Dalits and Adivasi communities become the easy target by the government when it comes to the encroachment of the forest lands for dams, mining operations and steel plants (Nayar 2001). In rich mineral resources states like Odisha, Jharkhand, and Bihar, steel and mining corporations exploit the people, and protestors are arrested for their 'anti-development' activities. Such disempowerment and violation of their human rights do not occur accidentally rather is a deliberate design to polarise the people (Roy 2013).

The primary source of evidence for this chapter are data collected through interviews with journalists, schedulers, stringers, media personnel and television audiences. Field notes from respondent observation in QTV studio, its archives and other reports of public enquiries into the media are made use of to substantiate my arguments. I moved between meeting rooms, editing studios, and the field with reporters to understand what these media professionals have to say about their work and their lives. While I conducted twenty formal and semi-formal interviews with QTV staff—recording and transcribing them—my most valuable insights about QTV came through eight qualitative interviews with the various department heads and associated professionals. The interviews explore how the media professionals imagine their audiences and what strategies are employed to have a good number of 'loyal' audiences. It also gave me insight into their notion of development (*vikasha*—the local term for development) and how they link it with the region, nation and the globe. Their selection of development news was a joint effort by an entire team of media professionals who cover it for political gains to secure revenue for running their channels. This chapter also engages with other secondary sources to relate the regional coverage of 'developmental' events with the other 'mainstream' national media coverage of different developmental issues of a similar nature.

This chapter is divided into three sections—the first section gives a background of the study mostly regarding the use of culture as 'soft' power, corporate takeovers of media networks, mergers and acquisitions and cross-media ownership and its impact on the representation of news on development. Such a political economy approach to understand media is essential as it reveals the linkages between capital, politics and broadcasting of news on development. However, the chapter does not limit itself to this perspective rather extends into the cultural politics involved in the construction of news. The second section limits itself to a case study of QTV and its coverage of news on developmental projects supported by the government, specifically the POSCO project. It maps the construction of news by entering into the terrain of various departments of television channel entrusted with the task of making the news. It demonstrates the strategies deployed by different media personnel to do the coverage of a 'positive' story of development by linking it with the dreams and aspirations of the citizens. The main focus of the third section is to engage with the television audience who are the victims of development and how they perceive the news on development. The encoding and decoding of the development news through television channel provides an understanding of how cultural appropriation is done by linking cultural identity with development by the media and how the cases of disenchantment among the viewers create a conflict between real and virtual.

The Corporatisation of Media and Dramatics of Development: Background of the Study

Media production is an interlinkage between culture and economy and also a platform for political gain. The period of the 1990s in India witnessed the import of 'foreign' TV programmes. India signed a MoU with South Korea for expansion of economic infrastructure of both the countries. The economic relationship gave way to the cultural expansion of Korea's media items in India. Korean TV series was shown on state-owned television channels in India. This was known as the 'Korean Wave' in popular terms. There was a phenomenal growth and spread of Korean popular culture ranging from its cuisine, movies, music, games and cartoons.

In the initial stage, the Korean wave entered Odisha mainly through economic investments and the number of jobs it created. The proposal of the Pohang Steel Company (POSCO), a steel giant of Korea, to invest 12 billion US dollars in integrated steel plants at Paradip in Odisha is the largest ever foreign investment in India and the single largest overseas investment by a Korean company.[3] However, the project was received with much criticism from certain sections of the state as it was alleged to ruin the source of livelihood of many tribals and poor people. The state government with its pro-development agenda turned a blind eye to this problem at the initial stage. With the intensification of protest against the project, specific rehabilitation measures were undertaken, which were inadequate and mostly remained on paper. Felix Padel and Samarendra Das (2008) link the exploitation of aluminium and steel companies and the state government to a sort of 'genocide' where there might not be physical death of the tribals but a psychic death, which they term as 'ethnicide', that is, killing-off of culture. It is worth noting that certain sections of the government and media label the activists who fight for the rights of the tribals as 'Naxalites' or 'Maoists' to justify police brutalities against them. When the victims of development protest against the state, they are labelled as terrorists, killed or arrested under Prevention of Terrorism Act (POTA). In Odisha, Adivasis have been reported to be killed for protesting against a bauxite mining project in December 2000 (Kumar 2001).

Local newspapers like *The Dharitri* and *The Samaja* carried stories about the sufferings of the villagers of Dhinkia, Gadakujang and Nuagaon of Jagatsinghpur district where POSCO plans to set up its steel industry. In various local newspapers, there were also the images of public protests against proposed POSCO steel plant. There were reports of police violence against the people sitting on dharnas. The clash between the police and the protestors took place when the police forcibly lathi-charged the people so that the district officials can acquire the land for the POSCO project. Biplav, one of my respondents, fighting for the cause of the beetle leaf cultivators in the POSCO site said:

> Police have filed false cases against the protestors though it was an entirely peaceful protest. Several houses were burnt to scare the villagers and to convey the message that this will be the fate of those who oppose the POSCO project. The state government is also taking the help of the local goons.

During this stage, the media in Odisha saw a significant change. It was only in the local Odia newspapers and few national dailies that reported the stories about the people who would be affected due to the POSCO project. The QTV, on the other hand, included the POSCO story, not from the viewpoint of the protestors rather as a progressive step taken by the ruling BJD party for the development of the state.

While there was a massive protest against the Korean Steel giant, simultaneously, on the other hand, the Korean cultural expansion was manifesting itself in Odia Television Channel as well. The first Odia channel to show Korean TV series dubbed in Odia was DD Odia, a state-owned television channel. The Korean series titled 'Maya' was telecasted in DD Odia in 2006. Maya was the story of a girl who was famous for her brilliant farming techniques. It was something new to Odisha Television. Unlike other Odia television serials, all the characters in this serial belonged to

South Korea, and they were showing the Farming Community of South Korea. Only the voices of the characters have been mute and dubbed over in Odia language so that the people of Odisha can understand it. It should be noted here that 'Maya', primarily a South Korean serial which has been produced by the South Korean Television Channel MBC (Munhwa Broadcasting Corporation), has found its place in Odia television channel because the chief minister of the state has full support for the POSCO Company.[4] There has been a demand by the opposition parties for his resignation as the chief minister seems to be indifferent to the environmental hazards and livelihood issues of the people in Odisha due to the POSCO and Vedanta, another developmental project supported by the state.

Despite such controversies related to the livelihood of the displaced and project-affected people, the state government continued its effort to bring in POSCO in Odisha. Culture was used as a soft power to legitimise the coming up of POSCO through the import of South Korean TV programmes and tailoring it for the people of Odisha through programmes like 'Maya' and producing a feature film for QTV (which is discussed below). This is a case that shows corporatisation of media and how a multi-national company has its say in the media matters of the state albeit with the full support of the ruling party in the state.[5] Though 'Maya' went off the air without being noticed, QTV took centre stage in the state.

QTV broadcast a feature film entitled '*Tamasoma Jyotirgamay*' (From Darkness lead unto light) produced by POSCO. It implied subtly that Odisha is in a state of darkness or underdevelopment and industrialisation due to POSCO would bring light or happiness into the lives of the people. The film was made with an intention to influence mass opinion in support of the project. There were dialogues used in the movie that promoted the disparity between Odisha and other states:

> where were these 'baharia loka' (outsiders/other state) activists and leaders who are now showing their concern for Odias and are encouraging them to oppose the POSCO project?
>
> These outsiders are very pretentious and are jealous of the development of our state. They do not want Odisha to become a developed state. It might be a fashion for them to call a protest against any such development project, but it is a question of our Odia identity as a developed state.

These discussions were intended to create an 'Other' to safeguard the pride of Odisha and Odia identity. Interestingly, the category of 'Other' includes other states in India and even people from Odisha, who have been raising their voice against POSCO. The 'Other' is portrayed as a threat to the developmental work undertaken by the Odisha government for the state. The professionals involved in the film were Odia actors, paid to speak these scripted dialogues and were not affected by the project in any case.

The film did not touch upon the livelihood issues of the people who would be affected due to the project. The activists from other states and also from Odisha, fighting for the basic rights of the project-affected people, were labelled as 'envious outsiders'. If the film were for internal viewing of the corporate house, it would not have been a problem, but the question arises how could QTV promote the film at the level of public broadcasting that does not pay heed to the needs of the project-affected people.[6] It is surprising that such projects are being carried out in the name of 'development', 'national interest' and 'public purpose'. One can also witness huge billboards, another form of media, of POSCO and Vedanta in major parts of Odisha claiming to have brought happiness into the lives of millions of poor and underprivileged people.

Staging of Development: Mapping the Construction of News

In this section, I would like to extend my argument regarding the controllers of media image, where one finds a dispersal or diffusion of media power. The main idea is to convey that it is not only the owners who decide the content of media programmes but also several other departments involved in running a programme. Taking an example of how QTV produces news about a particular issue, this chapter looks into five formal departments that play a significant role in this process of news making. This is, however, not to deny how patterns of ownership determine the political and economic interests of media organisations. The other media workers may influence the content or visibility of the QTV programmes, but it is always the chief executive officer or the managing director who has the final say in most prominent matters. This should not sound contradictory to my argument. I want to underline 'prominent matters' over here which refers to those terrains supposed to be untouched by other formal and informal players in media production. The other players might play with the small stories of corruption of crimes in the news or even content of serials, but they are not supposed to cross the threshold set for them. They are not expected to cover any story that goes against the ruling party in the state or even those companies who provide a high source of advertising revenue to the channel.

During my fieldwork in QTV studio/office, I realised that the field of media production is a site of a struggle having its autonomous logic. The struggle is not over the meaning of the televisual images and stories but other things like status, authority, money and identity. Pierre Bourdieu (1993) observes that in the field of cultural production, the struggle is over the various forms of capital, be it linguistic, socio-economic and symbolic. It is the possession of these forms of capital that determines one's position in the field of cultural production. Since the social actors in this field continuously engage in improving their position in the hierarchy while safeguarding their interests, the struggle and competition take place among them. For example, a reporter who needs permanent employment in QTV requires to file stories acceptable to an editor—that is, meeting formal standards of news-worthiness, objectivity, and timeliness. According to Bourdieu (1998), to understand what a journalist writes, one must evaluate his/her place in the journalistic field, and the status of the media for which he/she is writing. One's competence as a writer, he argues, is determined by how well one can discipline oneself to the constraints of the journalistic field.

The way journalists create a patterned account of the description of any event can also be understood by invoking Foucault's notion of power. Here power is seen as primarily productive (of pleasure, of knowledge, of discourse) rather than being repressive. In this view, social actors (reporters) discipline themselves. They produce valued goods and services (media texts) and simultaneously get the rewards—pay, promotion, regularity of job—that derive from their action. Power, for this reason, is a productive network, leading to disciplinary regimes.

One advantage of examining media production from this vantage point is that it allows us to look at the constant struggle and negotiations by the social actors while producing a media text. Media content gets negotiated as producers and directors employ various forms of authority, from appeals to budgetary limitations, to objectivity, to the tradition of representation, to aesthetics, to personal experience. In addition to this, discourses about audiences' needs and desires cannot be discounted. Producers repeatedly refer to viewers to justify particular creative or technical choices. They shift positions back and forth between suggesting what audiences will want to see and what they should see. Thus, media production in QTV takes place not only within a social field but within a constellation of fields that can together be described as comprising 'media worlds'.

When Boardroom Controls the Newsroom

The merging of larger media companies with the regional networks adversely affects the diversity of news flow. In a multi-lingual and multi-cultural country like India, the real challenge is to ensure that the growing concentration of ownership in an oligopolistic market does not lead to a diminishing level of heterogeneity and plurality regarding media content. In the absence of restrictions on cross-media ownership[7] and secondly, government policies facilitating corporatisation of television have aggravated the privatisation and commodification of information, which rarely remains a 'public good'. It has also affected the nature of editorial content as it is difficult to identify who are the real owners and what powers can they exercise in controlling the media content. There are multiple stakeholders in the new mergers and acquisitions making the structure complicated as the investments are made not by a single individual or company but through layers of subsidiary companies. The owner can exercise an influence on the news content. The appointment of the editor is through the owner's decision and as such exercise enormous influence over the editorial page. When the editor and the owner have different views, the editor does not risk upsetting the owner. Such shifting of power equations details the way news is handpicked by the reporters and editors suiting the interests of the owner of the media industry.

Apart from the dependency on advertising revenue, there has been a remarkable increase in relying on the state. It is more evident through the 'FICCI-KPMG Indian Media and Entertainment Report 2013', which states that the growth in revenue advertising has decreased significantly compelling the media organisations to cost-cutting practices and ultimately increase in state dependency. Such a situation gives an opportunity to the elite few to enter into the terrain of the media industry. All these have ended in making the owners of the media industry be the chief deciding agency of news content rather than the editors.

News operations have ceased to be democratic. It has become a rare sight to find editorial and news floor meetings where possible multiple ideas and angles of the same story or event were debated before it goes for the public consumption. The studio has become the site where 'consent' is manufactured on behalf of the existing power relations. It sounds similar to the propaganda model, as propounded by Chomsky and Herman, that ensures the marginalisation of dissent and 'allows the government and dominant private interests to get their messages across to the public' (1994: 2).

To give a clear picture of the working of different factors involved in the field of media production, I looked at five departments in QTV that are responsible for the construction of news related to POSCO issue starting from the CEO office to the HR department.

1. *The CEO Office*—The crucial editorial decisions, including deciding daily news agendas, programming content, show timings, the inclusion of particular stories to the exclusion of others, are taken by the corporate office. The CEO, Mrs. Patnaik (name changed), has the final say in both editorial and corporate matters. Her role as CEO and also as head of the editorial team meant that she had tremendous control over everyday functions of the office. She not only had to undertake the job of making profits (she is answerable to the shareholders) but also of balancing this with the ethics of journalistic practice and the production of a news channel. She confided that the editorial practice is affected mostly due to different stakeholders in the channel that has grown up due to cross-media ownership. When the story of POSCO was to be shown, all the parties agreed to represent it from a pro-developmentalist approach.

2. *Advertisement Sales*—The primary function of the sales team was to sell advertisement slots on the news channel to clients. Revenue earned through advertisements, as Mrs. Patnaik puts it, contributes to 70% of QTV's gross revenues. Most corporate clients of QTV who purchased advertisement slots did it indirectly through the media planning wings of advertising agencies that handle the media policies of their customers.

Mr. Behera, Head of Advertising and Sales unit, expressed in an interview to me how stories were created regarding the development that the government defined for its citizens to garner support for the POSCO project. The reporters were asked to create a story by linking all the perspectives on growth and prosperity as mentioned by the leaders who were in support of the project. Such instances point of how the corporate take on the key editorial functions. Certain things, which do not qualify as 'news', are strategically made into news.

The news studio thus becomes the site for 'manufacturing' news, and the reporter has become marginal to the news-gathering process. They have to follow the instructions and comply with the policies of the television channel while reporting an event.

He adds further 'Certain news about POSCO are highlighted while others like the protest around these developmental projects are not mentioned. We have a long unwritten list about which politicians to invite in discussion-based programmes related to POSCO or any other event, depending on their proximity to the owner of the channel. That is the reason you can see the same faces in every discussion of our channel. Though we claim that the views of the politicians are personal and QTV channel does not subscribe to their views, the thumb rule is Boss is always right'.

3. *Marketing News*—The primary job of marketing departments in QTV is image management, i.e. finding ways in which a particular perception of the channel can be created and maintained among the audience and the media market. This is achieved by three broad means: influencing the content, through promos (promotions) and placing of advertisements, and finally, through public relations exercises.

According to Ms. Rath, Marketing Head of QTV,

> The impression of a customer-oriented channel is continually reinforced through content. This requires collaboration with the editorial team. Marketing also regularly came up with programme ideas that furthered the desired image of the channel.

Giving an example of how 'positive' news about POSCO was created by QTV, she stated that QTV had a programme that was entirely developed by the Marketing team:

> It was called '*Apana Eka Nahanti*' (You are not alone). Viewers were encouraged to share their problems. Our team would help them in solving their problems, mostly in cases of proper monetary compensation for the land taken up by the government for the project, non-receipt of pension, ration card, LPG cylinders, cleaning of drains in the locality, sufficient electric and water supply. Even though there was (intentionally) no proper follow-up regarding critical cases of monetary compensation due to POSCO, the viewers felt empowered through us. We also suggested the tagline for the channel—'We Report. You Decide' implying that the news was for the audience and that they have a say in it. Also, on the top of the channel logo, we suggested putting the three words—Free. Fair. Unbiased.

A new development in QTV during my study was its strategic tie-up with the Odia film industry. It allows movie producers to have 'unlimited' air-time on the news channel to promote their movies. Also, QTV has rights to 'exclusive' interviews with the actors, access to film footage and other exclusive rights. Ms. Rath was responsible for making these strategic alliances with movie producers, thereby controlling a large amount of time in every news bulletin. The close alliance with the Odia film industry made it easier for QTV to produce a short film on POSCO (*Tamasoma Jyotirgamaya*, as discussed in the previous section) involving the Odia film stars. Such instances show that the Marketing team of QTV not only asks for specific stories but organises new content. While it can be pointed out that programmes like '*Apana Eka Nuhanti*' (You are not Alone) do not strictly fall into a 'news' category, film stories are included in the general news cycle in QTV news.

Both the Sales and Marketing departments depend heavily on data and inputs provided by the Research team at QTV. This team also plays a vital role in content management. It provides an analysis of the ratings on which the Sales, Marketing and Editorial team rely to maximise their impact, as well as revenue.

4. *The Research Team*—In terms of control over the editorial content and in providing inputs to them regarding programme timings, its market viability, the need for changes in the shows, the power to suggest new shows and to scrap existing ones, the research team perhaps has the most say among all the corporate teams that work with the Editorial team at QTV. The research team's inputs on editorial matters are based on its analysis of data provided by Television Audience Measurement (TAM), a private company that measures audience ratings or TRPs in India. Besides this data, the research team also sometimes employs private firms to conduct audience surveys. In an interview, I asked Ajit Parida, the Head of the Research team, to share his views on news and how his department contributes to content management about POSCO issue amidst such controversies around it. He replied thus:

> In the news nowadays there are enormous possibilities. Programmes are completely slotted based on viewership data, and also on past experience and on what the competition is showing at that time. We try to put some average figure regarding the future development of the state that will be possible with the coming up of POSCO like the increase in the number of employment, and that will take care of everything like poverty, education and health.

The attempt, he reiterated, was to provide a 'tailor-made product' targeting specific audience groups. The Research team also used the TAM data to reorganise or scrap existing programmes and shows.

5. *The Human Resource Management*—The HR team is responsible for the management of the personnel at QTV, their recruitment, promotions, punishment and rewards. This broad range of powers allowed the department to attempt a change of profile in the recruitment of journalists and also to promote a certain kind of news content with an eye on the profit margin. Mr. Sahoo, commenting on the need for changing the profile of journalists at QTV, said that he aimed to recruit news producers from the most affluent sections of society. He felt that it would be better if he hires media personnel who has a better understanding of the 'core' audiences' likes and dislikes.

Besides this clear management policy of changing the recruitment profile of journalists to suit a new kind of audience, there were other subtle strategies that the HR team employed to ensure journalistic compliance for a particular editorial policy, especially the way rewards and bonuses were handed out. The HR team, Sahoo stated, proposed firmly to link the increments and annual salary hikes of journalists to a corporate structure of bonuses and performance-based indices. He said that it was the TRPs that decide the worthiness of journalists. This means that if a story fails to get a high audience rating, the journalist's worth gets diminished within QTV. This also indicates that the editorial judgement of a good or bad news story, however erroneous, was being replaced with the fortunes of TRP ratings. Sahoo stated:

> While recruiting the reporters, I tell them precisely that they should collect at least five or six good stories in a month. They are told to do something 'different' from what others are doing. They are supposed to work in a way that should not hamper the image of the channel nor anything against the interests of the media organisation.

The policies and vision of the HR team at QTV sought to alter and significantly tailor news content. Apart from these formal departments, there is an entire gamut of other informal and semi-formal structure, which also operates in the news production in QTV and is very significant.

The ways of collecting and making news have also transferred. One of the primary sources of news content is through the stringers who have replaced the reporters and are willing to contribute to the news making by sending some footage of the event to the news channel, which could be genuine or rigged. There is more dependence on digital graphics and visual effects. Stories are told even through sophisticated animation, which has opened the gates for skilled technicians and young reporters who are replacing the senior and older journalists. This deskilling of media labour is accompanied by scrapping the more extended format of investigative reports and in-depth stories. The only skill that is praiseworthy is the ability to cover events by buying footage, presenting the story through animations, creating a discussion panel of people known to the owner of the media organisation.

The news is also determined by what the rival channels are showing. The same is replicated in the news channel and as such leads to homogenising of news content. Apart from manufacturing news as per the rival channels, digital platforms also become a significant source for constructing news. The posts on social media platforms like Twitter and other blogs done by politicians are regularly followed and incorporated within the news content.

The result of such shifting in power relations compels one to relook into the category of news. What constitutes news? It has come a long way from the older understanding of news being objective to something 'subjective', fact filtered and processed by the owner. There has been a 'top-down' construction of news, which establishes the centrality of the owner. It has become largely dramatic where the performance of the anchor is more valuable than the news content. It is noteworthy that the period after 2008 has witnessed the proliferation of what Bhushan (2013: 12) calls as, 'studio-based performers' rather than news professionals. He laments that we no longer find journalists instead have performers ranging from opinionated anchors, endless talking experts, academicians and politicians who transform the manner in which news is manufactured and delivered to the consuming audience.

Interpreting Development: The Act of Seeing

This section focuses on how the audiences receive such messages about development and how does it constitute to their formation of an Odia identity along the lines of being an insider or outsider. This process of constructing the Other along the lines of being an 'insider' or 'outsider' is played out by QTV differently in various contexts. My second argument is to understand media power by examining the direct interactions between media organisations and non-media people. At one level, the media people are the 'insiders', and the audience constitutes the 'outsiders'. At another level, the label of 'outsider' extends to categories of people within the audience. For example, those Odias who supported the anti-POSCO project were constructed as the outsider.

As mentioned earlier, QTV did not take cognisance of this disruptive dimension involved in the POSCO deal. It conveyed a message to the protesters that there goes a politics of representation in media reporting of news as well. The protesters, who were earlier only the consumers of media images, became the subjects of media representation. They were exposed to the entire process of news making interacting with the journalists, giving byte for the TV camera, posing for the press photographers and gazing at the satellite transmission dishes on the QTV crew vans.

Manjulata, a 42-year-old woman, is a social worker in Bhubaneswar. She worked for the betel leaves cultivators whose land will be usurped by the POSCO steel plant. She was one of my interviewees. She had a trust in media, particularly television news. She shares her experience of being misrepresented:

> I have been with them in their protest and sat on dharnas near almost all protest sites in Odisha. I am an eyewitness to the atrocities done by the police on innocent people. One evening, in the QTV news, which I regularly watch, the newsreader said that the anti-POSCO protesters became violent and threw stones at the police due to which the police had to use tear gas and lathi charge. I know the ground reality. The protesters are scared of the police, how can they attack the police in the first place? I wanted to call the television studio and tell them that this is not true. The TV story does not gel with what happened in reality.

This was one of the many conflicts between her or other protesters' accounts of the protest and media reports. It was the acutest because it revealed directly how the media report is constructed from a police press briefing. In other words, Manjulata experienced for herself the role of primary definers in news production that Hall et al. (1978) analysed. Most importantly, Manjulata realised that she was powerless to alter the report.

When around the same time Manjulata saw pictures of several protesters whom she knew personally on the television screen, surrounded by police, apparently involved in the conflict, she was concerned that people who didn't know them would misunderstand and misinterpret these images and assume that they were committing violence.

She was apprehensive:

> I know who they are, but nobody else would, those watching the news. They [the media] can put any story about them and create an entirely different story.

Manjulata felt forcibly the power of media, which stereotypes the agitators as the ones who are creating trouble and disturbance in the state. As she puts it:

> Social workers like me and the protesters are said to be building an internal rift within the state through this anti-POSCO struggle. The media report that we are the 'outsiders' who cannot tolerate the development of Odisha with the coming up of POSCO. We are shown as people doing that sort of thing [violence/disturbance]; we are represented as mobs.

After having lost her trust in QTV news, Manjulata's reflections bring out vividly the normal background assumptions about the media (and the media's social authority) which those disruptive events had dislodged:

> *Me*: What effect do you think it had on you, as you were a regular QTV News viewer?
>
> *Manjulata*: I think it ultimately took away all the respect I had for the media, especially 7 o'clock news bulletin.
>
> *Me*: And why do you feel so?
>
> *Manjulata*: We know that serials and films are done purposively for entertainment. The news is something, which I thought is a serious business. They will not be doing any manipulation. News is always fair…. That is what I used to think. But now when I am a witness to what they could do to a news report, neglecting all evidences, believing in the story of the police, I am surprised! Earlier I had so much respect for these media persons considering them to be strong, gathering news report from the sites of conflict but now all that has faded.
>
> *Me*: Why has it changed? Just because of this incident?
>
> *Manjulata*: Yes, they let me down, I think. My story of the actual events at the protest site was never heard. I wrote a letter to the QTV studio mentioning them that the news about the protest was one-sided. I never got any reply. My letter was not included in their 'chitti-patra' programme. They entertained only those letters that demanded change in the timings of some serials or to introduce some other new programmes. We never got to see the real story of the protest site. I think we are totally at the

mercy of the media. How they misrepresent us, the anti-POSCO protest is something that the common man will believe. They will think us to be 'outsiders'. They will never understand that things on the television are not always real.

Manjulata's interview shows how people's accounts of being close to the media's workings can reveal background assumptions about the media and its authority.

Sanjay, another supporter of anti-POSCO agitation, has also joined several protests for the cause of formation of a separate state in Western Odisha. He became active in the anti-POSCO agitation during his college days. He uses a camcorder to film the protest sites. Sanjay was a self-employed university graduate in his mid-thirties. He had gone with a friend in 1998 to a protest against the setting up of steel industries in Odisha displacing the landowners, which received considerable media coverage:

I had never protested or anything of this sort before. We just saw the TV coverage of the protest and decided to join this. After all, this is for our Odisha. When I saw on television so many normal, ordinary people in the rally, I told my friend why we couldn't join them. We can also do that kind of protest.

Sanjay had an image of protesters, who might be the unemployed and uneducated ones. Seeing images of 'ordinary people' protesting flatly contradicted this. He felt the ability to act, to protest. Initially, he was timid in front of the camera and avoided it as he believed that being seen on the television screen in the demonstration sites will bring bad publicity for his business. However, he was so upset by what he saw, including police behaviour in the protest sites, that he decided to buy a camcorder to 'capture it all on camera'. He went to Dhinkia village in Jagatsinghpur district, which was to be the most affected village due to coming up of POSCO:

If we keep on protesting in Bhubaneswar(capital city of Odisha), nobody will care or understand the problem. I wanted more people to join this cause. So I decided to go to the project affected villages and film their problems and show it to people to gain their support. You know we are not media people. We are ordinary people, but we can make a difference too.

His emphasis on being 'ordinary' yet having the potential to create a difference reminds one of social psychologist Michael Billig (1997), who argued that it is partly in the 'small words' of people's talk—'the unnoticed little words which seem beyond rhetorical challenge, and which are routinely and widely repeated' (1997: 225)—that power relationship are subtly revealed. Being 'ordinary', Sanjay suggests, normally means not going and making a difference. But now the camcorder provided the purpose which enabled him to spread the message of state violence and exploitation: 'it's only because we know that is happening, we are recording it all the time, and that's what makes a difference'.

So far, he was using the camcorder purely to gather evidence. He did not regard himself as doing anything connected with the media. This changed when a journalist he knew from the protests, who suggested that his work might interest the local media channel:

> The whole idea of going to the local media channel, giving them my work, which is not nicely recorded as I am not a professional journalist or reporter was a bit strange. The local newspaper also approached me as my recordings could be used as a backing for their stories about these protests. I was worried because that's going to be printed; they might take my interview. My purpose was never to come in contact with the media.

The advice to use the media had made no sense before to Sanjay because he understood himself and the media to belong to mutually exclusive categories. The media operated in a different world from him, the other side of a boundary policed by restrictions and fears. His story did reach the local press and media channel, and he received regular coverage for a while. Subsequently, he became active in generating storylines for the media. What is most important for my argument is Sanjay's changed understanding of his relationship to the media world? Once he came into contact with the process of production of news (first as a witness of mediated protest events, and then as a camcorder user himself), his account of that change reveals an earlier set of background assumptions about his lack of a place in the media world—assumptions that previously he had not challenged.

The analysis of interview accounts of people's dealings with the media brings out people's usual background assumptions about the media and their status. Each case study (Manjulata's and Sanjay's in particular) has raised the question of power—the massive concentration of symbolic resources and authority in media organisations—and with it the issue of hierarchy. Just as Sanjay considered himself an 'ordinary' person who, therefore, had nothing to do with the world of media production, similarly Manjulata once had a sense of respect for people working in media. In a sense, media is seen by them on an entirely different level from themselves, quite different from ordinary status ranking.[8] The understanding of being an insider or outsider does not remain confined to the debate about development—supporters and anti-POSCO—but also the relationship between people and media. In the case of Manjulata, she felt to be an outsider in relation to media, but in the case of Sanjay, he asserts to be an insider about media, particularly local channels and newspaper.

'Images on Television Are Not Always Real': Concluding Remarks

A free media is one of the necessary conditions for the existence and survival of liberal democracy. In India, as mentioned earlier, the primary engagement of national broadcaster was with development, mostly regarding disseminating state's objective of educational, agricultural, scientific and technological advancements. It created and supported an educated and prosperous citizenry. The problem arose when the developmental goals of the state got combined with the propaganda of the ruling political party. It gave a reason for growing suspicion about state-controlled media and paved the way for the opening of the airwaves to private players. There was much rejoicing with anticipation that private channels will provide independent and well-reasoned news and plurality in media content. However, the assumptions about private media proved to be wrong, especially when Indian mediascape, barring few, became characterised by jingoism, sensationalism and tabloidism. This chapter exemplified this scenario by taking QTV, a private channel in Odisha as a case study to understand the working of the media industry, the politics behind the making of developmental news, and the way audience decodes such media texts. The media packages development within the everyday discourses of the people through images of infrastructural facilities, employment opportunities, and improved educational and other changes in the lifestyle. The audience is brought under a magic spell of development, and the media does not leave any stone unturned to sustain their version of development. However, not all are enchanted by such developmental propaganda; instead, there are individuals like Manjulata who question such media texts. Manjulata's loss of trust is a complex shift in her attitude towards media. She felt that the media is not putting across the right story about the protest, though she had a real story to tell. One phrase that sums up the conflict between her old trust in television news and her new doubts: 'images on the television, is not always real'. This should not be seen as a picture of dismal rather an opportunity to challenge and initiate a process of constant questioning, thereby claiming a potential possibility to bring about a change in media representation about development.

Notes

1. However, it should also be noted that many of the Catholic countries, including France, Italy and Britain were also doing better in terms of development in comparison to their Protestant counterparts (Sen 2001: 11)
2. Even websites/internet is also being controlled by large media corporations.
3. *The Economic Times* (13 February 2009) quoted Mr. Pradip Kumar Amat, steel and mines minister of Odisha, as saying that POSCO-India to have spent around INR (Indian Rupees) 176 crores in the proposed mega steel plant in Odisha. Though POSCO-India has signed a MoU with the Odisha government in June 2005, it has failed to acquire the land for the project in the face of stiff opposition from the local residents who will lose their agricultural land due to this mega project.
4. In the Odisha Assembly on 4 December 2004, referring to protests against POSCO and Vedanta Project, the Chief Minister stated (as shown on TV news): '*No one – I repeat no one - will be allowed to stand in the way of Odisha's industrial development and the people's progress*'. However, what remains unanswered is who defines what is people's progress?
5. This reminds one of Adorno who in his work 'Culture and Administration' (1991) talks about the cultural politics of the state and not of the market wherein he says that we cannot separate culture and administration.
6. A fact-finding team of People's Union for Democratic Rights (PUDR), Delhi in their study of parts of Rayagada and Kalahandi districts of Odisha in April 2005 found that there is a struggle between the inhabitants of the region with the paid goons of the mining companies. The peasants of the land, tribals and Dalits, are at the receiving end where the process of usurping their land for the project involves coercion and manipulation.
7. Cross-media ownership has resulted in a kind of vertical integration in Indian mediascape. The large media conglomerates are usually groups that own many different companies ranging from textiles, chemicals, automobiles, etc. This allows them to have controlling stakes both in broadcasting and distribution through acquisition of licences under the name of the subsidiary or associate companies they own, enabling them to hoodwink the current restrictions and defeating the very purpose of their existence.

8. This distinction between media and oneself can be thought in terms of Durkheim's absolute distinction between 'sacred' and 'profane' in his analysis of the elementary forms of religious life. However, this is not to push the comparison between the media's authority and forms of religious authority very far but to suggest parallels between media power and symbolic power of religion.

References

Adorno, T. W. (1991). *The Culture Industry: Selected Essays on Mass Culture*. London: Routledge.

Bhushan, S. (2013). Manufacturing News. *Economic & Political Weekly, 48*(23), 12–15.

Billig, M. (1997). From Codes to Utterances: Cultural Studies, Discourse and Psychology. In M. Ferguson & P. Golding (Eds.), *Cultural Studies in Question*. London: Sage.

Bourdieu, P. (1993). *The Field of Cultural Production*. Cambridge: Polity Press.

Bourdieu, P. (1998/1996). *On Television and Journalism* (P. P. Ferguson, Trans.). London: Pluto.

Chomsky, N., & Herman, E. S. (1994). *Manufacturing Consent: The Political Economy of Mass Media*. London: Vintage Books.

Dhawan, B. D. (1972). Television in India: What Role in Economic Development? *Economic & Political Weekly, 7*(42), 2119–2122.

Hall, S., Critcher, C., Jefferson, T., Clarke, J., & Roberts, B. (1978). *Policing the Crisis: Mugging, the State, and Law and Order*. London: Macmillan.

Hanmer, L., de Jong, N., Kurian, R., & Mooij, J. (1997). *Social Development: Past Trends and Future Scenarios*. Stockholm: SIDA.

Kale, P. (1973). Developing a Tool for Development: Television in India. *Economic & Political Weekly, 8*(28), 1255–1257.

Kumar, S. (2001, November 6). The Adivasis of Orissa. *The Hindu*.

Nayar, K. (2001, November 28). Pushing the POTO. *The Hindu*.

Padel, F., & Das, S. (2008). Cultural Genocide: The Real Impact of Development-Induced Displacement. In H. M. Mathur (Ed.), *India: Social Development Report 2008. Development and Displacement* (pp.103–115). Delhi: Oxford University Press.

Pieterse, J. N. (2000). After Post-development. *Third World Quarterly, 21*(2), 175–191.

Rahnema, M. (1997). Towards Post-development: Searching for Signposts, a New Language and New Paradigms. In M. Rahnema (Ed.), *The Post-development Reader*. London: Zed Books.

Reddy, C. R. (2001, May 27). At Loggerheads Over Resources. *The Hindu*.

Roy, A. (2013). *An Ordinary Person's Guide to Empire*. India: Penguin Books.

Sachs, W. (Ed.). (1992). *The Development Dictionary: A Guide to Knowledge and Power*. London: Zed Books.
Schuurman, F. (1993). *Beyond the Impasse: New Directions in Development Theory*. London: Zed Books.
Schuurman, F. (2000). Paradigms Lost, Paradigms Regained? Development Studies in the Twenty-First Century. *Third World Quarterly, 21*(1), 7–20.
Sen, A. (2001, December 13). *Culture and Development*. Paper presented in World Bank Tokyo Meeting.
Thomas, A., & Allen, T. (2000). *Poverty and Development in the 21st Century*. Oxford: Oxford University Press.

CHAPTER 5

Crafting Development and Developing Craft: An On-Going Dialogue

Ektaa Jain

Introduction

The popular song '*Mera joota hai japani, ye patloon Hindustani... Sar pe laal topi hain par, phir bhi dil hai Hindustani...*'[1] from the 1955 Bollywood movie, 'Shri 420', reiterating the *hindustani* (Indian) identity amidst the global conundrum. The post-independent epoch of 1950s saw development and progress as the light at the end of deep dark tunnel that was plagued with myriad social problems like poverty, unemployment disparity of income levels. Clothing can be seen as an important and visible tool of projecting a desired image revolving around the ethos of development. The theme of development is centred in this post-independent era. It is in this context that the paper seeks to understand the journey of 'development' through the lens of craft. Spinning, weaving, printing; all are activities that seep naturally into the Indian fabric of life. According to Gevorkyan, 'transition economies' should be studied more efficiently in order to garner an understanding of development. The so-called transformational experi-

E. Jain (✉)
Centre for the Study of Social Systems (CSSS), Jawaharlal Nehru University (JNU), New Delhi, India

D. N. Pathak and A. K. Das (eds.), *Investigating Developmentalism*,
https://doi.org/10.1007/978-3-030-17443-9_5

ence is interesting. Crafts in India provide this opportunity (Breckenridge 1989). The idea of development is in tandem with the journey of Indian handicrafts along with the pivotal role of the state. Craft, in context of India, can be seen both as a cultural marker and as a vent out for creativity.

To begin with, it is crucial to understand how crafts are generally understood. The Development of Commissioner Handicrafts (DCH) came up with a very lucid definition of 'handicrafts' in 1989. The handicrafts were, '…Items made by hand, often with the use of simple tools, and…generally artistic and/ or traditional in nature They include objects of utility and objects of decoration' (Liebl and Roy 2004: 5367). It is important to note that the Indian textile industry, in particular, has always been a key player in context of development. The economics of textiles and crafts is crucial for the state to progress.

In the past, Indian handlooms had been signifiers of Indian culture, and the hand-woven fabrics of India made Indian cotton 'king' in the world.[2] However, over time there has been a substantial change in this scenario especially in terms of the newly emerging notion of 'development'. Indian craft and textiles now for a long time have been caught between the devil and the deep sea (Gillow 1991). While it is a sector which has the potential to bring in craftsperson to the central economic terrain, it still stigmatises the person with ideas of 'old', 'out of date', and 'backward'; the exact opposite of 'development' and 'modern'. The craft domain is one space ridden with this absurd duality (Jain 2014). This idea of development of fashion from craft becomes important for the craft to sustain itself. So while khadi may not retain its popularity in terms of Gandhian hand-spun cloth, the journey of khadi from 'Nehru jacket' to 'Modi jacket' brings intrigue to the idea of development.

A lot of this is also owing to the increasing use of machines and complicated technology (Saraf 1998). Mechanisation has always brought major changes in the production of crafts, for instance wooden blocks were used to print patterns on cotton, but these were superseded by screen printing. There came in cheaper quicker inks too. Modernisation and cost-effective production lies in the direction of powerlooms and jet-looms, while pristine culture and Indian aesthetics are best reflected in handlooms (Riello and Roy 2009). Very interestingly, India's political, moral, aesthetic or spiritual decline due to modernisation became quickly linked to any kind of slip in design, quality or reduced markets for crafts in view of eminent scholars like Birdwood, Coomaraswamy and Havell. Industrial reformers like Ranade viewed this destruction of Indian crafts as a threat to viability of

India at an international level. The journey that the craft domain has undertaken is interesting to understand the changing notion and adaptation of the blurred idea of development.

Envisioning Craft in Indian Context

The Indian Craftsman (1909) by Coomaraswamy can be seen as one of the first and a near complete work expressing the idealised vision of Indian crafts. It is a work devoted to the idea of craftsmanship rather than looking at the products or practices involved. There existed a school of thinkers for whom Indian crafts should be celebrated for their marked difference from the West. However, for every such thought, there was a diametrically opposite thinking of scholars for whom the crafts in India were leftovers of the past which were 'archaic' and stuck in age-old traditions that were in dire need of being replaced with the more modern factory production and newer techniques. For them, even though the machine goods represented a certain sort of aesthetic ugliness, one couldn't argue against the fact that these were markers of progress.

In his seminal work, Coomaraswamy highlights the centrality of caste within the Indian artisan system. According to him, the caste-based division of labour and association to a particular craft made that craft more than just a vocation. It was a kind of devotion for the artisan as he/she was totally inclined to the idea that it is this activity 'through which alone he can spiritually progress'. 'The craftsman is not an individual expressing individual whims, but a part of the universe, giving expressions to ideals of eternal beauty and unchanging laws, even as do the trees and flowers whose natural and less ordered beauty is no less God-given' (Coomaraswamy 1909: 48). This provided craft production the support of emotional entrenchment which was extremely crucial in Indian context.[3] Also, he adds, that such an engagement with work and caste affiliation provided 'assurance' to the artisan; assurance of his position as well as of his purpose and value. There was absence of anxiety which helped in producing quality work, 'quality of leisure so characteristic of true works of art and crafts can appear in them' (ibid.: 59). However, the gradual change of this understanding can be seen as craftwork being regarded as something not so worthy or reputed especially economically.

Following caste norms at all stages of craft production involving the usage of technology, employing people, diversifying products and so on; caste would thus restrict progress in the larger production keeping artisans away from freely responding to the newer market demands. This is evident from the speech by Wardle in Peshawar in 1890 where he insisted an indigo dyer to dye some cotton fabric red (McGowan 2009). Though Wardle offered a good price for the work, the dyer remarked after a very respectful salaam that he shall dye only blue. To Wardle's amazement, no money or reward could change his decision.

Whatever footings caste had for artisan community, government surveys generally suggested otherwise. For instance, in 1908, the Khatri dyers started moving to different occupations like silk and cotton weaving, wood turning, etc. This was also because of the introduction of chemical dyes that allowed people with lack of skill of mixing natural dyes to enter this arena. The cheap chemical dyes led to a very tough and implausible competition for the natural dye artisans who started getting forced out of this trade. According to 1885 Poona gazetteer, the Jingar caste, who were known to be saddle makers traditionally, started pursuing different crafts like casting metal, making figures of clay, wood carving and so on.

Apart from its hereditary understanding, caste also held great economic ramifications. Labour was trapped into hereditary occupations as stated above thereby shutting doors to different opportunities of work that might be more suited to their skill and talent. Thus, while caste made sure that individuals would stick to pursuing their own craft, it also made switching to crafts pursued by lower castes very difficult. Crafts were mainly dominated by lower castes. Consequentially, craftwork was deemed as work with lower social status. The natural reallocation of work according to the concepts of necessity and profitability was thus prevented due to caste principles. This also prevented pooling of knowledge. Fellow artisans and intellectuals from different caste groups could not share knowledge, use and understand scientific developments together, nor could collaborate on newer design products. Creativity was thus painted with restrictions. However, most craftsmen were not even interested in doing so. This was because of lack of education among the artisan groups wherein the people themselves lacked the understanding of their own work (Pal 1978). The artisans tended to be secretive of their work. Most of the times, there was a jarring inefficiency due to indifference to profitability lacking the quality of industriousness among artisans. The conditions seem to be quite similar even with the so-called movement towards achieving development goals.

The portrayal of village is also important when talking about the artisan community. While a very treasured and beautiful image of a village is at times portrayed in works of scholars like Birdwood and Coomaraswamy, such romanticisation was not entirely true. Villages, even before the nineteenth century, were not entirely 'republic'. They had connections with regional and pan-regional economies and networks of production. Artisans thus were not entirely independent to pursue their own creative choices. Social and economic relationships involving debts, duties, interdependence existed within which the creativity was deeply entrenched. One may assume that a rural setting would give higher independence to the artisan; exchange here was based on relations of power, hierarchy and patronage. The urban networks, on the other hand, had artisans producing for merchants and moneylenders who could hold their own dictates over designs, colours, styles and other specifications.

The period gradually ended with creating a situation of flux for concepts of caste, community and landholding. New criterions were thus being adopted by the elites to uphold and give leverage to their prominence. They emerged as the champions of education, science, technology and rationality. All stereotypical characteristics that marked the artisans including both the positives and negatives like traditionalism, being communitarian, conservatism, disregard towards economic gains were all rejected by this new modern Indian elite. The industrial activists as they were set their goal for the future while artisans remained rooted in the past. The idea of crafts difference basically served political goals: it helped in dramatising the issues and challenges society was facing under the British rule that made it possible to justify the emerging Indian elite leadership within the national culture. Such crafts difference also led to the interventions that the realm of craft was to witness. However, the transition is not as plain as one would assume.

Understanding Craft: *The Gandhian Way*

The notion of development in association with crafts can be seen as Gandhi's brainchild. In his weekly paper Young India of May 1919, Gandhi displayed his disappointment towards the lack of attention paid to crafts in India (Gonsalves 2010). According to him, the arts and handicrafts have always been considered to be inessential, and the authorities on economics have tended to ignore these. For them, national wealth could never be measured 'in terms of life', and thus they couldn't establish a link between "art and industry" thereby not being able to 'appreciate the value of quality or a high standard of workmanship'. Gandhi continuously suggested measures that would help crafts to survive and flourish. These included exhibitions which could act as a platform to showcase high standards of workmanship, state-sponsored collection of crafts to document product diversity and efforts that would increase collaboration of designers with artisans.

He made it quite evident in the article that 'crafts mattered'. Crafts were thus seen as part of the national culture made by artisans coming from varied backgrounds. Crafts also became part of the national economics; they could be seen as a mode of production that was rooted in the past. Crafts in totality became reflective of 'national society' (McGowan 2009: 2). One can trace this importance laid on crafts by Gandhi in his campaign for the hand-spun khadi. Manual labour and the idea of self-sufficiency became important and appreciated through the spinning of khadi. Simultaneously, it helped in atoning of the deterioration of the handloom industry.

Following khadi, crafts in general had twin occupancy in people's mind. It was central to the critiquing of British rule as well as was integral to the constructive programme of Gandhi. Boycott of foreign goods was accompanied by crafts being used as potent force for protest movements (Ramagundam 2008). They helped in highlighting the deficiency of colonial policies. It was through journals, newspapers, books as well as official reports that writers were continuously documenting traditional designs and techniques also discussing the problems that crafts were facing. Gandhi's call for swadeshi thus became a vehement symbol of protest against British imperialism; it also acted as a shining point for the numerous weavers and spinners of India. Indian handicrafts thus witnessed a new phase of appreciation and pride.[4]

The promotion of crafts as an expression of national culture and an obstacle to the rapid modern industrialisation was happening everywhere. The popular Arts and Crafts Movement is one of the biggest examples of this.[5] Ideals of Ruskin, Morris and others were integral to this (Jayakar and Irwin 1956). The renewed public interest in India was not only an influence of what was happening in other places but also was a creative project within the colonial society as Indian reality could now be negotiated through global ideas. Spaces like schools and laboratories were used to develop and disseminate newer technologies for making crafts. Newer styles of goods were also being produced to access wider markets for artisanal products. These were the initiatives that could be witnessed in the late nineteenth century. This was a time when crafts ceased to be just an individual artisans' concern or individual consumers' desire for satisfying taste. Crafts now began to be synonymous with India as a whole including its economy, polity, social and cultural matrix.

Craft's embedded nature in an artisan's life is apparent in Ramaswamy's poignant work '*The Song of the Loom*' (2013), wherein a weaver and the cloth he weaves have a relationship no less intimate than that between the spider and its web. All crafted objects were earlier seen as an extension of the personality of the craftsperson (Chatterjee 2014). Kamaladevi Chattopadhaya, who was instrumental in salvaging Indian crafts from the twin onslaughts of colonialism and consumerism, defined this symbiotic relationship (Chattopadhaya 1982). She envisioned craftsmanship as a way of village community, something that marked 'its joys and burdens, the change of seasons, the memories filled with song and verse, legends, myths and local romances, from the core and sub stance of their daily existence... they wove a rough and forceful art' (Chattopadhaya 1975: 126). According to her (1964), 'to understand Indian life is to understand Indian handicrafts, or vice versa to understand Indian handicrafts is to understand Indian life'. Such a relationship meant that no problem was individual (Chattopadhaya 1984). For instance, a potter still using the older wheels was no longer a matter of personal convenience or choice, it automatically became a part of national heritage.

The nineteenth century with its earlier influences most evidently became a period that saw an increase in the power of knowledge of crafts. Here craft went beyond being just a product and began to be understood as representing the larger Indian society (Dhamija 2007). It was that part of visual culture, which could explain social organisation, represented intellectual traditions and was a snapshot of an engagement with the global world. Though grounds were laid down for development of crafts here itself, the confusion that this domain is still fighting with soon surfaced up.

The Duality of Craft: Idealist Vis-À-Vis Moderniser

The Arts and Crafts movement with leaders like William Morris, Walter Crane, C. R. Ashbee was of the argument that the beauty in work is what coincided with the beauty in design. Thus, in their view, the big complicated system of factory production left artisans with no control over their designs that gradually resulted in ugliness resulting from the machines, a gift of development (Collingwood 1938). On the other hand, production within small units gave a say to artisans who could then work in tandem with designers thereby reiterating the grace of craft. Objects made through this understanding were beautiful and better than their machine-made alternatives (McGowan 2009: 79).[6] Birdwood in fact went a step forward in explaining capitalism as anathema to artisan way of life. For him, 'what is chiefly to be dreaded is the general introduction of machinery into India' (Birdwood 1980: 334). For Coomaraswamy (1964) too, the Indian craftsman was a portrait that emerged as being free from any shackles of employment competition or the stringent markets that were a hallmark of the West. In fact, in the rural understanding, artisans were regarded with respect and acted as valued members of the community.

There thus existed two clear strands of thought. On one hand existed the craft 'idealists' while on the other were craft 'modernisers'. The idealists made their problems with commercialisation apparent as according to them this affected the craft's quality, authenticity due to which the Indian handcraftsmanship could lead towards extinction in wake of exploitation. Contrary to this, the modernisers complained of stagnation and lack of change. They were concerned with the conservatism that the craft community showed which could lead to problems of adjustment with the changing world consequentially leading to lack of work and economic deprivation of individuals and gradually of the entire nation. The literature then made artisans look in dire need of help, as people who just could not pace up with modern changes and were succumbing into external pressures. The educated elites were thus considered crucial for helping this group of pitiable craftsperson.

The late nineteenth century thus conjured an understanding of crafts that had fractures within itself. Thus as McGowan comments, 'for every potter throwing clay in perfect communion with his self-contained village community, there were many more thoroughly integrated into broad market structures. For every wood carver toiling in isolation, there were many more working in various forms of association… for every dyer who refused to switch from indigo to red, or weaver who could not adopt to a new loom for fear of being excommunicated by his caste, there were others who led change from within crafts by adopting new technologies or shifting to new occupations altogether' (McGowan 2009: 93). This throws crucial light on the significance of the multiple meanings of development. The word thus exists differently for different people and communities.

Glyn Barlow (Principal of Victoria College, Palaghat and former editor of *Madras Times*) remarked in 1904, 'India's old fashioned ways of working, as it were, bow and arrows, with which she will vainly compete with the foreigner with his machine guns. India, for her salvation, must get rid of her bows and arrows and must learn to use machinery-guns too'. Dutt, on the other hand, contrasted the happiness of Indian weaver to the suffering of a British mill worker in the following manner: 'The individual man is at his best, in dignity, independence, and intelligence, when he ploughs his own field or works his own loom than when he is a labourer under a big landlord or an operative in a huge factory... The Indian village weaver, working his loom with the help of his wife and children, and selling the prepared cloth in the village market, is a more responsible and dignified being than the Lancashire operative, working in crowded noisome factories, and leading a life in which all the natural instincts of human nature are crushed out in one eternal round of factory work'. According to Dutt, any shift from crafts to a factory mode of production would thus be accompanied by exploitation.

Interestingly enough, the entire modernisation 'project' overlooked the artisans and kept them away from any kind of prominent leadership roles. According to Dutt, the knowledge that Indian elites were harking on was mainly drawn from all state produced surveys and statistics and rarely went out themselves to gather information (Bayly 2002: 50–51). This kind of lopsided documentation served the interests of officials as well as the elites equally. According to Ludden, this commitment to economic development was majorly about power, particularly state power (Ludden 1992: 252).

Many of the weavers have put away their loom frames; they either work as landless labourers during agricultural seasons, or they eke out a living as rickshaw pullers.[7] They have moved away from their villages and seek employment in cities—living their life out in slums in order to send money home to their families. Theirs is a dual alienation—from their habitat and from their crafts. The tragedy that has hit these craftsmen, who had once upon a time reigned as masters of the weaving craft, is a combination of crass commercialism, an insensitive urge to modernise and globalise and contrarily, also ironically, over-enthusiasm on the part of 'culture vultures'. (Ramaswamy 2002: 119)

It is quite bewildering to notice the lack of attention of industries, design centres, design schools towards the local markets which keep handicraft products at their heart. The attention is rather directed towards stores at Milan or Paris. Jaya Jaitly looks at industry as only a site of organised production (Symposium on culture-based development strategies, September 2005). This organised production is a result of managed and systematic work of man along with machine. Industrialisation is understood as authority and prominence of machines and capital over any kind of human potential and labour. Such an understanding of industry is quite opposite to that of crafts.

The dilemma of the central and state governments in the context of traditional designs versus consumer demands has resulted in ambivalent attitudes towards indigenous knowledge systems in the sphere of designs. Traditional floral and geometrical patterns were woven into traditional colours which combined to produce textile designs which were cultural signifiers. Consumerism and computerisation are thrusting on the weavers designs which may reflect popular tastes but are at variance with patterns reflecting their cultural ethos and aesthetics. The use of computer-aided designs by handloom weavers has resulted in setting another major trap for themselves (Ramaswamy 2002). Unlike traditional designs, many of which could be woven only on the handloom, the 'received' designs from craft centres could be easily created by the powerlooms at half the cost.

The growing commercialisation has, on the one hand, kept craft alive while the other end of the bridge sees this as exploitation of the existing traditions. Thus, a part of the responsibility lies with the state to choose whichever side of the mirror and accordingly frame its policies. This has been a difficult task. The difficulty gets multiplied also from the fact that the actual creators of the craft are not involved in constructing such policies and plans. A very different set of people are behind such policy planning with varied set of interests. For example, for those involved with cultural history, the traditional motifs become central to be preserved, for market the consumer demand is paramount, while for policy makers within the government, crafts become a domain existing on subsidies.

Industrial growth has been an important factor for nation-building since a very long time. The commitment to crafts at a public level was somewhere a part of this industrial concern. Since 1870s the industrial activists actually began propagating the idea of industry as being beyond the narrow pursuits of profit and loss linking it with humanity, culture and social fabric of the country at a larger level. It was argued that industry could be understood as a political matter the ideological claims of which may have national repercussions and acts as a material expression at the international level. Craft is a site where the capitalist lacks the power to exploit due to its decentralised set-up. Jaitly encourages one to not get constrained and jarred by the terms of 'cottage' or 'village' industry. Industry with its meaning of standardisation, automobile production and a wearisome activity has led to numbness of human thought. Governance intervention may lead to some kind of creativity in this arena. Also, with the growth of technology and globalisation, one may try to find newer ways to create and promote crafts.

In case of India or elsewhere too, the new forces of globalisation have created new ethos of consumerism, an ethos that seeks to deny all cultural memories and reduces the richness of life into images of mass consumption (Pathak 1998: 157). The logic of the market is to promote consumer culture. Everything is available for consumption by one who can pay for it. It was in the 1960s and 1970s that the government started viewing crafts as a 'sunset industry'. The approach shifted from perceiving it as a sector with economic potential to a sector meant to survive only through welfare schemes and plans.

There is thus indulgence in consumerism. Under the given complex of state-market relations, we have become crassly individualist without developing the new morality and losing out that which formed the bedrock of Indian culture and civilisation. If one looks at culture, it is a meaningful zone that every community needs to evolve to make sense of the world. Commercialisation can be seen through two lenses. While it may lead to major changes in the original craft, it may also help to retain the craft for a longer period of time and infuse it with new vigour. The old techniques may be revived and managed through newer machines and tools. This can also be a source of attraction for the producers and trainers of the craft to innovate. Interestingly, commercialisation of ethnic crafts may also result in becoming the 'cultural marker' for the ethnic community in the eyes of a global audience as mentioned by Cohn (1996). This is an image of identity, a symbol of identification thereon. Thus, a yearning to embolden this identity shall eventually help in getting involved with craft policies in a more interactive manner. Any attempt lacking with such thought shall lead to exploitation of the existing skills and styles as pointed out by Cohn. As understood, an ill-advised conservation would do no good in context of conserving crafts and helping to maintain a decent standard of living for the craftsperson (Cohn 1996: 168).

All scholars like Dutt, Birdwood, Coomaraswamy, Gupta, Barlow unanimously agreed that changes were seen in art and crafts due to external factors. The European designs that had entered the Indian bazaars were degrading the skills of Indian artisans. Preservation of crafts was seen as an imperative thereon. However, this idea of preservation did not emerge from the concern that artisan products would shift to factories; it was the fear of disappearance of traditional crafts that led to preserving them. It was understood that modern machinery would not be able to supply of material needs of India. Craftsmen thus needed to adapt to this machinery. However, this transition was like walking on a double-edged sword

(Vasanthi 2010). Crafts retained their negative features like isolated workers, backward technology, etc. and started embracing the newer features of modern industry like alienation, exploitation, etc. Thus, the positive aspects of crafts were somewhere getting lost. The effects of such a transition went way beyond the individual artisans and affected the national and cultural matrix. The solution was to battle the evil twins of westernisation and capitalism according to the preservationists. Interestingly enough, all change was not ridden off. Efforts began to accommodate newer technologies with existing artisan techniques in order to produce and innovate products that could meet the modern day demands. Market exigencies could be seen as replacing the earlier patronage. This however helped artisans to retain individual autonomy to some extent. This marks the hallmark for the development agenda in the contemporary form, if taken forward in a reasonable and honest fashion. In other words, for example, if metamorphosing a craft like block printing to aprons or kaftans from ghagras could retain the craftsmanship; this emerged as a sought after avenue. The attempt should be to bring a common melting point for the idealist and moderniser for crafts to exist and development to function holistically.

Conclusion

In a country like India, craft industry makes a crucial component of development. With the changing times and increasing role of the designer, the designer must be a part of learning process of the craft. This can be seen in case of khadi becoming a fashion fabric. Also one needs to understand the relationship of the craftsperson to the product avoiding any situation of alienation. The product should answer the question regarding its creator's whereabouts (Steel 1888). The skills of the person should be made relevant for contemporary use. With room for innovation and modifications, the craft products should be made a part of the contemporary lifestyles. Answers only in terms of 'aesthetic value' may not be enough. A craft needs to survive beyond its aesthetics (Jaitly 1990: 171). Involvement of designers and design firms by government and NGOs to liven up the craft sector maybe a good strategy, only if the craftspersons' interest is at the heart (Kasturi 2005: 69).

Amartya Sen in 'Development as Freedom' (1999), as quoted by Bir Kasturi, mentions that 'An adequate approach of development cannot really be so centred only on those in power. The reach has to be broader, and the need for popular participation is not just sanctimonious rubbish. Indeed, the idea of development cannot be dissociated from it'. Kasturi further questions if there is any other design could help in providing any alternate method of engaging with crafts apart from its existence as just 'packaged design' which would get reproduced recklessly time and again (Kasturi 2005: 70).

It is known by now that there exists involvement of the government, private sector and other non-profit institutions in the craft sector. A number of institutions, plans, policies and programmes have been developed by the government since independence. The private sector too has been an active player through creating retail chains which seem to provide shelter to these crafts to some extent. High-end fashion designers like Ritu Kumar, Tarun Tahiliani among others have been in the forefront regarding this too especially with the recent trend of social business. These designers have kept themselves close to the craftsperson. However, the product still does not become central to the designer's identity and is only a part of it, and is rather integrated into their own work. This is thus an indirect action on their part, yet an important one. Retailors like Fabindia and Anokhi are name that sprung up when talking about developing and expanding crafts at a global scale. These can be seen as socially conscious business models integrating artisanal craft with commercial end.

Like every work domain, a healthy intervention can help the domain of crafts too. This intervention then becomes important on two major grounds. Firstly, the craftsperson themselves shall not get their due benefit until the intervention is done. Secondly, from the perspective of growth of the industry, intervention becomes relevant (Liebl and Roy 2004: 5374). The problem that exists is that most of the initiatives driven by a need for commercial attainment lack the mettle of helping crafts to adapt to modern needs in a more convenient manner. Various sources including the Government of India, India-based NGOs and other funding agencies are sources which help in bringing forth such efforts. Sufficient data and information on the linkages between culture and development, especially in case of India, seem to be absent. A more comprehensive documentation and well-coordinated research might serve as an answer to the gaps in such policies and efforts.

The era is caught between great specialisation of skills and creation of wonderful crafts on the one hand and mass production on the other. This can be seen even in terms of the fabric khadi which has set upon a journey of multiple meanings ranging from Gandhian governance to the uniform of a politics in the contemporary India. With independence, the Indian capitalism as well as democracy saw a change in the shade of the fabric. However, the choice still exists of how to amalgamate and make the best of the two to expand and thrive in the future course of time. There thus exist alternative modernity. This alternative modernity could be achieved through a combination of design with craft. Design can very much translate the transition of tradition to modern and make it visible. However, for this to happen successfully, design shall need to grasp 'true progress'. Nowhere else is such an 'embarrassment of riches' of craft history, one that has seldom been mapped, studied or understood along with its technology and politics. It is here that the role of the state in terms of development of technology and craft becomes increasingly significant. To argue in favour of preservation of traditional designs and exclusive handloom varieties is not to deny the imperative need for commercial viability if handlooms are to survive (Venkatesan 2009).

While apprenticeship remains as the major way of learning crafts, especially when it is a hereditary one, a large number of government-funded training programmes and NGOs have entered the field to expand the learning of crafts. The sad part of the story is the craftspersons are not yet provided with understanding innovation and learning it. The designer marks their foray here. What has fallen on the craftspeople is the incessant commercialisation and an urge to embrace the so-called modern world. It must not be forgotten that Gandhi made the Charkha or spinning wheel the symbol of India's freedom struggle. Therefore, handlooms have survived and can continue to flourish in the next millennium only if they follow the principle of appropriate technology (ibid.: 124). Technology is however very much a part of the traditional handloom industry. However, technological inputs have been most effective only when the initiative has come from below, that is from the weavers or master-weavers themselves. To paraphrase Neil Postman, 'Can a nation preserve its history, originality, and humanity by refusing craftsmen access to creativity, innovation, knowledge, and fun?' (Postman 1992: 183). In all this, it is also important to note that crafts in India have meant more than something to please our aesthetics only.

Craft industry has been significant to the country for reasons more than one. Economically speaking, crafts are an important source of providing employment and generating higher export results. In terms of culture, crafts were a potent force for nation-building (Sennett 2008). The stress of rootedness of crafts within Indian culture labelled them as being 'national' that were representative of a collective conscience crossing diverse strata. Simply put, crafts could speak beyond linguistic barriers unlike stories or songs. Chattopadhyay very rightly remarked, 'the toran being hung over the doorway to welcome visitors, the colour painted on the horns of the cattle, the artistic shape in which the scythe is made… a hundred and one simple articles touched gently, delicately, aesthetically' (Chattopadhyaya 1964: 3).

Craft is a unique decentralised industry. The products may not be mass produced. However, if artisans are provided with an environment to sell products at a large scale to yield profits, helping the national economy; human mind and thought can become more prominent and crucial than small machines or other equipment. The machinery is then a product owned by the craftsperson and not vice versa. In this case, the sector is free from much undue exploitation. Thus, industry may still exist without being an exploitative mechanism, crafts may then try to come out of the shadow of being a diminishing sector and realise its ample scope given the emphasis on development. The two can thus function innovatively leading to encouraging results. Development needs participation and innovation. Any focus that is one dimensional would be losing out on a fruitful opportunity of craft sustenance and development.

Notes

1. Hindi song from popular Bollywood Movie, 'Shri 420' (1955), directed by Raj Kapoor.
2. Daniel Defoe, the celebrated author of Robinson Crusoe, wrote that after the 1688 revolution when William and Mary landed in England, they were resplendent in Indian calico (Ramaswamy 2002: 120).
3. The centrality of caste in Indian society is undeniable. The economics, polity and cultural fabric; all find themselves rooted in the concept of caste and its underpinnings. Caste emerged as an answer to explain everything from occupation, financial holdings, dress and costumes to religious affiliations, to human capacities of thinking and action too. It is no wonder then that caste came to organise the entire artisan life.
4. At the same time, Tagore in Bengal too initiated a thrust on indigenous roots and culture. This was just the beginning which inspired others to follow the footsteps towards Indian crafts.
5. The Arts and Crafts movement was one of the most influential, profound and far-reaching design movements of modern times. It began in Britain around 1880 and quickly spread across America and Europe. The two most influential figures were the theorist and critic John Ruskin and the designer, writer and activist William Morris. Ruskin examined the relationship between art, society and labour. Morris put Ruskin's philosophies into practice, plac-

ing great value on work, the joy of craftsmanship and the natural beauty of materials. See, http://www.vam.ac.uk/content/articles/t/the-arts-and-crafts-movement/.

6. It is thus clear why Steel once remarked, 'Phulkari work is a true art, in so much that it must be the outcome of love and leisure, not of haste and greed' (Steel 1888: 71, 72).
7. Ramaswamy again mentions the paradox of the word 'Kadar Kadarudu', as mentioned by a weaver at Erode. The word 'kadar' meant khadi in Tamil while 'kadaral' meant lamentation. In other words, the weaver was trying to tell that handlooms were in the death throes (Ramaswamy 2002: 120).

References

Bayly, C. A. (2002). 'Archaic' and 'Modern' Globalization in the Eurasian and African Arena, ca. 1750–1850. In A. G. Hopkins (Ed.), *Globalization in World History*. New York: W. W. Norton.

Birdwood, S. G. (1980). *The Industrial Arts of India*. London: Chapman & Hall Ltd.

Breckenridge, C. (1989). The Aesthetics and Politics of Colonial Collecting: India at World Fairs. *Comparative Studies of Society and History, 31*(2), 195–216.

Chatterjee, A. (2014). *Can Our Future Be Handmade*. Fifth Kamaladevi Chattopadhyay Memorial Lecture. Centre for Cultural Resource and Training.

Chattopadhyaya, K. (1964). Origin and Development of Embroidery in Our Land. *Marg Quarterly*.

Chattopadhaya, K. (1975). *Handicrafts of India*. New Delhi: Indian Council for Cultural Relations.

Chattopadhaya, K. (1982). *Decorative Design and Craftsmanship of India*. Bombay: D.B. Tara Parevala Sons and Co., Pvt. Ltd.

Chattopadhaya, K. (1984). Crafts and the Future. *India International Centre Quarterly, 11*(4), 5–14.

Cohn, B. (1996). Cloth, Clothes and Colonialism: India in the 19th Century. In B. Cohn (Ed.), *Colonialism and Its Forms of Knowledge: The British in India*. Princeton, NJ: Princeton University Press.

Collingwood, R. (1938). *The Principles of Art*. Oxford: Clarendon Press.

Coomaraswamy, A. (1909). *The Indian Craftsman*. London: Probsthain.

Coomaraswamy, A. (1964). *The Art and Crafts of India and Ceylon*. New York: Farrar, Straus.

Dhamija, J. (2007). *Kamaladevi Chattopadhyay*. New Delhi: National Book Trust.

Gevorkyan, A. V. (2018). *Transition Economies Transformation, Development, and Society in Eastern Europe and the Former Soviet Union*. Oxon: Routledge.

Gonsalves, P. (2010). *Clothing for Liberation: A Communication Analysis of Gandhi's Swadeshi Revolution*. Los Angeles: Sage.

Gillow, J. A. (1991). *Traditional Indian Textiles*. London: Thames and London Ltd.

Jain, E. (2014). Khadi: A Cloth and Beyond. *Gandhi Marg Quarterly*, 223–240.

Jain, J. (1985). Saudagiri Prints: Textiles for Far-Off Siam. *The India Magazine*, 54–63.

Jaitly, J. (1990). *The Craft Traditions of India*. New Delhi: Lusture Press.

Jayakar, P., & Irwin, J. (1956). *Textiles and Ornaments of India: A Selection of Designs*. New York: Museum of Modern Art.

Kasturi, P. B. (2005). Designing Freedom. *Design Issues, 21*(4), 68–77.

Liebl, M., & Roy, T. (2004). Handmade in India: Preliminary Analysis of Crafts Producers and Crafts Production. *Economic and Political Weekly, 38*(51/52), 5366–5376.

Ludden, D. (1992). India's Development Regime. In N. Dirks (Ed.), *Colonialism and Culture*. Ann Arbor: University of Michigan Press.

McGowan, A. (2009). *Crafting the Nation in Colonial India*. New York: Palgrave.

Naylor, G. (1970). *The Arts and Crafts Movement: A Study of Its Sources, Ideals and Influence of Design Theory*. London: Studio Vista.

Pal, M. K. (1978). *Crafts & Craftsmen in Traditional India*. New Delhi: Kanak.

Pathak, A. (1998). *Indian Modernity: Contradictions, Paradoxes and Possibilities*. New Delhi: Gyan Publishing House.

Postman, N. (1992). *Technopoly: The Surrender of Culture to Technology*. New York: Vintage.

Ramagundam, R. (2008). *Gandhi's Khadi: A History of Contention and Conciliation*. New Delhi: Orient Longman.

Ramaswamy, V. (2002). Alien Weave: Crafts Verses Consumerism. *India International Centre Quarterly, 29*(2), 117–128.

Ramaswamy, V. (2013). *The Song of the Loom*. New Delhi: Primus.

Riello, G., &. Roy, T. (2009). Introduction: The World of South Asian Textiles, 1500–1850. In G. Riello &. T. Roy (Eds.), *How India Clothed the World: The World of South Asian Textile, 1500–1850* (pp. 1–27). Leiden and Boston: Brill.

Saraf, D. N. (1998). *Indian Crafts: Development and Potential*. New Delhi: Vikas Publishing House.

Sennett, R. (2008). *The Craftsman*. New Haven: Yale University Press.

Steel, F. (1888). Phulkari Work in the Punjab. *Journal of Indian Art, 1*, 71–72.

Vasanthi, R. (2010). *The Warp and the Weft: Community and Gender Identity Among Banaras Weavers*. New Delhi: Routledge.

Venkatesan. S. (2009). Rethinking Agency: Persons and Things in the Heterotopia of 'Traditional Indian Craft'. *The Journal of the Royal Anthropological Institute, 15*(1), 78–95.

http://www.craftrevival.org/voiceDetails.asp?Code=311. Accessed on August 27, 2017.

http://ccrtindia.gov.in/downloads/other/lecture. Accessed on August 30, 2017.

CHAPTER 6

Documentaries and the Development Project: Filmmaking as a Discursive Practice

Nivedita Ghosh

Introduction

The post-structural critique of the development project entails a scrutiny of the manner in which it operates like a powerful ideology or a 'historically produced discourse' (Escobar 1995: 6) that led many countries to see themselves as underdeveloped and acquire the label of being 'poor', 'backward' and 'dependent' (Arce et al. 1996: 156), in short, as the 'third world'. Scholars have argued that these labels have enabled a justification for introducing development-based projects into various third world nations by turning them into 'clients' of legitimate intervention (Schaffer and Wood 1985) and have resultantly assisted various global agencies to expand their political and economic hold over the region. Further, development has involved not only a set of practices and actions but also a systematic 'deployment of knowledge' (Banda 2004: 98) about the regions to be developed. This knowledge entails representations about the people and their cultures shaping the way in which their realities can be imagined and acted upon.

N. Ghosh (✉)
Department of Sociology, Jesus and Mary College, University of Delhi, New Delhi, India

D. N. Pathak and A. K. Das (eds.), *Investigating Developmentalism*,
https://doi.org/10.1007/978-3-030-17443-9_6

Primarily, it involves European and Western representations of societies belonging to Asia, Africa, Latin America and Eastern Europe as overpopulated, poor and backward. Escobar further argues that developmentalism finds a close ally in Said's Orientalism (1979), which involves making descriptive and authoritative statements about the Orient in order to not only manage but also discursively produce it. These statements operate to represent the orient as exotic, primitive and at times irrational, reducing it to be inferior and opposite to the west. Like Orientalism, according to Escobar, developmentalism too involves a 'regime of representation' (Escobar 1995: 6) comprising of descriptions, statistics, categories and images. Escobar borrows from Mitchell (1989) to add that the development model presents the third world as a set of pictures, which the European subject experiences as a visitor at an exhibition. The visitor/observer enframes these images through European/Western categories in order to make sense of them. The third world and its people are therefore presented as being 'out there', to be viewed more as a representation, and outside of this exhibition what is expected to be encountered is not 'the real world but only further models and representations of the real' (Mitchell 1989: 221).

It is against this backdrop that we begin to understand the role of documentary films in forwarding the spirit of developmentalism. The story of development is integrally tied to the manner in which it has used documentary films to communicate the challenges and successes of its projects, while also highlighting the need for intervention in various areas. The issues raised by these films range between topics pertaining to human rights, population, poverty, health, gender, sustainability, environment, in short, as Sachs (1992) calls them, 'keywords of the development discourse'. It is worth a mention that such development-oriented topics, especially based on the third world nations are able to draw a substantial amount of funding from several international agencies, a point we return to at a later stage. Now, to theoretically contextualise this argument, the present essay borrows from the work of scholars who have contributed to the field of discursive analysis around power, knowledge and technology. A key figure in this debate is Michel Foucault who conceives of discourse as 'a complex network of relationship between individuals, texts, ideas and institutions, with each 'node' having an impact, to varying degrees on other nodes, and on the dynamics of the discourse as a whole' (Olsson 2007: 221). For Foucault, no statement is true or valid in a random way. Rather, there are:

> A set of conventions of "discursive rules" - either formal or implicit, but widely recognised within the community - by which a "truth statement" can be evaluated or validated or repudiated. These discursive rules not only shape the form that a valid truth statement can take in that discourse, but also, more fundamentally, they dictate, what can be said in the context of that discourse. (Olsson 2007: 222)

In the context of documentary films, this idea situates filmmaking activity as being contrary to the positivist approach, where knowledge/truth is considered to be based on an objective reality, which can be accessed by the filmmaker once she removes her inherent biases. In contrast to this, discourse analysis constitutes the practice of documentary filmmaking as a practice where meanings are not only shared and derived but borrowed from what Foucault explains to be archived. For Foucault:

> Members of a discourse community are connected not only by a shared engagement with a collection of texts but also by a set of interpretation of these texts that the members of the community share. The set of common "truth statements" held by a particular discourse community are known as the 'archive'. (Olsson 2007: 222)

In the present context, the body of work, texts, stories, locations and even equipment that filmmakers use or refer to constitute the archive. The archive allows the filmmaker to say something on a particular topic. It is the archive where the 'exotic', the 'difficult' and the 'problematic' are framed. Pollution, poverty, climate change, terrorism, exotic mythology, human rights, social movements, etc. are some of the common archival themes which, as we shall see are also able to draw more funding compared to other topics. Evidently, these themes are selected for filmmaking from what are understood to be the third world regions, one such popular destination being India. The following sections thus argue that the development project crucially depends upon documentary films to forward their cause and presents how the process of making these films remain problematic on several counts.

A Note on Documentary Film Funders

An important manner in which the direction of a documentary film is controlled is through the process of funding. Not only do topics like human rights, population, poverty, health, gender, sustainability, environment are able to attract more funds but interestingly, a number of major film festivals and documentary funding agencies (such as the Ford Foundation, IDFA Bertha Fund, Hubert Bals Fund, Movies That Matter, Alter Cine Foundation, etc.) demarcate grants for films and filmmakers from Asia, Africa, Latin America, and Middle and Eastern Europe as a separate category. In the call for applications section by the funders, we commonly see the use of phrases such as 'make a difference', 'invite [for] action and change', 'create stories that can change, heal, and enrich lives' and so on. The recurring use of such phrases presents the practice of documentary filmmaking almost as a 'call for action' to bring about social change and justice in the third world. As a result, we also witness a repetition in the choice of themes on which films are made from areas where intervention can be made or where one can 'make a difference'. Words like 'Asia', 'Africa', and 'Latin America' are themselves used repeatedly as archival words, demarcated as regions that evoke a specific range of film topics—broadly dealing with injustices of various kinds. A stark difference is visible when we look at the call for grants announcements for films based on America for instance. We find that, when it comes to funding documentaries from America, these grants are catered instead towards promoting the 'spirit of art' and refining the craft and technique of the filmmaker. These announcements do not define any specific theme, and even if they do, these themes focus on those pertaining to the strengthening of the democratic fabric of the American society. The announcement call for American documentaries treats the genre of non-fiction films as a source for providing entertainment to the viewer, and the practice of documentary filmmaking is seen as a means to express one's artistic side. This is in contrast to the funding requirements for the non-Western documentaries where the medium is seen as a tool to bring about 'change'.

Furthermore, for the American films, at no point, any specific topic for the documentary is spelt out and rather, the language of the funders presents the issues of the American society as 'complex', as emanating from the experiences of a 'diverse society'. This portrayal can be contextualised within the larger debate regarding the 'complexification' of the west as opposed to the 'simplification' of the non-west. Said (1979) for instance argued that the oversimplification of Eastern civilisations into stereotypical denominations was one of the pillars of the orientalist discourse, a practice that converted the region into mappable and understandable units. The process of funding can be seen as an extension of this exercise that in a major way, contributes to the 'enframing' of the third world as 'poor', 'dependent', 'difficult', 'problematic', 'populated' and as opposed to this, the west as 'democratic', 'diverse' and 'complex'. The funding process thus sets the non-west apart as a region that requires intervention, if not politically, at least visually. It needs to be highlighted at this point that this repetition in description of the west and non-west is not limited to the world of funding or the choice of film topics. Interestingly, the very understanding of what it means to be a documentary filmmaker can be drawn from the manner in which the professionals from this field describe the nature of their work and thus their choice of film equipment.

Equipment that Filmmakers Prefer

In November 2013, Public Broadcasting Service (PBS), an American Television Broadcasting Company, published the results of their survey[1] conducted on equipment that those involved in documentary filmmaking were using or preferred to use in their field. 83% of these respondents were based in the USA, 5% in the UK, 4% in Canada and 8% were 'others'. According to the survey, apart from the necessity of being Broadcast Compliant, the best cameras were decided on the basis of certain prominent features such as a long battery life, small size, light weight, low light shooting, image stabilisation and their ability to work well in 'difficult' environments. Such difficult environments included anything from harsh weather conditions to areas that required permissions to areas where there was a need for the filmmakers to be discreet. These documentary filmmaking requirements were incorporated in the survey in the form of reviews by professionals on their preferred make of cameras and other filmmaking equipment. These reviews were presented as being a result of the 'field experiences' of the equipment users, highlighting the performances, limitations and further expectations from these gadgets. In the reviews of the film practitioners, what we again find is a certain pattern or repetitiveness. Situations where documentary filmmaking takes place or is expected to take place are repeatedly defined as 'problematic', 'difficult' or 'abusive', and the preference of equipment is on the basis of its ability to stand up to such situations, thus the terms used for them are in the likes of 'sturdy' or 'indestructible'. Through the reviews in the PBS survey, we are reminded of Rosaldo's (1986) article, where he critiques E. E. Evans-Pritchard's classic text *The Nuer* (1940) by asserting that the fieldworker, in his attempt to create objective descriptions about his field is really constituting himself as the voice of reason, removing the context of political inequalities. A running theme in the Nuer descriptions, according to Rosaldo is the suffering that the fieldworker endured while attempting to cross-cultural boundaries. The following quote by Evans-Pritchard is strikingly similar to the concerns repeatedly pointed out by the documentary filmmakers in the above survey,

> My total residence among the Nuer was thus about a year. I do not consider a year adequate time in which to make a sociological study of a people, especially a difficult people in adverse circumstance. (Evans-Pritchard 1940: 14)

Rosaldo argues that Evans-Pritchard presents the fieldworker (himself) as 'a man endowed with calm presence of mind under the most arduous conditions' (ibid.), describing the endurance of his hardships, which he has 'lived to tell… despite all his trials and tribulations' (ibid.). The remarkable similarity between the descriptions of Evans-Pritchard and the documentary filmmakers about their field throws light on the very nature of contemporary documentary practices. Documentary filmmakers while talking about their work often share such hardships that went into the making of their films, a point evident also through the description of their choice of equipment. The PBS survey highlights how documentary filmmakers are presented as people who step into the problematic areas (often of the third world), and after heroically acquiring film footage, return with equipment, which remains unharmed if it is 'sturdy' enough. Filmmaking activity itself is seen as an achievement, an adventure of sorts where filming equipment is also named as Heros and Pros, precisely to highlight this adventurous role that is seen to be played by the filmmaker. Furthermore, with such repeated and matter-of-fact descriptions of the field as 'difficult', the film location emerges as a site, which has the character of being difficult, independent of the filmmaker. However, as we shall see through subsequent case studies, the difficulties faced by the filmmakers are also tied closely to their own negotiation skills and networking decisions. These difficulties are very much shaped by the filmmaker's knowledge about the people being filmed. The survey however does not bring out the dimensions of these difficulties and rather socially neutralises the filmmaker along with the equipment they use. The equipment too is presented as being untainted by the political context of its use and is portrayed as innocently doing the job that it is meant to do. Thus, in the language of the funders, in the choice of filmmaking topics, in the descriptions about the field, we find an emerging pattern, similar to a Foucauldian discursive formation. Foucault writes:

> Whenever one can describe, between a number of statements, such a system of dispersion, whenever, between objects, types of statement, concepts, or thematic choices, one can define a regularity (an order, correlations, positions and functionings, transformations), we will say, for the sake of convenience, that we are dealing with a discursive formation… (Foucault 1972: 38)

Discursive formation is the enunciative principle on the basis of which something can be said about an object. Such statements and groups of statements acquire a relationship even if they do not have the same author, or even if the authors are unaware of each other's existence. Such discursive statements can be understood to appear within a field (which is albeit not definitive or absolute), in order to grasp the rules of their appearance. Within that field, the statements refer to the same object, enabling its unity, thus constituting a discourse around the object. The result is a body of heterogenous statements that coexist, depend upon one another, interlock and even exclude other statements. Thus, the object, which may not be permanent, may acquire an appearance of permanency during a particular period of time. Further, these objects are shaped in their daily practice, through a certain style or constancy in the descriptions regarding them. Thus, the discourse not only constitutes the object but also may transform it altogether.

Accordingly, it is argued in this study that the practice of documentary filmmaking is a discursive field, within which, one may find a certain consistency in descriptions about the film location, film equipment, choice of topics or even those who will be filmed. This consistency not only characterises what has been already said in the context of documentary films pertaining to the third world, but 'what will be said' or, to be more precise, 'what can be said'. This argument will be further substantiated with the help of data drawn from documentaries shot by Western and European filmmakers in India. The chapter argues that the discursive nature of the development paradigm which presents the third world as 'problematic' and in need of intervention, harmoniously befits the discursive practice of documentary filmmaking which presents the filmmaker as that courageous individual who can tread this problematic territory and respond to the 'call for action' made by the funding agencies. In this process, we get to see not only how certain development issues get more attention than others, but also how certain issues get identified with the certain regions specifically.

Making of the Discursive Documentaries

The subsequent sections of the chapter examine three broad themes that operate as 'keywords' in the context of development related issues in India, namely *poverty*, *population* and *mythology*. It presents cases from the field that highlight the manner in which these were filmed by some of the major international documentary production houses, channels and filmmakers. The identity of those involved in the filmmaking process or the films themselves has not been revealed wherever I did not receive consent or where the participants showed discomfort. Names of actual locations however have been retained since much of the analysis of the filmmaking process is tied to the character of the location where the shooting is conducted. Real identities have been disclosed only of those who consented to be named. A final comment necessarily required before discussing the film shoots is that this chapter does not attempt to generalise the experiences of all westerners filming in India but only tries to bring out through specific case studies, the limitations of certain kinds of documentary filmmaking practices.

a. Filming Poverty

India is one of the favourite places for filmmakers trying to depict poverty and in the world of documentary filmmaking there is rarely a confusion regarding what it means to 'show' the poor. Images of people living in slums, under bridges or on the streets are some of the quintessential portrayals of the poor and can be repeatedly found in films that try to bring out this reality. Not surprisingly, therefore, during the course of my fieldwork, I got sufficient opportunity to interact with filmmakers and fixers about their experiences of filming the poor in India. What gets revealed through their accounts and experiences is how ideas regarding poverty and backwardness dominate not simply the storyline but the very process of filmmaking. As we will see, perceptions about the Indian poor as being 'needy', 'difficult' and even 'dangerous' define the experiences of Western filmmakers filming in India. This especially comes out in the manner in which compensations and payments are handled and negotiations are made with those intended to be filmed. In this section, we thus look at instances of how 'the poor' are approached by Western filmmakers on their shoots in India, problematising the very process of depicting poverty.

In this exploration, the accounts of the fixers become particularly important because many Western filmmakers hire the services of fixers or some sort of a guide to negotiate their way through the country. In a way, the fixers help the filmmakers sail through the 'difficulties' that they encounter in a foreign land. In order to find suitable fixers, the filmmaking teams get in touch with Indian film and TV production companies who assist them with research on their film, location scouting, searching for experts for filming interviews, production and finance management, liaison with government and non-government agencies, etc. Many of these tasks are undertaken by fixers who travel along with the film crew on shooting locations. The fixers have a wide network of contacts amongst equipment dealers, location assistants, transport suppliers, hoteliers, etc. and are also required to have the ability to make friends and acquaintances wherever they go, just in case they need to get in touch with people for the films. Usually, it is the relationship that the fixer has been able to develop with, e.g. the equipment supplier that ensures a speedy replacement of troublesome machinery.

The accounts and experiences of Indian documentary film fixers become crucial in developing an understanding about how filmmakers from the West approach their subject matter in India, and what they feel are problematic and difficult situations. It also allows us to delve into the manner in which Western filmmakers negotiate their way around, especially when they try to film 'the poor' in India. One such interesting trend observed during fieldwork was that it was the fixer who would undertake the task of befriending the poorer respondents and thanking them, without the filmmakers having to speak to them at all. The fixer's presence in a way released the filmmaker/crew from 'dealing with' people directly such that they could focus on the composition of the shot instead. This process can be understood as *delegation of rapport building* to the fixer, and one of the reasons, this was done was to save time for foreign filmmakers who did not want to engage in discussions and translations with people especially when they were on a tight shooting schedule. Because rapport building required conversations that centred around knowing one another, understanding the issues around the story, and also keeping in touch with respondents (especially if one needed to return to the field), filmmakers would delegate this task to the fixer whose qualification was enhanced by her ability to 'chat with people'. In such cases, the fixer also managed gratitudes and promises by getting back to the respondent with gifts, thank yous and updates. This instrumentality is significant since what becomes evident is, just because someone is being filmed, does not mean that the filmmakers have necessarily built any rapport or relationship of consent with them directly.

To substantiate this point, a brief example from a Delhi-based shoot can be used. An American-based film production team had hired a local fixer to assist them during the shooting of their film, which can be presently referred to as *Poverty in India*. The filmmaker wanted to project the problem of poverty in India 'in a visually interesting manner', by depicting some of the poorer localities in Delhi. This particular shoot took place in the Okhla region in a slum colony situated next to railway tracks. In this shoot, the idea was to capture a passing train with people hanging out from the doors and windows. The team also wanted to interview some slum dwellers about how they felt living next to a railway track. While the team got busy setting up its equipment, fixer Natasha started chatting with some local boys to see if they would be willing to give the team a sound bite, as required by the filmmaker. Seeing that the camera was being set up right next to where people slept, one of the boys shouted:

> *Hamari gareebi pe aap roti khane aaye ho? Yaha koi shooting nahi hone denge.*
>
> (You have come to earn your living by showing our poverty? We will not let your shooting happen here.)

Looking at this, the filmmaker suggested that perhaps they could be paid some money so that the boys don't create trouble for the crew as they appeared (to the filmmaker) to be non-cooperative and aggressive. Natasha however decided to speak to a few elders from the locality and tell them that the film was merely trying to bring out problems of people in the area. The elders convinced by this shooed away the 'aggressive boys' and asked another boy to go and give a sound bite before the camera. Natasha then thanked the elders as they made it possible for the shoot to materialise. What Natasha did was negotiated on behalf of the film crew while the latter chose to maintain a distance and instead focused on the setting up of the equipment. Furthermore, the filmmaker understood the boys to be 'uncooperative' and 'aggressive' and overlooked his own decision to set up the camera in a space that the boys saw as 'private'. Furthermore, the decision to pay the boys for gaining access needs to be within the larger documentary filmmaking context where compensations are often used by filmmakers as a route for easy access to a location, in which one does not have to get involved in lengthy negotiations. Monetary compensations not only highlight but are also used to reinforce the power relation between the filmmaker and the subject, such that the latter is expected to behave in a certain way, after being paid off. In a conversation with Shernaz Italia (a former fixer, but now owns her production company), this aspect of documentary filmmaking is further highlighted. In the following conversation, Italia describes how an important part of the fixer's work profile is to lend an ear to some of the difficult demands and expectations made by the filmmakers.

> One day we got a call from a British film company. The lady on the phone asked me...brace yourself for this... 'Can you fix a Sati for us'? At first I thought I heard her wrong. But then she said again, 'Can you fix a Sati for us'? I told her if she was aware that Sati involved the murder of a person and no, it was not possible for us to fix a Sati! They were willing to compensate well they said. Can you believe how ridiculous things can get in this line? Then another time, we had an American filmmaker wanting to film the Dakhma, the Parsi cremation ground. But it is such a sacred place and you cannot film there. He thought I could easily make that happen because I was Parsi. I refused him outright. You would think that as documentary filmmakers, these people would be more sensitized to the beliefs and customs of other cultures. But some of them just don't care and are willing to go to any extent to get that shot. I will tell you one incident Nivedita, but I cannot name this filmmaker because he is very renowned. We were shooting on the *ghats* of Banaras. There is this particular *ghat* where they float the dead and the water used to be full of flesh eating fish. This filmmaker wanted to show how poor Indians have to brave these fish and swim in these waters to float the dead bodies. Obviously no such thing used to happen because no one in their right mind would get into the water with deadly fish in it. So this filmmaker got hold of this poor, frail rickshaw puller, paid him money and asked him to get into the water. And in India, you know for some money, you can find enough poor people willing to do stupid things. I cannot forget the look on that guy's face when he entered the water. He was so scared, he kept shaking. On that day I experienced one of those moments when I just felt like quitting this line.

An understanding of the practice of documentary filmmaking through the accounts of the fixers allows us to critically delve into the production culture of these films. These accounts constitute documentary filmmaking as a practice that has the potential to feed on social misfortune, which is then portrayed through eye-catching gimmicks. Furthermore, while compensations may be seen as an easy way to get the required shots, not all filmmakers believe that they can access their respondents through payments. On the other end of the spectrum, there are filmmakers who feel payments may not be the best way to 'access the poor', since compensations make the situation even more difficult for the filmmaker. According to a renowned American Ethnographic Filmmaker (name undiscosed):

> As a documentary filmmaker, you will, in all probabilities be filming people poorer than you. But as a westerner, when you film in countries like India, the difficulty is that people quickly start to expect things in return. They feel you can either help them monetarily or by taking care of some bureaucratic hurdles for them. It is important to keep in mind that you must not start paying them. This will only build expectations of more payment, and eventually you will run out of funds. You have to tell them from day one that you have no money and you cannot help them in any way. If they still give you their time, you're in luck!

The above remark of the filmmaker feeds into the image of the poor Indian subject as 'needy', and waiting for the western figure to extend a helping hand. It also reflects an orientalist thought process that functions through a presumed centricity of the Western/affluent filmmaker, to whom the practice of documentary filmmaking is understood to belong. On one hand, the practice of documentary filmmaking can be seen to carry and reproduce the same ideological manifestations as that forwarded by the development discourse. In their bid to represent poverty, backwardness and hardship, several filmmakers seem to be reproducing similar kinds of imagery as that which is 'expected' from the region, thus continuously feeding such images to the larger development discourse. On the other hand, their actual engagement with the poor remains mediated, distanced and eased out by the presence of the fixer, thus making the development films as encashing upon and reinforcing the very ideas that they claim to challenge.

b. Filming Population

The next keyword discussed here fits into the classic example of what W. J. T. Mitchell refers to as the 'emergence of a world picture' (Mitchell 2007: 50). Mitchell argues that the world today is increasingly being scanned into images that are propagated not through Hollywood films but realistic documentary-based spectacles. A global distribution of images through mass media is contributing to a discourse of globalization by circulating images of different parts of the world as 'modern', 'militarized', 'poor' and so on. These spaces according to Mitchell are symbolic and carry larger global meanings, and are transformed into what he calls a 'heterotopia', 'a region set aside from use to transform a specific place into an emblem of the world' (ibid.: 58). It is argued here that the development apparatus, which presupposes a justified need for intervention, borrows heavily from these images, which effectively work as a 'call for action'. India too contributes to many of such 'world pictures', ranging from poverty and gender to health. The one we discuss here today is equally quintessential to the region, namely population.

To present an example that will enable us to understand the production of the 'world picture of overpopulation', we refer to a Delhi and Uttar Pradesh-based shoot for a film depicting the problem of increasing population in the world, and how India was a major contributor to this. To film this, the filmmaker had shortlisted two shooting sites in India, one that could aptly depict the problem of population, the other which could tell the viewer about the success of measures undertaken by the Indian government in order to tackle it. To visually depict the 'problem of population in India', the shoot location was decided by actively finding crowded areas. And since the base of the crew was Delhi, somehow it was not surprising that the site chosen was Old Delhi. In the congested lanes of Old Delhi, the idea was to shoot, what in film parlance refers to as GVs or 'General Views'. Wadsworth explains that GVs are 'shots of general nature, which can be used to set a scene or establish a location - establishers, in other words' (Wadsworth 2016: 25). He further explains, 'GVs are the types of shots that documentary filmmakers shoot all the time to allow a future edit to have as many options as possible' (ibid.). Thus, filming in Old Delhi would primarily entail making general shots of crowded marketplaces, traffic snarls, busy streets, etc. The second shooting location was decided on the basis of the solutions it had to offer, and thus, a sterilisation centre in Shahbad, Uttar Pradesh was shortlisted to see how effective these truly were in convincing people to opt for family planning. In the final edit, scenes from the sterilisation centre would be combined with Old Delhi GVs, and a narrator's voice would be added to show the viewer, how India was dealing with the menace of rising population. Interestingly, this problem-solution format of filmmaking, rather than being a mere choice of the filmmaker is in fact a requirement of several funding agencies. According to filmmaker Priyanka Chhabra:

> The (problem-solution) format is said to make the film viewing process simpler as it clearly identifies the issues and their possible resolutions, without confusing the audience. The voice narration guides the viewers towards the direction where the filmmaker wants to take them. However, a possible fallout of this format is that it ends up simplifying complex issues because sometimes the source of the problem is not that simple and clear.

Chhabra's remark reiterates how this type of documentary film's format attempts the simplification of complex 'third world' issues. Furthermore, a common reason for finding a range of documentary films on similar development-oriented topics, and based on a similar format can also be ascribed to general outlines put out by the funders. Documentary films that draw more funds and viewership are those that are somewhere able to deploy the problem-solution model in a simple and effective manner, as attempted by the current population shoot in Delhi/Uttar Pradesh. The monotony of such standardised depictions of complex issues is often not missed by the filmmakers themselves. During the course of my fieldwork, I met a number of filmmakers who engaged in a much prevalent practice of taking up these 'well-funded' projects to channelise a portion of the grant towards their own 'more meaningful films'. Thus, it is not surprising to find filmmakers who choose to make these development-oriented films as being quite disconnected from the complexities of the issue.

Interestingly, the problem-solution model for shooting this film was so standardised that it enabled the crew to shoot this film without the presence of the filmmaker. In the production of this particular film in India, the filmmaker was absent from the shooting locations and a cinematographer was hired to film on behalf of her, who would film by taking online instructions about the material that has to be shot. The American filmmaker was guiding the Indian-origin-US-based cinematographer Ashish by going over the material shot by him during the day telephonically and via emails, and then providing further inputs about the remaining shoot. While shooting, Ashish intermittently consulted the notes given by the filmmaker the previous day to understand what he needed to film next. The material shot during the day along with the general shooting experience of the crew would be emailed to the filmmaker in great detail. On the basis of that, she would give further filming instructions. Following is an excerpt from the shooting instructions sent to the fixer and cinematographer by the filmmaker:

> We are looking for a couple who is considering the sterilization procedure, but there's a bit of conflict, either a personal struggle with the decision or a struggle between two or more people about making the decision. It would be great if you found a few options for families and we could see photos, video and/or descriptions prior to shooting and decide who would be the best to follow…The ideal scenario for would be to find a couple that has all female

children – possibly many of them. The wife wants the sterilization procedure, but her husband does not want her to do it because he wants a son.

Apart from the written instructions, the filmmaker from USA had also forwarded images of what kind of 'crowd' shots she wanted from India. These were in the likes of 'over crowded streets', 'too many passengers on a *rickshaw*', 'traffic jams', 'trains overflowing with people', etc. Interestingly, some of these places in the images were from Old Delhi itself, e.g. worshippers offering prayer in Jama Masjid. These images were sent to Ashish as indicators of the kinds of shots he needed to take from India. While speaking to Ashish about how the experience of shooting without the director was, in his response, yet another aspect of the development-oriented documentary practice comes to light. Ashish said:

> See Joanne, the director of the film is a very open person and completely trusts my decisions, but still her not being here is also one reason why I can film this way. Western films are not made like this, with such flexibility and openness. There would have been a lot more scheduling and planning had she been here. The other thing is, documentary filmmaking is a lot about seeing what's happening and going with the flow. Lets say if I were to make the same film, I would have taken a very different approach. See, we are here in Old Delhi, and what I see is how there is so much of recycling going on here. Look at all this junk, which is brought here. The basic problem is that westerners think that just because India has all this population, it is depleting world's resources. And so even this film is trying to raise the issue of limited resources and rising population of the east. But Indians are surviving on so little! In fact, a third of world's resources are being used by the wealthiest in the west, whereas, the largest of the numbers are surviving on scraps. That's a more interesting story for me. So when you are directing a film from a distance, I guess you really miss out on the opportunity to see the story unfold before you.

The presence of the filmmaker on the filmmaking site thus leaves some space for modifying the narrative on the basis of what is available, rather than what is 'planned'. Her absence thus leads to the making of a film in which images will only be fitted into a larger, already available narrative. What we thus encounter is a process where already existing images and notions about sterilization and rising population (as provided by the filmmaker) contributes to the production of more of such similar imagery and discourse around population growth in India—e.g. son preference of the father. *Rather than art being mechanically reproduced, as argued by Benjamin, it is being discursively reproduced, in the Focauldian sense.* It is in this way that we also understand the production of heterotopic images of the world that Mitchell talks about.

To explain this point further, one can focus on certain important moments from the Old Delhi shoot. On the day of the shoot, the crew reached the location by 10:00 a.m. Cinematographer Ashish explained that usually they would start early but since they wanted to film crowded areas, it would be pointless to come before, as the shops would not have opened. As directed by the filmmaker, this shooting was going to be in crowded areas and the equipment was set up in the corner of the busy street right opposite the Red Fort. As the equipment was being set up, and just as the camera was mounted on the tripod, curious people started to gather around, stopping to see the shoot. Overhearing the conversations between the crew about not finding enough crowd, two *rickshaw* pullers who were hired to carry the film equipment in the lanes of Old Delhi, also gave their suggestion to the fixer:

> *Aapko bheed chahiye na? Yaha nahi milega.. woh Darya Ganj mein milega.. ekdum khacha khach bhara rehta hai. Hamari suniye, aapko tower ke upar leke jaate hain, pura purani dilli ka nazara milega, pura bheed.*
>
> (You want a crowd right? You wont find it here. You will find it in Darya Ganj. That place is pact! Listen to us, we'll take you to the top of the tower. You can see the whole of Old Delhi from there…the whole congestion.)

The crew took the suggestion of the *rickshaw* pullers and decided to move towards Darya Ganj. The camera was set up again at Darya Ganj and again the crowd started to accumulate. While still discussing what would be a good shot to take, a man approached the crew and started chatting with the fixer and me:

> What is this film about? Traffic? Are you trying to show how much public inconvenience happens because of the traffic jams? In that case you should wait for some time since morning is not the right time to see traffic. In the afternoon once the schools close, hundreds of children gather on this main crossing. The whole road gets blocked. While you are at it, you might as well film the causes of traffic jams.

The crew didn't quite pay attention to what the man was saying and continued to go by Ashish's decisions. Ashish, throughout most of his filming, had put the camera at a slightly lower angle, such that it was not at the eye level of the people. By doing this, the viewer would look at *rickshaws*, traffic and people walking from a mid-torso-level. Ashish explained his decision to film from a lower angle in a discussion later. He said that low-level shots are supposed to make images appear imposing and would make the crowd overpowering to the viewer. Similarly, the shot he had taken from the straight crowded lane of Meena Bazaar opposite Jama Masjid was a perspective shot from a slightly high angle. This shot was taken to create a sense of numbers of people spread out over a vertical distance. Similarly, some of the shots of the crowd had been blurred to create a sense of confusion, more people, and more hustle bustle, than there actually was.

A word on the camera angles and effects becomes interesting here because, in this depiction of a 'populated area', it was not enough to merely show to the viewer 'a lot of people', but it was equally important to make the viewer experience certain feelings about those visuals. The visuals were captured in a way to create a sense of confusion and overbearingness for the viewer, something that those present while taking the shots were not quite experiencing. Rather, the crew, because of the time at which they were shooting, had to struggle to find the overcrowded moments they were truly looking for. Thus, we see how GVs are guided by the discursive constructions around the topic to be filmed, not only by reproducing images that are already 'out there', but also by attaching effects that further reinforce the Western descriptions about the region as being 'confusing' and 'overbearing'. Furthermore, Ashish did not try to film the possible reasons for why the place becomes overcrowded on certain times of the day, as being pointed out by the onlookers. The exploration of the reasons was not a part of the instructions sent to the cinematographer who was primarily supposed to 'stick to the instructions'. In the final edit, these standardised images are going to be 'fitted' into an already existing narrative, without really having the need to understand for instance why a particular locality faces traffic snarls? Accordingly, the locality of Darya Ganj will acquire the characteristic of 'any locality whatsoever' in India, thus generalising a very local problem. In such development documentary films trying to depict overpopulation in India, we see how discursive imagery and narrative is only being re-created and re-presented, rather than contributing to the production of newer modes of knowledge around the topic.

Filming Mythologies

The final case presented in this section highlights how documentary filmmaking undertakes exotic representations of a region or people, attempting to present the respondents as if they were frozen in a period of time. It was Edward Said, who offered a systematic critique of the Western discourse of the Orient and scratched the surface of a vast pool of writings and imageries that had both dehumanised and exoticised the non-Western. Several decades of overly simplified portrayal of the third world has found legitimacy in both fiction and non-fiction films. When we speak of India, both have actively participated to create a visual imagery of the region, carefully guiding the imagination and the thought process of the west. Images of yogis, saints, tribes, peasants, people in their traditional costumes, making traditional handicrafts, etc. have been commonly used to describe the 'idea' of India. In this section, we look at the manner in which these exotic representations find their way in documentary films. It is argued here that a very effective tool through which exoticism innocuously enters the film is through its *script*. Das (2007) clarifies that:

> A map helps you on your way and prevents you from getting lost. A shooting script is a conceptual map for your shooting journey. It consolidates research and outlines the film's story, providing a visual guideline for the shoot. (Das 2007: 3)

What goes into the making of a script especially for filmmakers wanting to film in other parts of world, many a times is inadequate secondary research. Limited funds and time make filmmakers depend upon these secondary sources, which frequently depict a reality very different from what is finally available to the filmmakers. This is a concern often raised by the fixers, since it is them who more often than not are allotted the task of finding the respondents and locations pertaining to the script, and on several occasions, these seem to be missing from the ground. Thus, as we will see, the script has a serious impact on the ground especially because, in order to mend the gap between what is required and what is available, filmmakers may resort to staging and fakery. The theoretical use of the script also exists in contrast to how it plays out on actual shoots especially because film crews visiting from other countries are often on a tight schedule and have little time to engage in primary research and develop their stories. Sticking to the script thus works well for them as it enables the crew to be on schedule and at the same time access some relevant visuals. The script, as we will see also on occasions removes the necessary presence of the filmmaker from the site of shooting, such that the filming process is heavily guided by the script itself. This is not to say that exotic representations cannot be made without a script, but through such inadequate scripts, documentary filmmaking emerges as a practice that reproduces serious and at times offensive misconceptions about the people being filmed.

To substantiate this argument, we refer to a documentary shot by a British film crew in the Kutch region of Gujarat. This was a partly historical partly mythological documentary where the British filmmakers wanted to film tribes who still were connected/rooted to the Indus Valley Civilization. The research on this film was carried out in advance as part of the pre-production stage. However, this research was secondary, based purely on popular texts and reference material available online. The research team itself had never visited India for developing the story, finalising the interviewees or rekeying the location. No one from the research team was present during the actual shoot of the film either and the crew had to rely majorly on the inputs of the fixer provided by the local production company that they had contacted for production assistance. The film team was in constant touch with the fixer, and via emails had sent the personnel and technical requirements for the shoot, along with an operational script. Following is an excerpt from the script sent to the fixer, which was forwarded to me on the filmmaker's consent:

INDIA

1) TRIBE

We want to discover that there are still tribes (with roots in the IVC) exporting traditional handicrafts today—just as the IVC did. We want to hear about their oral traditions, particularly any about floods (flood in Rann of Kutch 2010). If they are Hindu (this could lead to the introduction to Manu), Mona would like to 'camp' overnight with the tribe, get an intimate insight into their life, oral traditions, etc. but this has to look authentic (not touristy feeling!).

2) HINDUISM

We want to discover that the Indus Valley Civilization practised an early form of Hinduism. We want to learn about the Hindu Trinity (parallel to Christianity)—Brahma, Vishnu and Krishna and that the last 'Kalpa' (Uni-

> verse) ended with a deluge. Then hear the story of Manu. But: * Who can tell us about the above in a simple, fluent way?

According to Said, one of the most significant constructions of Orientalists is the idea of stability and durability of the Orient. In the above script, a search for 'unchanged communities' that are rooted in traditional forms of livelihood, whose lives can be experienced through an overnight stay, is perhaps one of the most striking aspects of orientalism included in the document. Because the script carried a portrayal of people derived from stereotypical ideas about how these tribes would be, some of the scholars and professionals who had an authority to speak on the subject matter eventually refused to be a part of the film as they did not wish to participate in such an exotic portrayal of the local craftsmen. Apart from this, yet another equally problematic characteristic of the script was its need to find a subject who could speak 'fluently' (in English), a request that was raised several times in the remaining script. This criterion was so crucial for the filmmakers that many of the experts lined up for this film were rejected or edited out later because they were not 'fluent' enough for an English audience. Interestingly, this was the case even after making use of subtitles for Easterners speaking in the film. This shows how the film was being made strictly keeping in mind the English viewer, who shouldn't have to struggle too much to make sense of the audio. The film was to be directed by British documentary filmmaker (referred here as) Paul R. The actual shooting would be carried out in several locations around Bhuj, including Mandvi, Ajrakhapur and Dhola Vira. The research and location rekey for the film would be carried out by fixer Ritu, with whom the filmmaker was in constant touch via emails. It was Ritu's responsibility to finally arrange for the experts to be interviewed for the film. And interestingly, the first expert, Ritu got in touch with, was a textile curator, Yazeer Bhai, who was my respondent from another film. It was through Yazeer Bhai that Ritu got my contact and I ended up being a part of this film project, not only as a researcher, but interestingly, as another 'expert' to be filmed. Upon meeting me, Ritu explained that:

> (1) The team was actually not looking for someone who knew too much about this. They were looking for a more general view so that it is easier for the 'Brits' to make sense of something as vast as Hinduism.
>
> (2) They were just really looking for someone who could speak all this in English, fluently and in a simple way.

As I agreed to be the 'expert' for this film, Ritu handed me some literature, pictures/plates depicting Vishnu's various avatars. Guided by the script, now Ritu had to locate the remaining experts and communities, as close to the directions forwarded by the film team as possible. She could not arrange for Mona's night camping with the 'tribes' or them speaking about Manu. The secondary research of the film team had made the assumption that Hindus would know about *Manu* and *Manusmriti*, but not that in this region, the tribes were not necessarily Hindu and even if they were, they did not necessarily know much about Sanskritic Hindu mythologies. In fact, Ritu herself admitted that she could not locate any local from the area who knew anything significant about the *Vishnu-Matsya* myth or *Manu's* background. Apart from this, yet another inaccurate demand by the script that could not be arranged for was the expectation that the craftsmen should speak about the connections between their craft and IVC. Accordingly, Ritu asked Yazeer Bhai to speak on IVC crafts and artefacts, though ironically, this interview, with the only genuine expert on the topic would not make it to the final film since his English was not clear enough for the filmmaker. The interview with me, however, a 'fake expert' would be retained in the film.

On the day of the shoot, I was dropped to the local *Swaminarayan* temple where the sequence was to be filmed. I was briefed that I was supposed to welcome Mona to the temple for the camera and show her around the premises, even though I had never myself been to the place before. Prior to the team's arrival, I quickly took a brief tour of the temple and started rehearsing some things I could say. The team arrived in half an hour and Mona and I performed our 'first meet' sequence a couple of times. We shook hands, exchanged hellos and welcomes and the shot cut! I was then briefed that I had to talk about the temple and then quickly move on to the discussion on *Manu* and *Vishnu,* while showing Mona some of the picture plates that were given to me by Ritu. Although these pictures belonged to the film crew, I had to present them on camera as part of my 'expert' documents. The shooting continued and I started explaining to Mona, aided by her prompts about the Hindu Trinity; about the temple; about the pictures; about the myth; and about the Hindu conception of the circle of life. Paul kept calling cuts and rolls at the end of the day, I had apparently done a good job. After this, the team went on to shoot some of the final scenes such as the temple *aartii* (prayers), where Mona appeared to be mesmerised by the sounds and colours of this exotic ambience. The team eventually thanked me, as did I and left.

The filming of the temple sequence allows us to understand the process of developing a scripted story and the ideas and assumptions about people that the script itself may carry. The script as we see in this case, thus merely becomes a 'to do list' of things to be done/found/filmed and whatever is unavailable, keeps getting dropped out from it. Interestingly, this dropping out does not make any substantial difference in the larger story, and rather, then story is then constructed on the basis of what material could finally be shot. *The final film story therefore does not develop overtime chronologically, but rather develops episodically, depending upon what could be ultimately filmed.* And in moments when any item from the list becomes unavailable but required, it can be 'fixed', as in the case of the temple sequence, which incorporated two moments of staging—one with 'expert' on Hindu mythology and the other with the anchor, who was shown to be mesmerised by the evening temple *aarti*. Both the scenes incorporated the act of repeating—be it a gesture, a sentence or a look. In fact, the *aarti* scene presented the anchor as though 'feeling moved' by the sounds of the chants and bells of the temple. The scene was a classic attempt to exhibit India as a romanticised land where one could find peace and tranquillity. In fact, during several such uncomfortable moments of staging while shooting this film, the filmmaker clarified that:

> Usually things are not so staged. Right now it is required because the time is so less…we have only two days to film here.

Interestingly, the concern of the filmmaker that there will be some fakery and it should not be visible to the viewer reflects an important critique of the documentary practice. It raises a question on what really has the reflexive turn in documentary filmmaking been able to achieve? *Reflexivity is in fact reduced to a 'choice' or style exercised by the filmmakers depending upon the project they are a part of.* Thus, the same filmmaker could be reflexive and polemical in one film (usually their personal projects) but not in another. This practice is in fact more common than it appears to be. However, despite these limitations of the script, the film was shot, and the film was completed and released. The film would be presented in the form of well-researched and authoritative images and words, given that the filmmakers were associated with a major and reputed English TV and film production channel. It is in this way that we understand the Foucauldian nexus between power and knowledge, such that the former produces the latter. Documentary filmmaking, in such cases rather than being 'creative treatment of actuality' (Grierson 1933), can instead be seen as a discursive practice, through which a dominant understanding about actuality comes into repetition. The script in the present shoot exists as an object far removed from a filmmaker's experiential level and instead comes into existence by borrowing from already discursive constructions about the field and the people to be filmed. The making of this mythological documentary film thus shows not only how orientalist assumptions make way into the script but also into the final film.

Concluding Remarks

The departure point for this essay has been the manner in which the practice of documentary filmmaking carries forward the discursive project of developmentalism. International agencies make use of documentary films as a tool for justifying political intervention into the third world nations. A study of the making of these films however reveals a gap in the understanding of the complexity of some of these issues by filmmakers and in this process, what we repeatedly achieve are films that recreate the already existing discourses around the topic. This recreation entails production of similar kind of imagery, as that which is 'expected' from India, thus making Western documentary filmmaking an exercise that primarily caters to the imaginations of the Western audience. Furthermore, this chapter establishes how the documentary filmmaker is understood to be someone who enters into problematic, difficult or exotic areas of the world, where filmmaking activity itself is seen as an achievement. The PBS survey, by drawing on heroic experiences of filmmakers, lists the equipments which they may use in such difficult and challenging environments. Filming equipment is also named as Heros and Pros, precisely to highlight this adventurous role which is seen to be played by the filmmaker. What transpires in this process is a neutralisation of the filmmaker's own understanding of the field and her negotiation skills during the filmmaking process. Rather than understanding 'difficult environments' as problematic areas of the world 'out there', the essay establishes how the filmmaker's own ideas about the field contribute to the creation of these assumptions about specific regions. This is not to say that the field location never offers any resistance, but in what way the filmmakers navigate these resistances depends upon their own understanding and experience. Finally, the essay can be seen as an analysis of the work of Western and European documentary filmmakers, especially in the field of development, filming in India, to show how many of them continue to take an Orientalised approach towards their subject matter. A close scrutiny of this practice has allowed us to understand the discursive constructions about the field, the filmmakers, and those filmed. The essay initiates a discussion into the extent to which these constructions translate into the practice, shaping and influencing documentary filmmaking towards a particular direction. It allows us to see how the films catering to the development project, rather than contributing to newer forms of knowledges, heavily depend upon the circulation of pre-existing discourses and ideas.

Note

1. http://www.pbs.org/pov/filmmakers/.

References

Arce, A., Villarreal, M., & de Vries, P. (1996). The Social Construction of Rural Development: Discourses, Practices and Power. In D. Booth (Ed.), *Rethinking Social Development: Theory, Research and Practice*. Harlow: Addison Wesley Longman.

Das, T. (2007). *How to Write a Documentary Script*. New Delhi, India: Public Service Broadcasting Trust, UNESCO.

Escobar, A. (1995). *Encountering Development: The Making and Unmaking of the Third World*. Princeton, NJ: Princeton University Press.

Evans-Pritchard, E. E. (1940). *The Nuer: A Description of the Modes of Livelihood and Political Institutions of a Nilotic People*. Oxford: Oxford University Press.

Foucault, M. (1972). *The Archaeology of Knowledge*. New York: Pantheon Books.

Grierson, J. (1933). The Documentary Producer. *Cinema Quarterly, 2*(1), 7–9.

Hannigan, J. A. (2014). *Environmental Sociology*. London: Routledge, Taylor & Francis Group.

Mitchell, T. (1989). The World as Exhibition. *Comparative Studies in Society and History, 31*(2), 217–236.

Mitchell, W. J. T. (2007). World Pictures: Globalization and Visual Culture. *Neohelicon, 34*(2), 49–59. https://doi.org/10.1007/s11059-007-2005-7.

Nichols, B. (2010). *Representing Reality: Issues and Concepts in Documentary*. Bloomington, IN: Indiana University Press.

Olsson, M. (2007). Power/Knowledge: The Discursive Construction of an Author. *The Library Quarterly: Information, Community, Policy, 77*(2), 219–240.

Ranaweera Banda, R. M. (2004). Development Discourse and the Third World. In *Proceedings of the Second Academic Sessions*. http://www.ruh.ac.lk/research/academic_sessions/2004_mergepdf/98-103.PDF.

Rosaldo, R. (1986). From the Door of His Tent: The Fieldworker and the Inquisitor. In J. Clifford & G. E. Marcus (Eds.), *Writing Culture: The Poetics and Politics of Ethnography*. Berkeley: University of California Press.

Sachs, W. (Ed.). (1992). *The Development Dictionary: A Guide to Knowledge as Power*. London: Zed Books.

Said, E. W. (1979). *Orientalism*. New York: Vintage Books.

Schaffer, B. (1985). Policy Makers Have Their Needs Too: Irish Itinerants and the Culture of Poverty. In G. Wood (Ed.), *Labelling in Development Policy: Essays in Honour of Bernard Schaffer*. London: Sage.

Wadsworth, C. (2016). *The Editor's Toolkit: A Hands-On Guide to the Craft of Film and TV Editing*. New York: Focal Press; London: Taylor and Francis.

Wood, G. (Ed.). (1985). *Labelling in Development Policy: Essays in Honour of Bernard Schaffer*. London: Sage.

CHAPTER 7

'Tayyari Jeet Ki': The Production of Childhood as a Cultural Trope of Developmentalism

Lakshita Malik

Introduction

Lofty debates around *development* are fought in either ideological or quantifiable terms, even if they aren't always fact based. The concerns around GDP numbers and per capita income dominate the discussion and even the more critical voices measure development, or the lack thereof, in terms of missing yardsticks or theoretical shortcomings. While significant, these perspectives have produced a sterilized understanding of a concept that has had a culturally entangled life of its own. 'Development' is after all a value loaded term with a promise of a better life and even as its meanings may vary, the allure envelops intimate spaces of existence to become

'Prepare to win' is the slogan for Bournvita, a popular malted and chocolate malt drink mixes for children, manufactured by the parent company, Cadbury.

L. Malik (✉)
University of Illinois, Chicago, IL, USA

D. N. Pathak and A. K. Das (eds.), *Investigating Developmentalism*,
https://doi.org/10.1007/978-3-030-17443-9_7

a durable motif. In this chapter, I explore the enchantment with *development* through the aspirations and anxieties surrounding child-rearing and the social production of childhood. The everyday interest in development, not simply as a collective but also a personal journey of upward mobility has allowed for mystification that cannot be explained through numbers. I focus on the contemporary, cultural emphasis on the *child* as someone more than in need of discipline to inhabit the civic world. The child undergoes complex individuation where the process of growing-up is temporally magnified in visual representations, marking significant shifts in how new paths to development are paved.

Development develops a mundane aura in the promise of individual, upward mobility, as both the affect and effect abstract policies. *Developmentalism* is an affectively loaded space that operates in the web of jargon laden theoretical debates that are made alive and actively reproduced in public discourse through aspirational investment in maintaining class, status and power. Childhood becomes a dynamic space of performing class/caste-based differences that bear the mark of a distinctly indigenous developmentalism. This developmentalism is the stage for showcasing a distinctly *Indian* global competence that prides itself in a grounded liaison with 'modernity'. At the same time, this Indian global developmentalism is coded with class/caste-based exclusions that make this developmentalism an emulsion of desperate desire and unattainable by just anyone. Much like the *X* factor that cannot be replicated in mimesis of material conditions, this developmentalism is laced with enchantment in the contemporary Indian context. In the wake of educational access expanding beyond the grasp of the middle-class alone, the investment in childhood now goes beyond producing upstanding citizens. The familial spaces are not simply the spaces of passive growing-up but active sites of performing childhood in a way that embodies class- and caste-based differences. These differences determine who gets to the rightful, upstanding citizen who embodies the nation itself.

Intimate Spaces of Development

The idea and imagination of development are injected through various methods in the society. For example, in a 1981 edition of the *Dharmyug* magazine, an advertisement for Calcium Sandoz states that बाद में कितना ही कैल्शियम क्यों न दिया जाये, वो बचपन की कमी को पूरा नहीं कर सकता (*No amount of calcium intake later can make up for the lack of it during childhood*) (*Dharmyug*, October 1981). This was a famous advertisement which has been extracted from an ad for 'Calcium Sandoz', in the above-mentioned magazine. The above health warning is part of a larger text that emphasises the significance of calcium among growing children. The dense text is displayed along an image of two smiling boys in shorts and t-shirts; one jumping over the other in a presentation of superior physical fitness. The ribs and arm bones of the boys have been accentuated, animatedly so. Apart from the obvious onset of marketing for products specifically designed for children, the ad is part of a larger gamut of material in the magazine that fixates childhood as a specific and significant stage in the physical growth of man. The caution spelled out in attempts at compensation during adulthood demarcates the nurturance during childhood as a special and an unretrievable moment.

My intent in this chapter is to approach the notion of *developmentalism* through a focus on childhood. I espouse a recognition of the logic that the grand ideologies require subjective transformations which are (re)produced through bodily and spatial dispositions (Foucault 1977; Bourdieu 1984; Lefebvre 1991; Munn 1992). The question of subjectivity is also pertinent in understanding the contextually derived meanings of development. The Indian rendition of the development saga has been shaped by its colonial encounter; closely tied to the idea of the nation and recently to ideas of globalization and transnational movement. The complex entanglement of the idea of development with that of national interest has been historically produced with close connection to the changing interpretations of 'modernity'.

The purpose of the chapter is not to reiterate the changing nature of Indian modernity and concurrent understandings of development but to explore the cultural dimension which naturalizes these political ideologies and makes them durable. I wish to explore how dry political terms become imbued with enchanting properties that render them self-referential. This attempt is by no means novel. Cultural tropes of Indian nationalism (in both colonial and post-colonial contexts), for instance, have located both feminine (Chatterjee 1989; Sarkar 2000; Srivastava 2004) and masculine (Sinha 1995; Haynes 2011) selves, which are produced as the cultural iterations of nationalism (necessarily embroiled with categories of caste and class).

Childhood has emerged as a relatively new space of cultural prominence, continuing to gain visibility as a site for investment for the 'future'; and the terms of this 'future' are set by the narrative of (economic) development. Therefore, before going any further, I would like to briefly pose the problem of development for the purpose of this chapter.

The evolutionary understanding of human development which structured the colonial as well as post-colonial relationships between Western and non-Western societies found one of the earliest critics in the Latin American dependency theorists. Apart from spelling out the structural inequality inherent in the development processes underscored by capitalist expansion, the logic of development itself was situated in the historical specificity of the European experience of modernization (Grosfuegel 2000; Soja 1989). Accordingly, the hallmark of any developed society was modernity (in thought and practice) and within the context of colonized societies such as India, this was to be achieved through a violent break with 'tradition'. This break with 'tradition', of course, was neither absolute nor always welcome as a number of scholars have suggested. Women, especially, within the bounds of the 'home' became the embodiment of 'tradition', as sacrificial wives and mothers, placed under the authority of the Hindu men (Sinha 1995; Chaudhuri 2012). This became a nationalist take on the Western nuclear family. The Indian appropriation of 'European' nuclear family continued well after independence, within the Indian family planning policies to parallel the ethos of a planned economy at 'home' through the planned and small family (Chatterjee and Riley 2001).

The 'modern' nuclear family (Löfgren 2003) was therefore appropriated as the site for asserting nationalist subjectivities rooted in 'tradition'. This 'resistance' to modernity was representationally limited to the 'home' and the embrace of modern, scientific temperament reflected itself in the heavy industry-driven development of the Indian nation post-independence. Srivastava (2015), in his analysis of the cinematic representation of state-driven, rational development, suggests prominence of the doctor or the engineer, (what he refers to as the Five-Year-Plan-Hero) as the protagonist of this post-colonial Indian modernity. In the wake of economic restructuring in the 1980s, however, the legitimate habitation of the national spaces was identified as the right of the 'consumer citizen' (Harriss 2007; Lukose 2005; Srivastava 2015). The state-driven investment in heavy industry began to give way to market-driven economic growth in the national imaginary.[1] Leela Fernandes (2006), with reference to this shift suggests,

> The four members of the state-sponsored family model (man, woman, son, and daughter) have been replaced by man, woman, child, and car. In this vision of the modern Indian family, the commodity reworks older ideological narratives that have been deployed by the nation-state with the caste-and class-based aesthetics of the new middle class family. (pp. 61–64)

I focus on this changing terrain of economic development, through the changing subjectivity of the *child* and the changing sentiment towards childhood. Through a range of material including cinema, magazines and advertisements, I locate the growing notability of childhood beyond its implications for producing as desired 'future'. While that is certainly significant and is the backdrop of this investment in childhood, the child himself becomes conditionally agentive in producing class- and caste-based differences (and consequently national identities) through processes of commodity consumption which tie into aspects of education and leisure. The process of growing-up becomes a performative space, with a showcase of greater individuation of the child and the natural tenets of his personality, paradoxically being steeped in regimented educational and recreational training. This naturalization of difference (Bourdieu 1984) cements superior stakes in the claims to national development, both in terms of contribution to production as well as consumption.

Childhood: The Age of Innocence and Impressionability

Childhood is considered to the symbol of innocence. They are projected as buds and flowers. This popular line portrays them as the facilitator of prosperity. 'नन्हे मुन्नो की मुस्कान से आबाद है जहान' (*With the smile of the young ones the world prosper*). This kind of narrative attracts the attention towards the blossoming of children. It creates an imagination to pay due attention towards the childhood in the popular media. If the nationalist narrative reinvented the woman as the idealized and sacrificial mother, represented in the mythical imagery of Yashoda and a young Krishna (Jain 2007) as the bearer of tradition, then childhood became the site for modernist intervention. However, childhood was a relatively new modality; it required specialized systems of care-taking, even within the European context and was a modern idea (Aries 1962).

With the 1929 Child Marriage Restraint Act abolishing child marriage, the apolitical category of childhood was formally introduced in the national vocabulary at the site of articulating superior modern ethos (Pande 2012).[2] There was a marked shift in the discourse on adult attitude towards children. The notion of the 'child' as a discrete age set, embodying innocence, vulnerability, lacking agency and therefore dependent on the adult for disciplining and preparation for successful participation in a 'civilized' society, became prevalent.[3] Education, specifically formal education, was central to this entry into civility and to produce subjects who would aid in the process of national development.[4]

This idea was also echoed in post-independence Hindi cinema. *Jagriti* (1954), for instance, is a story of a 'problem child', Ajay, whose glaring lack of discipline can only be corrected at boarding school. Ajay successfully becomes the disciplined child his family hoped he would become at the school, with the help of Superintendent Shekhar (an unorthodox teacher). Superintendent Shekhar is able to move past the mere practice of discipline and explicate the bigger picture to his students, especially Ajay: the legacy of the great nation of India. The Superintendent even escorts the boys on a train journey through India to educate them about the sacrifices that were made for India, to inspire them and help them understand the larger purpose of the disciplining.[5] The hopes of the nation are tethered to the child and his ability to grow up to become the 'Five-Year-plan-Hero' (Srivastava 2005, 2015).

Decades later *Taare Zameen Par* (2007) posed the boarding school as a similar, intended space for the disciplining of the child. The school continues to be the site of rigorous training. However, even as the notion of securing a brighter future through children is certainly intact, growing-up is not a simple coming of age story. Child-care becomes more complex, and progressiveness is embodied in the nuances of engaging with the child. The child is portrayed as the *natural* bearer of talent and creativity which require recognition, nurturing and understanding. Ishaan Awasthi, the protagonist of the film, suffers from dyslexia (which remains undiagnosed for the first part of the film) and is unable to compete with his academically accomplished brother, Yohan Awasthi. Though, unlike *Jagriti*, there is no clean break between the 'home' and the school, with the latter being the only space for educating the child. There is constant movement back and forth to hold the parents accountable for the care of the child in a way that nurtures his uniqueness and facilitates his individuality to take shape, and meaningfully so. The extra hours put in by the Ishaan's art teacher to help him through his work in classes is meant to be the job of the parents as not every child may be lucky enough to meet the talented teachers.

Similarly, instead of looking at Indian nationalist icons and the history of the Indian nation, inspiration is sought in international icons like Albert Einstein, Agatha Christie, Pablo Picasso and even Abhishek Bachchan. The list is not only of accomplished individuals who suffered from 'difficulty in reading and writing' but is also meant to represent the range of acceptable career options available to citizens of the transnationally visible and entrepreneurially active India. By now, the terms of modernity and the Indian conception of national development allow for different way of perceiving the future. The spectrum of aspirations extends beyond the staples of becoming doctors, lawyers and engineers (Donner and De Neve 2011).

It is critical to keep in mind that the bearers of duty of national development through self-improvement were a small section of nationalist elite residing in the metropolis (Donner and De Neve 2011; Srivastava 2004). The economic restructuring of the 1980s and the opening of the Indian economy and rapid globalization in the 1990s coupled with the affirmative action allowed by the recommendations of the Mandal commission fractured the ideological uniformity of the middle-class. The fruits of progress which were the destiny of a select few from the erstwhile niche middle-class have now opened up to a larger and more diverse section of society (Donner and De Neve 2011). Within this context, where the value of education as accumulated (cultural) capital is firmly understood by all, child-care can no longer be left to the schools alone, nor can opportunities within the state institutions be enough to accommodate new spaces of distinction for the elite (Bourdieu 1984). Just as the entanglement of personal aspirations (of a certain class) with those of an erstwhile colonized nation become evident, the family emerges as a much more fruitful site of emphasizing difference and reclaiming the mantle of producing rightful citizens.

The trajectories of national development and subjective biographies of upward mobility have always been entwined and with the porous borders of the new middle-classes, child-care is now a key site of performing difference that is naturalized to the point of no replication. The rhetoric of *Achhe Din* (good days) has affective resonance in so far as they imply palpable shifts in familial living accounted through upward mobility. The changing vistas of this familial living have child-care a crucial component of how these good days are defined.

The contemporary focus on the consuming citizen as the 'good' citizen has impacted the spaces of childhood, which may have earlier been taken for granted. The child must not only undergo linear disciplining at the school, the process of growing-up itself becomes a visceral performance implicating the child and his personality in unforeseen ways. The regiment of child care must now accommodate the values of 'proper' consumption and navigation of the market. Moreover, spaces of learning, which may now be available to a larger section of the population, demand an active involvement of the parents ('home') in the process of learning which goes beyond material provisions. Child care demands emotional and intellectual rigour on the part of the parent (especially the mother). The enchantment with developmentalism structures intimate relationships and experiences at 'home'.

The Disciplining of Children as Investment for the Future

Children are also targeted as an active consumers. These days along with the blooming of the kid's television channels, various advertisements target the children to lure them. This trend has started in the 1980s. One popular advertisement of Leo toy says ' वाह ! अब देखो लियो के और नए खिलौने भरता जा रहे है मेरा खज़ाना' (*Wow! Now look, Leo's new toys adding to my treasure*) (*Dharmyug*, May 1984). The above quoted line is part of an advertisement for Leo Toys which features a young boy in pulled up socks, a striped t-shirt and shorts, surrounded by a number of toys. Mostly these toys are miniatures of the modern technological achievements including cars and guns. Apart from the striking representation of young boys learning gender role, the ad marks the significance of the child as the consumer. However, this new consumer is very much placed within the idiom of contributing to the development of the nation-state.

Children are no longer the simplistic extension of the ideal conjugal unit, whose existence is limited to the aesthetic articulation of the family planning politics. The discussion on children is no longer limited to the appropriate number for a progressive family in the nationalist narrative. The contemporary focus on the child is structured through a paradoxical need to both claim the extraordinary abilities as a part of the child's natural makeup (to code these differences in caste/class terms) as well as forcing strict regimes in the form of preschool education, coaching centres, etc.

The May 1984 issue of the magazine *Dharmyug* which features the ad has it comfortably placed on page 4 and, with a cover story celebrating Rakesh Sharma's (first Indian astronaut) return from Space. The use of leisure for inculcating interest in academia, and science in particular, is by no means limited to this instance. The magazine also received regular advertising from *Junior Science Encyclopedia* ('well-known, entertaining as well as enlightening books'). A particular feature (*Dharmyug*, April 1986) also advertises for books on 'computers for beginners' and 'basic computer programming' in addition to 'Children's tricks and stunts', 'world-famous invention', 'world's bizarre flora and fauna' among others. The magazine also published a segment for children (which is markedly different from the youth section), featuring short length articles about general knowledge trivia (science with fun and games) and short stories of moral significance. There is also a focus on accomplishments of children in academia, sports as well as arts like photography. There are complex ways in which consumption, leisure and inculcation of nationalist ethos come together to produce the middle-class child. Clearly weaved into the narratives of both motherhood and fatherhood, one can see the notion of childhood becoming more nuanced and layered. Especially through consumerist practices, the family is declared as a key space of producing 'gifted' children.

Family becomes the affective idiom for producing a progressive nation through complex personal journeys. Within the youth section of the magazine, one author recounts his coming of age story—'When I ran away from school' (*Dharmyug*, April 1986). He writes about his experience of cutting class up until he got caught in 8th standard and suffers harsh consequences but learns his lesson is ushered into responsible adulthood. Meanwhile the variety of different brands like *Cerelac* baby food, further differentiated childhood between early and later years. The mother is implicated directly into these nuances of familial and child care, evident in the imagery of most of ads, from soaps to toothpastes but in that child-care becomes its own concentrated space of knowledge. This knowledge is certainly class/caste-specific and therefore, even commodity cultures that locate the child as the consumer must be deployed for use in this project.

Douglas Haynes (2011), in his study of advertising in colonial India has suggested the criticality of the nuclear family, especially geared towards the male breadwinner in ads for insurance, for instance. The trope of the child in need of protection and care against the harshness of adult world was used to abet the significance of the father (and husband) as the provider of the family. Haynes points out how, in the 1930s, *Horlicks*, for instance, was advertised as an 'everyday product that men would see as crucial to coping with a competitive work world, and thus ultimately to perpetuating the nuclear family' (Haynes 2011: 35). This current of marketing was adapted after marketing to children was considered 'too narrow' (Haynes 2011: 35).

However, the child as the consumer of this nuclear family situated within bounds of caste is no longer part of a demographic that is 'too narrow'. Even in filmic representation, childhood is no longer glossed over, as something that is passive. In fact, there has been a marked increase in the variety of films focusing on the complex subjectivity of the child (and adolescent). *Taare Zameen Par*, for instance, changed the conversation on representation of children in popular Hindi cinema. Even as there were films that focused on the distinct innocence and vulnerability of the child (*Masoom* 1983; *Mr. India* 1987), the idea of care-taking remained rather vague and often involved deploying the generic category of 'love'. Childhood, now, emerges as the domain of elaborate care-taking with no place for general rules. What works for Yohan does not work for his brother Ishaan.

The film *Udaan* (2010) places childhood to forge a larger critique of the Nehruvian model of progress. 17-year-old Rohan is expelled from a prestigious boarding school and has to return home to an emotionally distant and physically abusive father who runs a steel factory in Jamshedpur, Jharkhand. Rohan doesn't want to be an engineer (like his father wants him to be) but continues with his studies in the arts. In the absence of a mother, who had passed away a while back, and whose pristine memories are interspersed with Rohan's violence-laced reality, his home becomes a claustrophobic space. Due to the lack of engagement on any front but monetary, but more importantly his father's inability to understand his individuality, the home reeks of a childhood that was lost and abandoned illustrating the failure of the parent. The failures of his father echo in the way his younger step-brother, Arjun, is being raised. Having only learned about Arjun's existence the day he comes back, Rohan meets him with the same anger with which his father meets him. The refusal of his father to acknowledge that Arjun requires special care that goes beyond providing him with food, shelter and education is the epitome of this failure. The climax of the film sees Rohan leaving his father's home along with his brother to be able to give him a 'future'. At one point, Rohan articulates to his uncle how disappointed and angry he was at his father for not being bothered to visit him even once in all the eight years he was at boarding school. 'I am his son, not a fixed deposit in a bank', he spits out. The film captures the new middle-class disenchantment with the old developmentalist Indian state and the former institutions that nurtured future citizens. In the wake of collapsing borders of these erstwhile fortified spaces (school), it is the private spaces (familial space) that must foster a distinguished ambiance for progress and upward mobility.

There are complex issues performing masculinities within domestic spaces at stake here and they warrant separate attention. What is critical for our purposes is the scoff in the face of Nehruvian modernity and notions of progress. The limits of this progress are spelled out in the charting out of Rohan's future by his father, which begins and ends by working in his factory. The yield from investment in heavy industry is now stunted and is rendered palpable in the techniques of child-care. The possibilities of progressing beyond the limits of what the state can provide are vested with within the space of the family.

The aforementioned story from *Dharmyug* about coming of age through disciplining the body and mind within the space of the school is problematized in the aftermath of the Mandal agitation. The recommendations for reservations based on caste were seen as a wild attack on meritocracy and have discredited the Nehruvian paths of progress. The distinction of the middle-class family can no longer be maintained just by simplistic routes of training at the school.

Srivastava, in his analysis of the changing hue of Indian modernity, historically locates the Doon School (the premier boarding school) as one site of producing nationalist, modern subjects (Srivastava 2005). The school became the site of reproducing the nationalist elite both culturally and socially. The modernist path to development was indoctrinated through introducing a child to the 'secular' public domain spatially embodied in the school. This public space was meant to be distinct from 'home' where lay the affective domain which was to be transcended (ibid.). Individuality was to be cultivated through the school as an institution, at least in theory, by limiting caste and religion to the private spaces.

However, the expanding (heterogenous) membership of this erstwhile enclosed middle-class complicates this iteration of the modernist path to development. Donner (2006), in her study of pre-schools in Calcutta suggests the anxieties middle-class parents feel about who their children socialize with, at school. The necessity of smoothing over differences has now been replaced with the need to articulate them in specific ways through performing cultural capital that cannot just be financially supplied and child-care is a crucial space for such a performance.

The Child Consumer and New Motifs of Developmentalism

It is interesting to note the transition of a child into the youth. The tag of a popular advertisement substantiates this with the line 'मेरे नन्हे साहबज़ादे की सालगिरह थी...और जनाब न्यौता दे आए ६३ दोस्तों को!' (*It was my little prince's birthday... and he invited 63 of his friends*!) (*Dharmyug*, April 1986). There has to be 'something else' that can neither be bought nor is only useful in the singular and responsible movement of the child into adulthood. The nicknames (Munni, Chunnu) that feature prominently in *Dharmyug* stories that are authored by adults highlighting the naïveté of childhood are now being replaced with names like Ayush, Kabir, Ishaan, which individualize the child. There needs to be something more than hard work (a prerogative available to *everyone*) that defines the child. Childhood becomes a complex space with different rules of parental engagement and care and significantly different public modes of performance. *Dharmyug* epitomizes the transition period from the 1970s and 1980s onwards. The strain of (scientific) academic achievement is particularly high, allowing the childhood to be trained to become proper future citizens. However, the commodity representations enliven this training as a performative act. With Calcium Sandoz and Cerelac and science encyclopedia, the child can train and prepare for adulthood in a truly unparalleled manner. In fact, childhood is not simply just everything before adulthood. The chasms between infancy, pre-puberty and post-puberty in addition to already existing gendered definitions of childhood make are a result of a unique historical trajectory.

Gendered socialization has been an academic and social concern for quite some time now, especially the restricted access to education as well as nutrition for girls. In fact, the policy focus on childhood has been in the spaces of health and nutrition with education for girls being of specific significance in the road to modernity. Procter & Gamble ran ads promising donations towards providing educational infrastructure for girls on every P&G product bought, with the tagline 'Padhega India, Badhega India'.[6] There are separate concerns about what education, in particular, means for girls and boys. Donner (2006), for instance, in her work on motherhood suggests the category of the mother's love requires intellectual engagement just as much as physical labour. The mother must not only put in the hours of work cooking can cleaning but more importantly nurture the child's curiosity and natural talents, help them consume morally (Srivastava 2009) and provide the 'something else' that the school cannot necessarily provide. One could argue then, that investment in the education of girls is then prompted by their future role as the modern wife and mother.[7] As Donner (2008) suggests:

> Thus, English-medium education has become a desirable trait in a bride-to-be, and campaigns for 'computer literacy' aimed at lower middle-class women whose ability to coach their children based on their own 'knowing computers' have substituted the familiar 'trained in classical dance/music' in matrimonial ads. (p. 131)

The changing terms of childhood can be read in the light of the post-Mandal climate, when the upper-caste monopoly over education was off-set. The middle-class child must now produce the difference, which goes beyond an access to the bare minimum education. The use of the child as a motif in suggesting qualitative superiority (which can only be enhanced and must be protected) is visible across a number of ad campaigns, such as those of Dettol and even the government sponsored *Swachh Bharat* ads.

In the Dettol ad, for instance, one can see a man sitting down for dinner, on a table already set and occupied by his sister, niece and nephew, is asked by the sister to wash his hands before eating. He replies saying (referring to himself), 'do lions ever wash their paws?' The nephew interjects and points, 'even rats don't wash their paws, Uncle', leaving him flabbergasted and the mother looking proud. The child appears, here, as having natural wit, something that is part of the natural character of the child. However, this increased focus of the rapidly individualizing child, capable of going beyond what the books can teach him, and exuding confidence in the face of competition from his peers, comes through increased training in coaching centres, focus on fluency in the English language as well as extra-curricular training (including music, dance or sports). Thus, while on the one hand there is interest in emphasizing the naturalness of the child's talent, material and symbolic resources spent on extra-regimentation that may allow the child to cultivate an 'edge'. Thus, the constantly evolving cultural capital (Bourdieu 1984), that sustains the middle-class, is now situated in the act differentiating the child both from the lower classes as well as the children who may be within the same economic class, given that the Indian middle-class itself is quite heterogeneous. This extra training prepares the child for a meritorious success which does not require the crutches of reservation either during higher education (in coveted Indian as well as Western institutions) or in getting jobs (within India and abroad). A whole range of consumer products have emerged to aid the child in the process for instance, energy drinks (Bournvita/Horlicks). An entire industry of pre-schools has developed in association with preparing children as young as 3 years for 'future participation global workforce, migration, and white-collar employment in particularly desirable industries' (Donner 2006: 373).

The 2012 Hindi film, *English Vinglish*, which traces the journey of housewife and caterer, Shashi, as she learns English to assert herself more effectively within the familial domain, where she is mocked by her husband and daughter for not speaking the language. In the opening scene itself, where the entire family is at the dining table, eating breakfast, the daughter (Sapna) tells Shashi to buy white bread for the house, instead of brown bread. Shashi, tells her she must have picked up these inconsequential discussions at her 'jazz' class, mispronouncing it. For this mispronunciation, she is immediately mocked by Sapna. Shashi's inability to speak English is interpreted by her daughter, as her inability to make 'proper' choices as her mother. The cultural capital that Sapna accumulates through her rigorous training in the school and 'jazz' class seems incommensurate with the performance of motherhood by Shashi. The mother must adapt and learn alongside this gifted child; she does not have the luxury to rely upon hours spent in the kitchen alone.

Bournvita advertisements have also morphed the spatial practice of motherhood. The mother must do more than just pour the glass of milk for her child. In one particular commercial, we see the mother training alongside her son under the harshest conditions, presumably for the child to become a professional runner.[8] Parenting becomes more than the provision of material conditions to succeed, and the childhood becomes the active site of performing difference.[9] Of course, the burden of excellence is felt tremendously as the child strays from academics, and if there has to be a career path from these athletic abilities, it cannot be carved out be mediocrity. In fact, Bournvita has similar iterations of these ads of children inclined to various sports and recreational activities, where they must strive for greatness (or it may not mean much).

The 'too narrow' market in the 1930s is now ripe with all kinds of products ripe for strategic use for the family unit. From laptops, printers, learning applications for tablets to leisure items like toys, flavoured drinks, juices that are allowed usage only for the singular purpose of enhancing their capabilities but as the palpable site of articulating the organic engagement of the child with global and consumer cultures.

The above-mentioned line 'It was my little prince's birthday… and he invited 63 of his friends!' has been taken from a Rasna advertisement from the April 1986 issue of *Dharmyug*. The woman, wearing a sleeveless blouse and a dark blue saree sits mildly amused, as her son is on her left and the daughter in the background to her left. There are streamers up on the wall behind them and gifts all around, one of which the son has opened and is looking at intently. The soft-drink concentrate, Rasna, becomes the mother's best friend in that it allows her to indulge her son and celebrate his special day in that his preposterous invitation to 'half the school' is not only tolerated but dealt with amusement and pride. It is significant for the child to be allowed to engage with commodity cultures to showcase the individuality of his thought encased here in his naiveté.

Of course, the child cannot rabidly consume, which is why care-taking underscores this venture into the 'outside' world. To remain rooted in 'tradition' and respect one's 'heritage' also becomes a significant component of childhood. *Kabhi Khushi Kabhi Gham* (2001) tugged at the heartstrings of the great Indian diaspora uprooted from 'home' in a 'foreign' land with a scene where the child (Krish) of an NRI couple sings the Indian national anthem with his British classmates and surprises his mother (and the audience). This culminates in a dramatic run from the mother to the stage to hug her child. The child is able to uphold his sense of belonging in the face of overwhelming presence of global and particularly Western cultures.

Conclusion

I have argued that the subjective interpretation of development in the contemporary India is staged through the performance of childhood with crucial emphasis being placed on child-care. What is at stake through this performative childhood is the quality of parental investment and the ability of the child showcase class/caste differences as innate and necessarily unattainable for 'others' and in the process keeping the allure and enchantment of developmentalism alive. The historical cultivation of childhood as the site of vulnerability, innocence and naivety is now more than just a critical stage of learning. Childhood is enlarged and temporally slowed down to become emphasized in representative imagery. Childhood becomes the robust site of performance of new ideologies of development (which are necessarily class and caste coded). In the wake of a fracturing 'old' middle-class and the anti-reservation temperament of the formerly caste-less elite (Deshpande 2013), the child cannot depend on the plebianizing space of the school to foster his ambition. 'Home' becomes the site of this nurturance. However, the child himself undergoes greater individuation and must become the bearer of a *natural* talent at which this nurturance can help him excel. The nurturance takes the form of rigorous training which must simultaneously be masked (Subramanian 2015).

The disillusionment with the developmentalist Indian state and the further disinterest in spaces of education that have lost the charm accumulated through years of exclusion have ushered in a new era of enthralment with development. The cultural capital of education must be imparted through convoluted and intimate modes that by no means can be duplicated through affirmative state policies. In the ever-evolving attitudes towards development, the contemporary interpretation looks towards more personal journeys of upward mobility as being representative of national development. The child becomes the centrepiece of the cultural narrative of development. Enchantment with a new modality of developmentalism is corporeally exhibited in the performance of the (middle-class) childhood; the child at once being the repository of natural talent (to sustain claims of merit) and requiring rigorous training at 'home' which is part of a complex web of affective and closely guarded cultural capital. The pressure to perform then amply falls on the child and now is not just at the level of learning but also showcasing his/her individuality but on terms already set as 'acceptable'. Developmentalism then should be seen beyond solidified policy discussions and understood for how it is weaved into ordinary lives to structure aspiration and imagination.

Notes

1. It is, of course, vital to stress that these notions of the national development are necessarily gendered and divided along lines of caste and class. Class, in fact, became a more serious centre for the analysis of the Indian imaginary from the 1970s–1980s, when the policy focus began shifting towards the interests of the middle-classes.
2. It should be noted that this protectionist attitude towards the child was coded in terms of gender. The condemnation of the Age of Consent Act 1891 by the Hindu orthodoxy gave way to the narrative of leaving barbarity behind by protecting the sexual innocence of the child instead of the woman. However, the act remained rooted in the need for sexual protection of girls as Ishita Pande has suggested (Pande 2012).
3. The use of the term 'civilized' here is to emphasize the centrality of socialization theories on the understanding of childhood as a blank slate upon which norms of gender, for instance, are scribbled only to become permanent during adulthood.
4. Of course, there were gendered idioms to the way in which education for boys and girls was approached with education for women, often being furthered as the step in the direction of 'improving' the 'home' within the appropriate bounds of tradition (Hancock 2001).
5. The crucial evasion of Mughal era as a moment of celebration in India's past, as everyone from Rajputs and Marathas were hailed for their sacrifice, is obvious. The scene is set to the popular song 'Aao baccho tumhe dikahae jhanki hindistan ki' (*Come children, let me show you the tableau of India*).

6. 'Educated India will lead to a progress of India' (https://www.youtube.com/watch?v=G8-PhzRkp7M).
7. This is not to suggest that career concerns are not significant for women, however, home and child care always placed at a higher pedestal in the understanding of 'respectable femininity' in the Indian context (Radhakrishnan 2009).
8. https://www.youtube.com/watch?v=OyRzWt1nPD8.
9. Arguably there are different spaces of parenting that the mother and the father occupy and that is significant for a complex understanding of anxious familial sites. The father, as the provider, for instance, may be seen as setting the moral agenda of the household as has been represented in films like *Dangal* (2016) where the terms of ambition and empowerment for the children are being set by the father, even if it is done so at the expense of what the mother (or even the child) may want. The mother becomes the executor of this vision. Ensuring that the child is physically and intellectually equipped to enhance his skills and represent the family. In the case of *Dangal*, the interests of the family align perfectly with that of the 'nation' when the medal for the nation's honour is won on an international platform.

References

Aries, P. (1962). *Centuries of Childhood: A Social History of Family Life*. New York: Vintage.

Bourdieu, P. (1984). *Distinction: A Social Critique of the Judgement of Taste*. London: Routledge & Kegan Paul.

Chatterjee, P. (1989). Colonialism, Nationalism, and Colonialized Women: The Contest in India. *American Ethnologist, 16*(4), 622–633.

Chatterjee, N., & Riley, N. E. (2001). Planning and Indian Modernity: The Gendered Politics of Fertility Control. *Signs, 26*(3), 811–845.

Chaudhuri, S. (2012). Interiors and Integrity in Nineteenth Century India. In C. Briganti & K. Mezei (Eds.), *The Domestic Space Reader*. Canada: University of Toronto Press.

Deshpande, S. (2013, April 13). Caste and Castelessness: Towards a Biography of the "General Category". *Economic and Political Weekly, 48*(15), 32–39.

Dharmyug. (1981, 1984, 1986). Advertisements from the Magazine *Dharmyug*.

Donner, H. (2006). Committed Mothers and Well-Adjusted Children: Privatisation, Early-Years Education and Motherhood in Calcutta. *Modern Asian Studies, 40*(02), 371–395.

Donner, H. (2008). *Domestic Goddesses: Maternity, Globalization and Middle-Class Identity in Contemporary India*. Farnham: Ashgate.

Donner, H., & De Neve, G. (2011). Introduction. In H. Donner (Ed.), *Being Middle Class in India: A Way of Life* (pp. 1–22). London: Routledge.

Dutt, D., & Dutt, C. (Producers), Kapur, S. (Director). (1983). *Masoom* [Motion Picture]. India: Krsna Movies Enterprises.
Fernandes, L. (2006). *India's New Middle Class: Democratic Politics in an Era of Economic Reform*. Minneapolis: University of Minnesota Press.
Foucault, M. (1977). *Discipline and Punish: The Birth of the Prison*. New York: Vintage.
Grosfuegel, R. (2000). Developmentalism, Modernity, and Dependency Theory in Latin America. *Nepantla: Views from South, 1*(2), 347–374.
Hancock, M. (2001). Home Science and the Nationalization of Domesticity in Colonial India. *Modern Asian Studies, 35*(4), 871–904.
Harriss, J. (2007). Antimonies of Empowerment: Observations on Civil Society, Politics and Urban Governance in India. *Economic and Political Weekly, 42*, 2716–2724.
Haynes, E. D. (2011). Masculinity, Advertising and the Reproduction of the Middle-Class Family in Western India. In H. Donner (Ed.), *Being Middle Class in India: A Way of Life* (pp. 23–46). London: Routledge.
Jain, K. (2007). *Gods in the Bazaar: The Economies of Indian Calendar Arts*. Durham, NC: Duke University Press.
Johar, Y. (Producers), Johar, K (Director). (2001). *Kabhi Khushi Kabhi Gham* [Motion Picture]. India: Dharma Productions.
Kapur, B. (Producer), Kapur, S. (Director). (1987). *Mr. Indian* [Motion Picture]. India: Narsimha Enterprises.
Kashyap, A., Singh, S., & Screwwala, R. (Producers), Vikramadituya, M. (Director). (2010). *Udaan* [Motion Picture]. India: UTV Spotboy.
Khan, A. (Producer), Khan, A. (Director). (2007). *Taare Zameen Par* [Motion Picture]. India: Aamir Khan Productions.
Khan, A., Rao, K., & Kapor, S. R. (Producers), Tiwari, N. (Director). (2016). *Dangal* [Motion Picture]. India. Aamir Khan Productions.
Lefebvre, H. (1991). *The Production of Space*. Oxford: Blackwell.
Löfgren, O. (2003). The Sweetness of Home: Class, Culture and Family Life in Sweden. In S. Low & D. Lawrence-Zúñiga (Eds.), *The Anthropology of Space and Place: Locating Culture* (pp. 142–159). Malden, MA: Blackwell.
Lukose, R. (2005). Empty Citizenship: Protesting Politics in the Era of Globalization. *Cultural Anthropology, 20*(4), 506–533.
Lulla, S., Balki, R., Rakesh, J., & Damini R. K. (Producers), Shinde, G. (Director). (2012). *English Vinglish* [Motion Picture]. India: Hope Productions.
Mukherjee, S. (Producer), Bose, S. (Director). (1954). *Jagriti* [Motion Picture]. India: Filmistan.
Munn, N. D. (1992). *The Fame of Gawa: A Symbolic Study of Value Transformation in a Massim (Papua New Guinea) Society*. Cambridge, UK: Cambridge University Press.

Pande, I. (2012). Coming of Age: Law, Sex and Childhood in Late Colonial India. *Gender and History, 24*(1), 205–230.

Radhakrishnan, S. (2009). Professional Women, Good Families: Respectable Femininity and the Cultural Politics of a "New" India. *Qualitative Sociology, 32*(2), 195–212.

Sarkar, T. (2000). *Hindu Wife, Hindu Nation: Religion, Community, Cultural Nationalism*. New Delhi: Permanent Black.

Sinha, M. (1995). *Colonial Masculinity: The 'Manly Englishman' and the 'Effeminate Bengali' in the Late Nineteenth Century*. Manchester: Manchester University Press.

Soja, E. (1989). *Postmodern Geographies: The Reassertion of Space in Critical Social Theory*. London: Verso.

Srivastava, S. (2004). Voice, Gender and Space in the Time of Five-Year Plans: The Idea of Lata Mangeshkar. *The Economic and Political Weekly, 39*(20), 2019–2028.

Srivastava, S. (2005). *Constructing Post-colonial India National Character and the Doon School*. London: Routledge.

Srivastava, S. (2009). Urban Spaces, Disney-Divinity, and Moral Middle Classes in Delhi. *Economic and Political Weekly, 44*(26/27), 338–345.

Srivastava, S. (2015). Modi-Masculinity: Media, Manhood, and "Traditions" in a Time of Consumerism. *Television & New Media, 16*(4), 331–338.

Subramanian, A. (2015). Making Merit: The Indian Institutes of Technology and the Social Life of Caste. *Comparative Studies in Society and History, 57*(2), 291–322.

PART III

Details of Discontents

CHAPTER 8

Development, Marginality, and 'Contested Space' in South India

Salah Punathil

This paper explores the disenchantment of development in the social life of the fishers in the coastal areas of Kerala state in South India. The essay has two parts. By following a political ecology perspective, the first part analyzes the historical and structural factors that condition coastal villages as a 'contested space' of disenchantment. The second part demonstrates how the disenchantment of development leads to various forms of routine conflicts and everyday crisis in the life of coastal communities. Though the entire coastal belt of the state has been referred in the study, examples are gleaned mostly from instances in the coastal belts of Thiruvananthapuram, the district under which the most of the field study for this paper has been carried out with the Vizhinjam fishing village area being the focal point.

S. Punathil (✉)
Centre for Regional Studies, University of Hyderabad, Hyderabad, India

Post Dcotoral Fellow at Max Plack Institute for the Study of Religious and Ethnic Diversity, Gottingen, Germany

D. N. Pathak and A. K. Das (eds.), *Investigating Developmentalism*,
https://doi.org/10.1007/978-3-030-17443-9_8

Social Development and Marginality in Kerala: The Historical Background

To begin with, 'marginality' is a key concept in contemporary social science often accompanied by concepts like backwardness, social exclusion, deprivation etc. Generally, marginality lies in the socio-cultural and political spheres where the disadvantaged groups are forced to struggle to gain access to the resources and full participation in social life. Such people might be socially, politically, and legally ignored (Gurung and Kollmair 2005). Being isolated and placed at the edge of the society, both in the material as well as in cultural sense, the marginalized are the essential 'other' of the mainstream. There are two major aspects that define marginality—the social and spatial—wherein the former is seen in the demographic, religious, economic and cultural conditions, the latter is primarily about the physical location/distance from the mainstream, which is increasingly referred as geographical marginality (ibid.). The geographical as well as social marginality of the fishers under this study could be located in the backdrop of three broader factors of Kerala's development history that played a crucial role in the social transformation in the state—(a) community mobilization in colonial period; (b) land reforms after the state formation in 1956; and (c) the celebrated 'Kerala model of development.'

The unique feature of the community mobilization-led social development in Kerala is that, it's traditional caste and religious groups got transformed themselves into 'political communities' (See Arunima 2006; Aloysius 2005; Menon 2002). That means, the socio-political transformation of the state and social development is uniquely intertwined or inseparable. For example, Aloysius (2005) highlights the importance of tracing the historicity of the region and community formations to understand the contemporary social development. The competition to grab the social, economic, and political opportunities which the colonial period provided, created a sense of collective bargaining among the subordinated groups like the Ezhavas, Muslims, and Christians and question the hegemony of the upper castes in various realms of life (Aloysius 2005). But it was not a wide sweep as the Dalits, the Adivasis, fisher folks, and women remained in a disadvantageous position from the development process, as they were excluded from the development initiatives since the colonial period. Although there were few leaders form the most downtrodden sections like Ayyankali and a few scattered movements in different places, the Dalits never emerged as a uniform political community unlike the Ezhavas or Muslims or any other backward groups. The Adivasis, being isolated in the hilly regions, were kept away from the modern socio-political process. The agency of women was also suppressed in the community-based assertions (Devika 2014). Likewise, the fisher communities known as the Araya Hindus, the Puislans, the Marakkayar Muslims, and the Mukkuvar Christians were never part of the political assertions during the colonial period and thus have no history of mobilization on their own or with the larger religious fold they belong to. This long and still continuing history of aloofness is significant in understanding the marginality of the fishers as the colonial history of community mobilization has greatly influenced the post-Independent democratic politics of Kerala.

The second major factor that brought significant structural changes in Kerala was the land reforms initiated after the formation of the state in 1956. The class- and caste-based political and social formations, which developed during the colonial era, were in the real triggers for the land reforms initiated in 1957 by the first Communist government of the state under E. M. S. Namboodiripad, which in fact led to the foundation of the celebrated Kerala model of development. But, some of the recent appraisals of land reforms excluded certain sections, including fishers, from the purview. It is true that a few sections, especially landless agricultural laborers, have benefitted to some extent from the land reforms. But most poorer sections have not benefited from land reforms (Oommen 1999; Tharakan 2007; Devika 2014). Also, more importantly to this study, the landless fishers living adjacent to the coasts were not considered as beneficiaries of the land reform policy, because the Left political movements and the land reform policy implemented by its ministry did not consider the coastal localities as part of the agrarian economy of the inland regions.

The distinct trajectory of Kerala's social development compared to other states has been a point of discussion not only among social scientists, but also in socio-political discourses and academics. Much of such discourses are anchored around the uniqueness of state's developmental policies adopted from the very beginning of the formation of the state in November 1956. By the 1970s, rapid strides the state has achieved in the socio-political and economic developments began to be monikered as the 'Kerala model of development' (Rajasenan and Groot 2005). The indicators of the 'Kerala model' are high life expectancy, low infant mortality, high literacy rate, social security entitlements, etc. The name is based on the claim that these developments are a collective result, mainly of the 'public action,' which has been supplemented with state initiatives (Oommen 1999). Therefore, this discourse on the 'Kerala model development' is largely confined to some social indicators of recent past which do not take into account other larger historical factors that have brought in radical social changes on the caste and religious lines helping drive the social development since the colonial era (Devika 2014; Punathil 2013).

However, when it comes to weaker sections, this so-called Kerala model is nothing but a story of utter exclusion (See Devika 2014; Rammohan 2008; Oommen 1999 and others). It has been increasingly proven that the Kerala model has failed to uniformly distribute the developmental benefits to all the needy, as it has been directed to some sections particularly the middle classes and middle castes (Harilal 2005; Tharakan 2007). They were able to corner further benefits making better use of opportunities emanating from education, organized sector jobs, migration, and remittances, thus pushing the already marginalized groups further into the 'outliers' (Kurien 2000).

Political Ecology, Modernization of Fishing, and the Crisis of Fishers

This section details how the fishing that has been mostly used by fishers earlier for their survival got transformed following larger socio-economic changes and how this change has impacted the lives of the fishers in Kerala (Kurien and Achari 1990). The idea of political ecology is a more significant concept in this context.[1] Political ecology in its minimal sense denotes how power influences human-environment interactions (Bryant and Bailey 1997).[2] Blaikie and Brookfield define political ecology in the following words:

> ......the phrase 'political ecology' combines the concerns of ecology and a broadly defined political economy. Together, this encompasses the constantly shifting dialectics between society and land-based resources, and also within classes and groups within society itself. (Blaikie and Brookfield 1987: 17, cited in Bryant and Bailey 1997)

Studies on political ecology show how local, national, and transitional economic and political changes impact the power relationship over various forms of natural resources. Political ecology shows that resources that is generally referred to as 'common' like water, forests, fish, etc. are increasingly becoming a site of contestations between individuals, groups, and other actors like state and global economic forces.[3]

The post-Independent era witnessed major changes in the fishing scenario across the country as a consequence of the larger polices adopted by the state to modernize the fisheries sector. After the 1950s, the vast fisheries resources of the country attracted policymakers and international economic forces to implement new fishing technologies and other innovative programs like building harbors. From the beginning, fisheries resource has been a major concern of developmental policies at national level as it reflected in the policies of the Planning Commission from the very first Five-Year Plan. The development initiatives aimed at transforming the 'backward coastal villages' by increasing the fish harvest through modernization (Kurien 2000; Mathew 2000; Subramanian 2003). The modernization program aimed at introduction of several major changes to conventional fishing methods.

Such a transformation called for drastic changes in the traditional methods of fishing using labor-intensive methods giving way to adoption of technology-driven and capital-intensive modern methods (Kurien 2000). The modernization project aimed at improving the socio-economic condition of the fishers, soon gave way to promotion of large scale export of fish to overseas markets thus transforming the traditional consumption-oriented fishing by individuals or small groups into a commercial venture of rich businessmen.

Kerala has been popularly known as a rich fisheries resource state, both nationally as well as internationally. This had the mark in terms of Central government's plan for the state's coastal localities in the first Five-Year Plan, and Kerala became one of first costal states to adopt development policies in a greater way. Importantly, it was the southern coastal belts of the state that witnessed more developmental experiments. The first developmental fishing project introduced in the state was the 'Indo-Norwegian Project for Fisheries Community Development' way back in 1956. The villages where the project was launched saw many radical shifts in the way fishing was done with the introduction of mechanized boats. But this has also led to a number of problems and much of the crises faced by the fishing communities can be attributed to the anomalies created by technological interventions in the coastal life (Kurien 2000; Thomson 1989; Aerthayil 2000).

The modernization project has subverted the traditional economic patterns and market forces, and modern technology has started to play an important role. The two contrasting forms of fishing and differential productivities created tension in the seas. Poor artisanal fishers, unable to buy motorized boats and ill-equipped to handle modernized fishing system, became more impoverished with exhaustive fishing even as outsiders who could appropriate the opportunities opened by the new policies thrived. Demand for fish abroad especially for prawns made an international market for local fishing and it has led to over-exploitation of the resource by using mechanized boats, leading to a faster depletion of the resources over a period of time. This led to pauperization of the economic system of average fishers. For the fishing community, the sea was their 'common property' to which the individual fishers have had 'open access' resulting in a greater degree of equality among them and giving the impression of a barrier-free access to resources. But mechanized trawling proved to be destructive as it led to decrease in production and monopoly by commercial interests. This led to a drastic decline in productivity, income, and the quality of life of the traditional fish workers, who were not only denied any benefits from mechanization but were also deprived of what belonged to them traditionally for centuries. Technology gave way to the emergence of a new capitalist class among the fishers supported by the state and merchants from outside (Arethayil 2000). Mechanization also created a strong element of uncertainty in their occupation as fishers with the same fishing gears and have been fishing in the same part of the sea simultaneously can end up netting either nothing or catching a different quantum of fish. The larger outcome of the modernization and capitalist interventions in the seacoast was the impoverishment of poor fishers living adjacent to the coast and depletion of their valuable fisheries resource. These changes have led to violent conflicts in the sea as well as on the coast between various stakeholders. The discrepancy prevailing between the 'community regulated' economic life of the coastal localities and the modern economic pattern of the mainstream has led to several conflicts over a period of time (Kurien 2000). There have also been many bloody fights between the traditional fishers and owners of motorized boats in many coastal villages of the state.

Despite the intense crisis of survival, fishers have been excluded from all political mobilizations and struggles for rights that the Kerala witnessed in recent decades[4] (Tharakan 2007). And wherever they participated, the impact was minimal. What is more striking is that even the Left parties, who otherwise have instigated and carried out several struggles and movements for the cause of the working class especially for the betterment of the agricultural laborers, toddy tappers, and coir and cashew workers turned a

Nelson's eye on the plight of the fishers (ibid.). Intervention of political parties was restricted to the vote bank politics primarily[5] (ibid.). Even the Left parties never addressed fishing as labor and the problems of fishers as a working-class issue. However, there were few attempts from the radical Left, but were of limited success, partly because they did not focus specifically on the problems of the fisheries sector, which are different from those of the land-based workers (Aertheyil 2000). The Left politicians considered fish workers as an unorganizable group. During the late 1970s, the CPI-M and the CPI separately tried in vain to rope in the fishers into their respective trade unions, the Centre for Trade Unions (CITU), and All-India Trade Union Congress (AITUC), respectively.

However, since the 1970s, there were independent fishers mobilising in various parts of the state. However, a collective voice, cutting across caste, creed, and political barriers could be heard only with the formation of the Kerala Swathanthra Malsya Thozhilali Federation (KSMTF) in 1980. The movement became very powerful in the 1990s with massive mobilization of members. But the movement, despite its secular claims, has remained restricted more or less to Christian localities and has been losing its earlier strength. It is seen that wherever political organizations are active among the fishers, they tend to polarize them on the caste and religious lines[6] (Aertheyil 2000). Overall, it can be argued that fishers have not been able to register their presence in the political sphere in spite of intense social problems they have been facing, primarily because their problems are not part of the agendas of the politicians. However, the independent organizations that emerged among the community though has been suffering from several limitations, they somehow succeeded in bringing about some transformations in in their lives at least in some pockets.

Social Indicators of Marginality

This section brings attention to various social indicators on fishers, revealing their highly marginalized condition. Firstly, the section deals with the geographical dimension of marginality. Across the state, the coastal strips are densely populated. The landlessness of coastal people, a condition ignored by land reform policy, forced them to continue to populate the coast. The limited and geographically bounded nature of coasts plays a major role in generating a congested, economically deprived, and even culturally segregated social life. Kalpana Ram, in her study on the Mukkuvars of Kanyakumari coast says the tremendous population pressure in the area, along with

Table 8.1 District-wise distribution of average distance of house from the shore

District	*Average distance (in metres)*	*Range*
Thiruvananthapuram	67	1–300
Alappuzha	161	2–1000
Ernakulam	136	1–1500
Malappuram	77	6.5–300
Kannur	284	10–5000
Kerala average	148	1–5000

Human Development Report of the Fisher Folks in Kerala (2009)

a precarious economy, leads to social and communal volatility and violence (ibid.). She opines that the closely packed dwellings and widespread poverty give the coastal strips an appearance more like a slum than a series of rural villages (Ram 1992) (Table 8.1).

One can note that on an average, Kerala's fishers are settled within 1 meter to 1 km of the coast. In Thiruvananthapuram and Malappuram districts, the houses are closer to the sea compared to other districts. In these districts, the average distance is under 100 meters and maximum is 300 meters from the seashore. An interesting observation is that about 87% of the total houses are under 200 meters from the shore. The proportion of houses under 200 meters off the coast constitutes 99% in Thiruvananthapuram. It is important to note that as many as 2000–8000 fisher hutments are damaged every monsoon across the Kerala coast.[7] The following table gives village-specific details of how these settlement patterns directly cause damages and death to the residents. The following table offers a glimpse of the landholding pattern among the fishers.

Table 8.2 shows that around one-fourth of the households do not own an inch of land, while nearly 40% have under 5 cents under their feet. District-wise data also reveal that most households do not own landed property and those who own have only below 5 cents. Again, Thiruvananthapuram has the worst story in this case too.[8] This is a result of the neglect by successive governments even as they went ahead and implemented another celebrated success stories of Kerala—the land reforms. Availability of drinking water is a grave problem in most coastal villages and often they have to pay private parties for this. In the coastal belts of Thiruvananthapuram, only 45.5% have access to public supply of drinking water.

Table 8.2 District-wise percentage distribution of possession of land among fishers

Category	*Thiruvananthapuram*	*Alappuzha*	*Ernakulam*	*Malappuram*	*Kannur*	*Kerala*
No land	68.0	4.2	18.1	5.0	56.0	31.0
Up to 5 cents	27.8	35.4	48.6	37.0	39.0	37.0
6–10 cents	2.1	49.0	25.0	43.0	4.0	24.5
11–25 cents	1.0	8.3	8.3	11.0	1.0	5.8
25–50 cents	1.0	3.1	0.0	4.0	0.0	1.7
Total	100.0	100.0	100.0	100.0	100.0	100.0

Human Development Report of the Fisher Folks in Kerala (2009)

The rate of morbidity is higher among the fishers compared to the general population. Higher morbidity rates are observed in Thiruvananthapuram, Malappuram, and Kannur. In Thiruvananthapuram, it is 124.4 per thousand. Due to the congested housing and wet soil conditions, toilet facilities become difficult along coastal villages. Only 60% of fishers households have toilets as against 84% for the rest as of 2011, indicating one of the main reasons for the overall poor health status of the fishers.[9] On employment front, again this community has the one of highest levels at 29%. The unemployed are mostly females and younger generation males.[10]

Apart from these, coastal communities are also deprived of getting access to resources and full participation in the political sphere. People without voter identity cards and unregistered houses are still common and unaware of the beneficial government programs meant for them. There is an acute discrepancy between the institutional programs of the government and the response from the fishers. From the above discussion, it is evident that the coastal regions inhabited by fishers is a 'fringe' space and they have been subjected to various forms of marginalities. These facts reaffirm that social development in Kerala is largely a story of the inland society, and fishers have been systematically deprived of most of the social development processes and policies, leaving behind them and creating a pattern of marginality across the coastal belts.

Contested Space—Insights from Vizhinjam

Das and Poole (2004) in the introduction of their fascinating volume 'Anthropology in the Margin of State' try to locate the question of marginality in the context of the 'state-margin' relationship where isolated and often excluded geographies and social groups are important ethnographic sites. Such geographical locations, according to them, are not only territorial sites, but also are places where rules and regulations of the statefail to penetrate. They cite the examples of Latin American countries where peasant communities exist as a cultural and social group 'removed' from the national culture and polity. This sort of territoriality, according to Das and Poole, assumes a central mode of spatial and social relations in which a 'margin' is imagined as something that can be located as the outer edge of a given social unit. This notion of territorial margin forms a part of a well-known anthropological account of the peasant families as isolated and marginal to the state. The Vizhinjam coast, the focal point of this study, resembles many of the features of such anthropological sites. It is explicit that Vizhinjam, like other coastal villages of the state, lies at the outer sphere of the inland society that makes it a micro-social setting on the fringes. The geographical location places Vizhinjam between the deep sea and the outlier of inland (Aerthayil 2000).

While located in the margin of the state, coastal localities like Vizhinjam are space of various forms of contestations. Here, the idea of 'contested space,' as proposed by Low and Zunika (2003), is significant in understanding the everyday manifestation of social life in marginalized seashore. Low and Zunika (2003) define 'contested space' as geographic locations where conflicts in the form of opposition, confrontation, subversion, and/or resistance engage actors whose social positions are defined by differential control of resources and access to power' (2003: 18). They further describe

> ....contested spaces give material expression to and act as loci for creating and promulgating, countering, and negotiating dominant cultural themes that find expression in myriad aspects of social life. Spaces are contested precisely because they concretize the fundamental and reoccurring, but otherwise unexamined, ideological and social framework that structure practice. (2003: 18)

The idea of 'contested space' is used in this study to understand how a coastal belt as a physical space becomes a site of conflicts, contestations, and confrontations between groups and individuals in the everyday life. The descriptions of the field experience from the Vizhinjam coast explore empirically the nature of 'contested spaces' in the coastal locality.

The Congested Inhabitation

The coastal land is divided into small colonies consisting of several tiny houses at the Vizhinjam village. Each colony has different names. The northern side, which is the area closer to the seashore, is dominated by the Marakkayar Muslims, is called Pattanikkolani, while the single largest Christian colony is called Pallithura. Pattanikkolani consists of small densely set hutments. Between the sea and the housing area, there is a small market where tea stalls, provisions stores, and other small shops are located. The Marakkayars have seven such clusters. Apart from Pattanikkolani, there is a place called Mathilpuram and five small clusters which fall under the Pullurkonam ward. The largest Christian settlement at Pallithura is also closer to the seashore. There are four other Mukkuvar Christian clusters at Kottappuram, which is a bit far off the coast. All except a few Christian houses are built on the community land governed by the church. In both localities, the houses are close to each other that there is nearly no place to move about. Narrow lanes, barely two or three feet in width, run through the maze of houses. While the majority population of Vizhinjam are fishers living in clusters, a minor non-fishing population and the upper strata among both the groups are settled off the cost.

The 'Kadappuram' (seacoast) of the Muslims is closer to the Pattanikkolani, where fish sale takes place round the clock. The families living in the thickly populated Pattanikkolani are without any basic infrastructure like bathrooms, toilets, piped water, etc. and most households have 8–10 members. The Pallithura Mukkuvar colony is just 100 meters away from the Pattanikolany domiciled where the Muslims have more or less similar features. The thickly populated area is full of small huts inhabited by 'extended families.' There is no drinking water facility as is the case in Pattanikkolani. Recreation activities are depended on the sea. Pallippuram edging into the sea is the most congested area in the locality dotted by huts, fish market, and a general market. The condition in other colonies is not dissimilar. The Lakshamveed Colony,[11] Rakavilakam Colony, and the Township Colony at Pullurkonam are dominated by the Muslim Marakkayars. In the Mukkuvar area too, there are other colonies adjacent to Pallippuram where a huge chunk of Christians live. At the Kottappuram junction, slightly off the coast is the Sindhu Matha Church surrounded by small shops, and from where one can access all other Mukkuvar neighborhoods. Near the church is the parish council hall and the auditorium where most of the marriage functions of Mukkuvars take place. Off Kottappuram and on the southern edge is the another Muslim area called Karimpallikkaras.

The congested spatial feature of the settlements at Vizhinjam generates a lot of tension and conflicts among people and sometimes results in violence. The land closer to the coast where families are hugely concentrated is owned by government as it is part of the coast. At the same time, the land which is slightly away from the seashore is under the ownership of the Church and the Palli-Jama-et, respectively. The possession of land is a highly contested issue in the village. Neither the government nor the authority of these religious institutions are fully accepted by the actual inhabitants which is clear from their narratives that reveal contesting claims over small areas of land which they occupy. Though the Mukkuvars and the Markkayars don't have any right over them, there is resentment against collective ownership by religious institutions of those land parcels lying a bit away from the seacoast. The resentment is also directed toward government ownership of the land that is located in the coast. Fishers have been demanding individual property rights from both the government and their respective religious authorities.

However, inter-family strife and conflicts ebb and flow all the time within the bounded space of both these communities and the living conditions are no way better than those available in urban slum clusters. During field work, I have witnessed many quarrels generated by what could be termed as 'imposed proximity.' The closeness of the houses in the limited space leads to quarrel over boundaries. More importantly, privacy for the family is very limited and it leads to many other conflicts including sex-related issues.

The pathetic living conditions are well reflected in their narratives. Ummer, the owner of a tea shop at the Muslim side of Kadappuram says, 'there is no toilet facility for the majority of the people. The main reason is the lack of space. All houses are so congested it is difficult to build toilets. Most of the people here depend on the sea to meet their 'basic needs.' Muslim women were hesitant to admit that they use the sea for 'basic needs.' There is also no drinking water supply. They pay Rs. 2.50 per kudam (a large pot) to the Water Authority for their daily needs, which works out to be Rs. 10–15 a day. Hassan Khan, the ex-president of the Vizhinjam Panchayat explains the difficulty:

> Here, we suffer from serious water crisis. A pot of water costs Rs 2.50. We don't have any facility here. Even if we dig wells, we get brine. So, every day

> we will have to buy seven to eight pots of water from the government truck which ferries it to us. There are a few wells in the township, but water is not available all the time. Even the water supplied by the government contains worms and insects. We have to stand in queue every day at the coast to get drinking water.[12]

Stephen, a local political activist from the Mukkuvar community talks about unemployment and the pathetic situation of the people.

> People are jobless here. Majority of them live in poverty. Some people live entirely on debts. There is always tension prevailing due to indebtedness. If you cannot repay a thousand rupees that you had borrowed from a friend on time, it will create problems for both the parties.[13]

The educational condition is also very poor among both communities. Among the Marakkayars, a madrassa and a primary school exist side by side and this is the only educational institution in the locality. Due to economic hardships, many parents choose schools that provide free uniforms and books even if the school is far away from home. The educational condition of the Mukkuvars is slightly better though as they have a higher secondary school of their own. Hassan Khan says:

> People hardly complete the 10th standard. Education is very pathetic among us. We only have a lower primary school in the area. Those who don't have money really struggle to go to places outside Vizhinjam. We don't have anyone to push for our demands from the government here. We wanted to upgrade this L.P school to a U.P (Upper Primary), but we are unable to do that. Politicians, wealthy people, and others support the management of the bigger schools nearby as they need students from everywhere.

Work-Related Fights

The work space of the fisherfolks is the most tensed space. The space is very limited, and the people, fishing boats, and fishing instruments are more than such types of space could accommodate all of them. This congestion makes these types of space an ideal ground for continuous quarrels and aggression. During the peak time of fish exchange, Kadappurams gives an impression of a quarreling place. The verbal abuse and the aggressive body language are routine. Aggressive behavior is a form of resistance and survival strategy. Use of physical aggression over the other becomes indispensable to get things done. Shouting and high decibels communication help establish domination while selling fish. Quarrels take place between people when some dispute occurs over space. When one boat hits the other; when somebody occupies the space in the shed where fishing instruments are kept; when someone encroaches upon the fish selling space or while bargaining for a price for the fish, they quarrel; and sometimes it leads to violence. In this way, Kadappurams are always a domain of conflicts and violence.

Beyond this everyday manifestation of conflicts, there are some deeper issues of intra-community conflicts at work space. The economic organization of fishing activity within the community has an exploitative dimension. It is well known that Lelakaran or the auctioneer plays different roles in a fishing village. Sometimes, he comes to the rescue of fishers especially during lean seasons, but his main intention is to claim a share of the fish and in that sense is an 'exploiter' (Thomson 1989). The exploitation of fish workers by middlemen happens at various levels. First of all fishers are forced to sell fish only to the middlemen to whom they are indebted and thus they lose their bargaining power. Naturally the middlemen control price to their advantage. Secondly, due to the accumulated interest on the loans taken as advance, fishers fail to pay back on time and it further impoverishes them. Unable to pay back the capital, their whole life is tied to the middlemen. Slowly, it develops into a relationship of bonded labor in which the fishers have their financial dealings only with the middlemen. But it is difficult to say whether traders and middlemen constitute a separate social class or caste like the groups well off than those who go for fishing. There is a loan system called *Udambadi Sambradayam* or *Kuru*, meaning an agreement or contract. In this system, if a fisherman wants a loan, he/she approaches a moneylender and enters into an agreement that they would return the loan within a stipulated period and that the moneylender would be allowed to collect 3 percentage of the daily catch as interest on the loan. The moneylender or his agent will be the middleman in the sale of fish in his catch, for which he would be paid 2 or 3% of the sales as commission. The moneylender is known as *Udambadikkaran* or *Kurukkaran*. He is spotted at the beach near the loading place from the morning till dusk. As soon as the fish is loaded, he moves as the middlemen of the sale and conduct the sale. The reason for this highly exploitative credit system is obvious, since the fishers have no resources to invest in equipment or have the means to acquire money for other urgent expenses.

In Vizhinjam, apart from the fishers, one can also see others dependent on fishing. These are the wholesale merchants, male retail merchants called cycle loaders, and the female retailers called basket sellers and those who specialize in selling fish at the beach to consumers who directly come to the beach. Since Vizhinjam is vibrant in fishing and marketing, the level of exploitation is very high. Apart from the fishers and intermediaries, there are several occupational categories like the small traders in shrimps and cuttlefish, head-load women vendors, the tax or Kuthaka collectors, those dealing with ice, kerosene and oil, repairers of outboard engines and plywood boats, or vallams, etc. Because of conflicting interests, quarrels between these groups are an everyday sight at Vizhinjam.

Gender-Related Conflicts

Inter-family conflicts also arise from various contestations related to marriage. Despite the poor economic conditions, the practice of dowry is very common and it generates a lot of problems. In most cases, parents of the girl fail to give the huge amount of money they had promised to the groom. Since both families are from the same locality, it leads to frequent quarrels. Sweeta, a women activist who works among the Mukkuvars, says 'one of the biggest problems at Vizhinjam is the family conflict over dowry.'[14] Mostly, the victims of such conflicts are women who suffer even physical abuse, which leads to temporary separation or divorce.'

The sufferings of women are more intense and visible in the coastal area. At the Marakkayar localities, women are not allowed to go for work and more or less confined to homes due to religious reasons. On the contrary, the Mukkuvar women work along with their men in fishing activities, mainly in selling fish. Among the Marakkayars, the gender conflict and subordination are more confined to the domestic realm, though the division between domestic and public is perhaps not very accurate. The congested community life generates many gender-related conflicts when patriarchal norms and practices entangle with the havoc of everyday crisis. The dispute over various issues between families and individuals generates subtle forms of violence over women and sometimes it leads to physical abuse.

The sufferings of the Mukkuvar women have some added dimensions as violence is not merely confined to the domestic realm, but it extends to the work space and the wider public realm as well as women are very much part of the economic life of the Mukkuvar community. The role of women in the economic function is invariably linked with violence inflicted by men.

Men in the market and other public places humiliate them. They are also victims of male misconduct when they bargain for fish in the Kadappuram. Women are always subjects of '*Pallu Vili*' (scolding), the verbal abuse of men when they attempt to buy fish at cheaper rates. Many women carry fish in baskets to sell in neighboring towns as not all of them can sell fish in the locality itself. When they enter a bus, they are scolded by the bus staff as their fish baskets are an eyesore. Sometimes the anger of the bus staff and the travelers go beyond verbal abuse and leads to physical aggression. There are a number of cases of abuses and utterances on women fish workers, which hardly get any serious attention from the male-dominated public or protectors of law, rather their patriarchal attitude and lack of sympathy further humiliate the hapless Mukkuvar women. When women go to the neighboring towns, the male fish sellers also create problems. The problem of violence on the Mukkuvar women by their own men is also very common. Narratives reveal that the heavy drinking habits of their men counterpart, they are being subjected to martial fidelity, disputes over dowry and property, all result in physical violence on women and this is one of the most severe problems in the Mukkuvar area.

Conclusion

By using the political ecology framework, the essay unraveled how the larger development policies and projects reaffirm the vulnerable economic positions and social life of the marginalized communities in India. The essay has shown how systematic exclusion from development turns margins of the state as contested space. The essay also demonstrates that the attention to micro context would yield a more nuanced understanding of the crisis of development in contemporary time. The idea of 'contested space' can be a useful ploy to understand the everyday manifestation of the disenchantment of development in comparative contexts.

Notes

1. The idea of social ecology is also important here. When the conventional models of society, premised upon the four basic pillars—namely economy, culture, social structure, and polity—are challenged, social ecology as a category gained significance in social sciences, particularly in sociology (Guha 1998). Social ecology talks about the interdependence of the biophysical and socio-cultural domains. By foregrounding ecological infrastructure that

is, soil, water, flora and fauna, climate, etc., social ecology links the natural environment and socio-cultural domains. From this perspective, political, cultural, social, and economic conditions and ecology are necessarily interacting with each other in shaping human relationships. It is noticeable that ecology has been given a greater emphasis in many studies on fishers across the world as they are one group which directly depends on the natural resources for the survival.

2. There are various strands within political ecology.
3. The well-known article by Garret Hardin titled 'Tragedy of the Commons' set a debate among social scientists on the relationship between human beings and the commons. While the article proposes a very pessimistic notion on the harmonious nature of usage of commons in a fast changing, individualist, and increasingly urbanized world, many tried to look at the history, present, and future of the 'commons' in terms of its collective meaning in different social and ecological settings.
4. The historical events in which fisherfolks in Kerala had some indirect involvement were the Punnapra-Vayalar Uprising and the Mappila Rebellion. The Punnapra-Vayalar Uprising was organised in Alappuzha in the 1940s as part of the Communist movement against the socio-political establishment.
5. They provided outboard motors, ring-seine nets and plywood boats and other fishing instruments for people to impress the fishers before the elections.
6. The Malsya Thozhilali (Fisher workers) Congress, trade union wing of the Congress Party mainly organized Mukkuvar Christians, who were its vote banks. This was because of political affiliation between the Congress and the Church. Among the Hindu fish workers of southern and northern Kerala, the Dheerava Sabha, a caste organisation had some influence. In north Kerala it was the Muslim League, which was influential among the Muslim fishers, who constitute the majority there.
7. See Human Development Report of the Fisher Folks in Kerala (2009)
8. See Human Development Report of the Fisher Folks in Kerala (2009)
9. See Human Development Report of the Fisher Folks in Kerala (2009)
10. See Human Development Report of the Fisher Folks in Kerala (2009)
11. Lakshamveed colony is a policy of government that provides houses for poorer section especially for Scheduled caste and Scheduled tribes. This is a rare case that a Muslim community in the state is living at 'Lakshamveed'. The Lakshamveed colonies constructed at Vizhinjam were to accommodate the fisher people families displaced from the sea side after the harbour project.
12. Hassan Khan, 56, 8 February 2011, Pallippuram, Vizhinjam.
13. Stephen, 42, 4 March 2011, Kottappuram, Vizhinjam
14. Sweeta, 46, 1 May 2011, Trivandrum.

References

Aerthayil, M. (2000). *Fishworker's Movement in Kerala (1977–1994): The Role of Non-party Political Organizations in Social Transformation in India*. New Delhi: Indian Social Institute.

Aloysius, G. (2005). *Interpreting Kerala's Social Development*. New Delhi: Critical Quest.

Arunima, G. (2006). Imagining Communities Differently; Print, Language and Public Sphere in Colonial Kerala. *Indian Economic and Social History Review.*, *43*(1), 63–76.

Bryant, R. L., & Bailey, S. (1997). *Third World Political Ecology*. London: Routledge.

Das, V., & Poole, D. (2004). *Anthropology in the Margins of the State*. New Delhi: Oxford University Press.

Devika, J. (2014). Deprivation, Abjection and Dispossession: Social Disadvantage in Early 21st Century in Kerala. *Economic and Political Weekly, 18*(420), 73–80.

Guha, R. (1998). *Social Ecology*. New Delhi: Oxford University Press.

Gurung, G. S., & Kollmair, M. (2005). *Marginality. Concepts and Their Limitations* (IP6 Working Paper No. 4). Winterthurerstr: Development Study Group, Department of Geography, University of Zurich.

Harilal, K. N. (2005). Confronting Bureaucratic Capture: Rethinking Participatory Development Methodology in Kerala. *Economic and Political Weekly, 48*(36), 52–60.

Kurien, J. (2000). Icelandic Fisheries Governance: A Third World Understanding. *Economic and Political Weekly, 35*(34), 3061–3066.

Kurien, J., & Achari, T. R. T. (1990). Overfishing Along Kerala Coast: Causes and Consequences. *Economic and Political Weekly, 25*(35/36), 2011–2018.

Low, S. M., & Zunika, D. L. (2003). *The Anthropology of Space and Place: Locating Culture*. Oxford: Blackwell.

Mathew, G. (2000). *Fisher Worker's Movement in Kerala*. New Delhi: Indian Social Institute.

Menon, D. (2002). Religion and Colonial Modernity—Rethinking Belief and Identity. *Economic and Political Weekly.*, *37*(17), 1662–1667.

Oommen, M. A. (Ed.). (1999). *Rethinking Development: Kerala's Development Experience*. New Delhi: Institute of Social Science.

Punathil, S. (2013). Kerala Muslims and Shifting Notions of Religion in the Public Sphere. *South Asia Research, 33*(1), 1–20.

Rajasenan, D., & Groot, G. (2005). *Kerala Economy: Trajectories Challenges and Implications*. Cochin: Directorate of Publications and Public Relations.

Ram, K. (1992). *Mukkuvar Women: Gender, Hegemony and Capitalist Transformation in a South Indian Fishing Community*. New Delhi: Kali for Women.

Rammohan, K. T. (2008). Caste and Landlessness in Kerala: Signals from Chengara. *Economic and Political Weekly, 43*(37), 14–16.

Subramanian, A. (2003). Mukkuvar Modernity: Development as a Cultural Identity. In A. Agrawal & K. Sivaramakrishnan (Eds.), *Regional Modernities: The Cultural Politics of Development in India* (pp. 262–275). Stanford: Stanford University Press.

Tharakan, M. (2007). *Kerala Model Revisited: New Problems, Fresh Challenges* (Working Paper No. 15). Kochi: Centre for Socio-economic & Environmental Studies (CSES).

Thomson, K. T. (1989). *Political Economy of Fishing: A Study of an Indigenous Social System in Tamilnadu* (Unpublished PhD dissertation). University of Madras.

CHAPTER 9

Resurgence of Community in the Midst of Despair: Development's Changing Course in Northeast India

A. S. Shimreiwung

Questions of development in Northeast India are generally presumed as a challenge for all the stakeholders. Reasons for this outlook come from the innumerable disadvantages that the region faces, such as political instability, inept governance mechanism, and located at the periphery of Indian state. However, the major point of contention in academic discourse on development in the region is whether those factors that have impede development process come from governance mechanism within the region or from the apathy of policymakers at the helms of the decision-making process (Verghese 1997; Bhaumik 2009; Nongbri 2014). 'Development is management of a promise—and what if the promise does not deliver?' (Pieterse 2000). These lines fit more aptly with various kinds of developmental promises made by both the state and non-state actors in Northeastern states of India. When it comes to problems that have emerged from within the region, the problem of insurgency is presumed as an overarching factor, besieging gov-

A. S. Shimreiwung (✉)
Department of Sociology, Tezpur University, Assam, India

D. N. Pathak and A. K. Das (eds.), *Investigating Developmentalism*,
https://doi.org/10.1007/978-3-030-17443-9_9

ernance mechanism in most of the Northeastern states. Thus, questions of development in the Northeast region are projected as intrinsically linked with the political solution, making it a prerequisite condition; as economic growth and progress require 'law-and-order' and stable government. On the other hand, numerous scholars and policymakers consider lack of development as one of the major factors for political turmoil in the region. Despite the best effort by the stakeholders involved in the developmental process of the region, which has come in varied forms and designs, the path toward development does not seem to have taken place as desired, and a sense of despair seems to prevail over the process of development among state agencies and community as well. As the Indian state continues to press for development of the region, the policy for economic growth of Northeast India still hinges on the idea of 'Look East' policy (recently changed into 'Act East'), where the emphasis is on connecting the region with East Asian markets. However, the communities in the region seem to have taken different perspectives to the path of development, differing much from 'policymakers' in New Delhi. This new perspectives on development have been marked by 'choosing development' in parts, accepting those policies that suit local politics and rejecting the others, and taking initiatives on development by themselves rather than depending on the policies framed by the government to be implemented. All these varied responses to the development indicate the larger outlook of the communities on what development ought to be from their view, and what actually happened in their localities. Besides the disjuncture between expectations and realities of 'developmental process' in the Northeast region, the challenges to the path of development have already appeared to be almost insurmountable in the view-from-below. At the national level, the concept of 'development' is becoming 'synonymous with the high rate of growth rate of gross domestic products' (Patnaik 2010). In the Northeast India, the common people see development primarily in terms of availability and establishment of modern infrastructure and industrialization, which does not directly relate with the state of Gross Domestic Products. Thus, unlike national policymakers for whom the contribution of Northeast India to India's rate of Gross Domestic Products play a pivotal parameter to measure the region's state of development, the common people and the local leader see the socio-political contentment and basic infrastructural establishment as the core aspects of development in the region.

Contours on developmental issues in the region make it imperative to analyze the interface between the state and local community, and their multifaceted dynamics of federal states relationship in developing countries. Dominant discourse on developmental process in the Northeast region has projected the state's role as 'provider' of 'development' to the 'people,' whereby the relationship between state and community has been posited as sharing an 'un-equal' power relations. However, in understanding the social and political dynamics of development in the region, one needs to re-conceptualize the role of the state and community by considering them as 'determinants' and 'agents' which acts and reacts to a given situation and not as passive receivers. While the Indian state may have been the only active agent of the development process in Northeast region in the past, the change in political atmosphere in the region has also made the community aware of their responsibilities and rights. There is a growing consciousness among the varied communities in the region about what they want for their localities to be in the process of development. Duncan McDuie-Ra (2007) has identified that in recent time, civil societies have become major determinants in deciding the direction of the developmental policies and processes in the state like Meghalaya. The involvement of community-based organizations, which have been acting as the guardian for the community, in the developmental process heralds a paradigm shift in the political space and governance process in the region. Apart from the interference and intrusion of civil societies in determining the developmental policy of the state, there are also varied situations where the states in Northeast region have deliberately shared its responsible to non-state agencies and communities in executing their plans and policies. These new changes in the Indian state's policy are projected as innovation in developmental process; however, making the community as partners in development has also given rise to the idea that common people are not only stakeholders but can also be an active agent for themselves and are arbitrators of developmental projects. When the state fails to fulfill the requisite demand and need of common citizens, whether in small towns or in far-flung villages in the Northeast region, the notion that 'community' has to take action for their own interest is predominantly becoming popular. However, the various initiatives taken by the community, in the form of civil societies or village community, are indeed a form of response to the despair and hopelessness on the pace of development implemented in Northeast India by the Indian state. The realities of development process in Northeast India have turn development as 'negotiated space' between varied stakeholders, mostly between the state and community. This study attempts to explore how state and community negotiate the path of development and design development to suit its own interest, and in turn determine their relationships.

State and Community in Northeast India: Unfriendly Postures and Intimate Struggles

The relationship between state and society in Northeast region has largely been shaped by political turmoil, which was marked by violent confrontation and conflict between rebels and the state agencies for a long period of time, eventually leading to an atmosphere of distrust and distance between the two. When the insurgency was at its height in the region during the 1970s and 1980s, the state has assumed a totalitarian posture, using violence as a medium to re-assert its authority as well as engage with the political rebels and public alike. The period of insurgency varies from one state to another, while states like Assam and Mizoram had experienced political turmoil for a decade or more, there are also states like Nagaland and Manipur which are still living under the shadow of political conflict and violent confrontation between the state's paramilitary force and rebel groups. The period of conflict and confrontation, whether short or long, seems to have made the same impact on state-society relationships in almost all the states in Northeast: that it creates distrust and animosity between the two. On the other hand, the state-making process in the region, during the colonial period and the post-independence era, has not changed, but it remains not as a mere administrative exercise but as forms of conflict resolution.

Diverse communities inhabit Northeast India, with variations in terms of language, race, religion, and culture, which can also be broadly categorized as distinctions between tribes and caste communities. In terms of political structure, there have been societies with the state, and societies without the state; however, during the colonial period, most of these variations in terms of political institutions were flattened as they all come under the authority of British Empire. Colonial rule had a cataclysmic effect on those societies that had remained stateless in the past, as the authority of the state was not only accepted by 'stateless-societies' in the region, and gradually state became a necessity for maintaining the welfare of society. In the post-independence era, what have been seen in terms of political movements for 'self-determination' in the region were actually serious attempt by the communities to create their own 'state,' rather than abolishing the state structure altogether. At present, most of the political movements in the region have either been incorporated through 'creation' of states on the basis of their ethnic identity or given succor in the form of 'Autonomous Councils.' Therefore, in terms of structural relationships, societies in the Northeast have accommodated the authority and relevance of state in their own terms, rather than rejecting it in totality. Taking the perspectives that have been put forward by James C. Scott in his book *The Art of Not Being Govern: An Anarchist History of Upland Southeast Asia* (2010), we may argue that the process of 'enclosure' of non-state communities in Northeast India within the 'state-space' has almost attained full circle.

The nature of relationship between the state and society is not similar in all the states of Northeast India. While comparing the state-society relations between Mizoram and Manipur, M. Sajjad Hassan has highlighted that in Mizoram the acceptance of the state authority is much stronger than Manipur, where the role of state appears as 'imposition' from outside (Hassan 2006). Some of the major factors that have created such differences between Mizoram and Manipur pertains to 'power-relations' within the society and the political dynamics of 'state-making' in these two states. Manipur's historical experience, as remaining in Part-C State for three decades where the administration was controlled directly from the center, has been a major factor for the creation of a volatile relationship between the state and society. Whereas, in Mizoram, the transition to statehood had taken much lesser time and the power of administration was passed on to local leaders within a short period after attaining the status of Union Territory in 1971. Further, according to Sajjad Hassan (2006), the key to a stable state-society relationship is also dependent on the state's capability -- whether state leaders have the authority (and the legitimacy) to act as the central force in society – determining, social, political and economic interactions or if they are hindered in these task by rival forces. Based on the experiences of these two states in Northeast India, we can assume that the nature of state-society in conflict zones depends much on the ability of the state to establish its 'authority' and 'legitimacy' among the communities being governed by it as well as creating a situation for economic progress and growth.

Development as processes of economic growth is not separate from 'state-making' process in the Uplands of Southeast Asian region, where modern states had tried to 'bring non-state spaces and people to heel' (Scott 2010: 4). This point has been asserted by James C. Scott who argues that 'the attempt to fully incorporate them has been cultural styled as development, economic progress, literacy, and social integration' (Scott 2010:

4–5). Thus, the developmental process is not only the objectives of a state-making process, but it has become intrinsic to the nature of the interface between state and society in the Northeast region. The response from societies in the region toward state-making and developmental process is determined by how it has been introduced and planned by the state and also seen in its political terms. Development stylized as a remedy to political conflicts and local politics in the Northeast region has been the predominant theme in India's policy toward this region. In the same way, the local community also sees development as simply an attempt to divert people's attention from identity politics to economic growth. However, over the years, what has happened in the region is that development has gradually become an integral part of identity politics in the region. Such is the extent of its integration into people's mindset that political claims and demands put forward either by the community-based civil societies or by rebel groups often include 'economic packages'. In some cases, political movements have emerged due to disparity in development projects between the neighbouring communities and localities. The status and perspectives that their 'locality' is 'undeveloped' are often derived by comparing with other locality within the same state, inhabited by their neighbouring communities. Thus the notion of being undeveloped is derivative and often relied on what the 'local community' has adopted. Again, the blame for inequality between the communities in terms of development goes to the attitude and interest of the state. Thus, the community's outlook towards development have come to determine the nature of the relationship between state and community in Northeast India, which is a result of presenting 'development' as an alternative to 'political struggle.' Therefore, it appears to be little choice for the community in the region between taking-up arm struggle and accepting development; the failure of one option eventually leads the people to choose the other. Not all responses to the failure of development have actually compelled the people to take the option of political struggle in the region, while we cannot rule out that some of the political movements have emerged out of despair over developmental policies or an attempt to attain it. The onus of negotiating and arbitrating on behalf of the community on development in the region seems to fallen on civil societies, and they seem to have taken the role with exceptional ingenuity.

Here, I want to focus on the modes of the interface between the state and society on development process; and, how communities in Northeast India have responded towards the role of the state in fulfilling its promises of development to the people. The process of development, in developing countries across the world, as argued by Jan Nederveen Pieterse is largely a game of 'management of promise,' and the questions arise is 'what if the promise is not delivered?' (Pieterse 2000). The outlook of local communities in Northeast India on development has largely stemmed from the development promises made by various political leaders and state agencies. Based on the local contingencies and situations, the diverse communities in the region have also reacted in varied ways to the project of state's development project in Northeast India. Looking at some of the major responses on development by the communities in the region, I have broadly categorized it into three different types, these are: (1) Anti-Development Posture, (2) Co-Partners in Development Process, (3) Public as agents of Development. The modes of the interface between state and society that has been identified are neither exclusive nor exhaustive and not restricted to a particular state or society, it is an attempt to interrogate how communities that are in 'zones of enclosure' are mitigating the role of the state in their everyday life.

Anti-development Postures

The emergence of civil societies as active arbitrators on developmental process in various states of Northeast region represents a new form of relationship between state and community, where the former has emerged as representative of people's voice as well as pressure groups. Duncan McDuie-Ra argues, 'In Northeast India, links between tribal identities and anti-modernity are still central to the politics of development' (McDuie-Ra 2007). Instead of simply reading and categorizing tribal movements as ecological movements and anti-modern, we need to rethink this long held perspective, as the relationship that people's movement shared with environmental issues are more complex than what we thought to be. Civil society actors in Khasi Hills, according to McDuie-Ra, have 'oppose developments when it fits into dominant political discourse,' while ecological issues remained unaddressed (McDuie-Ra 2007). Uranium mining in Khasi Hills has been opposed by various civil society organizations and taken up huge protests over the issue, whereas similar forms of protest have not happened on the issue of coal mining although it is causing severe ecological damage in the state. McDuie-Ra explains that the contradictory stand taken by civil societies in Khasi Hills in terms of ethnic politics. Uranium mining has been opposed as it fits the 'outsider' discourse, that it brings more 'outsiders' into the state, and also 'money from coal stays in Khasi

Hills while money from uranium would leave Khasi Hills' (McDuie-Ra 2007). Further, there are possibilities that the actual victims of environmental degradation and radiations are not been able to raise their issues, as they do not have the ability to do so. McDuie-Ra argues that development and environmental issues have been co-opted in the discourse on people's movement in Northeast region, whereas there is also a growing tendency of 'ethnicization' of the environment, which in one way or other have affected developmental process (McDuie-Ra 2007). The state's policy on uranium mining has gradually been influenced by the mass movement and protest that has emerged over the issue.

There are other public movements that are underway in Northeast region that may actually bring another dimension to the relationship between 'anti-development' movement and 'ethnic politics' in the region. In the early 2017, tribal civil societies in Nagaland raised opposition to the implementation of Nagaland Municipality Act 2001, which empowered the state government to established Urban Local Bodies (ULB) in towns and cities across the state with 33% reservation for women. While the implementation of this Act intents to bring development in various towns and cities in the state of Nagaland, Naga civil societies have protested and disrupted the state government from holding the elections to ULB on the ground that implementation of this Act will infringe upon their inalienable rights to natural resources, customary, and traditional rights. While the controversy soon erupted into a violent confrontation between civil societies and the state leading to loss of life, Nagaland state government was forced by mass protesters to halt the implementation of the Act and the Chief Minister was compelled to resign. Therefore, in Nagaland the civil societies made it succinctly clear that 'development' in any form that has been proposed by the state has to go through the approval of community. In one of the memorandum that was submitted to Chief Minister of Nagaland, the community leaders have stated that civil societies hold no malice or have any intention to suppress women's rights, however once again we unequivocally establish our clear stand that, we oppose the divisive policy of the Government to suppress the wishes and rights of the Nagas. Civil organizations in Nagaland have claimed they are not against women's reservation; however, their intentions to protect customary laws have been considered by women activists as a ploy to maintain patriarchal structures already in place in Naga society. On the other hand, their mode of confrontation with the government appears to be contestation over 'authority' and 'legitimacy' over the cultural practices and control of natural resources in the state. By staging a violent protest and stalling the electoral process, civil societies have made themselves clear that they are becoming an 'agent' in the developmental process of the state, and not passive receivers of state's policy. Further, we can discern that the elected government and political leaders may be legitimate authority under the Constitutional provisions, but their power has been restricted by civil societies on matters pertaining to development.

Co-partners of Development

The entry of Non-Governmental Organizations (NGOs) in developmental processes of Northeast region heralds a new dimension in state-society relationships as well as a governance mechanism. There have been concerted efforts by NGOs that have emerged from within the region, often aided by state agencies or foreign agencies, who have independently taken up varied projects for enhancement of livelihood, empowerment of weaker sections of society in the region. Here, however, my focus is on the partnership between state and other agencies in the developmental process, which can be considered as delegation and sharing of state's responsibility with other agencies. In its Annual Report for 2015–2016, Ministry of Development of North Eastern Region (MDoNER) declared that it has been implementing three Externally Aided Projects (EAP) in diverse areas such as livelihood to climate change in selected areas of the Northeastern region.

North Eastern Region Community Resource Management Project (NERCORMP), one of the EAPs in the region, is basically a multilateral effort of two International Organizations and North Eastern Council (NEC), and their operation area falls under three states (Assam, Meghalaya, Manipur), and six districts of Northeastern region. So far, their work is mainly focussed on the development of upland areas, villages in remote areas of the region, and it can be seen as an attempt to change the socio-economic conditions of the rural poor by empowering them through various schemes. In order to make this implement, MDoNER has created a 'regional level autonomous society' named as North Eastern Livelihood Promotion Society (NELPS) in 2012 headquartered in Guwahati. What actually can be put into questions here is that what is the necessity for the Central Agencies to establish an autonomous society for execution of plans and projects. Through concerted efforts, NERCORMP has penetrated rural areas of the region, by working independently from state agencies, and introduced new institutions and ideas to the rural folk. One of the major aspects of these projects is the introduction of Self Help Groups (SHGS) in communities, where the reach of the state's developmental activities has been minimal or nil. Although there have been various challenges and setback, in the implementation of this project, it certainly has made a certain impact on the livelihood of the poorest and vulnerable in society. Even though empowerment of women faces various challenges, the effort made by these projects seems to be making a positive impact on the lives of rural poor women in remotes villages of Northeast India.

The classic model where the partnership between state and society is the implementation of Communitisation Act in Nagaland in 2002. R. S. Pandey, one of the architectures of this model, has considered communitization as 'third way of governance,' where he explains it as 'to leverage the funds, the expertise, and the regulatory powers of the government with the social capital of the users 'community'' (Pandey 2010). Inefficiency within the system of governance and lack of motivation are some of the main reasons behind the transfer of power from the state to the community. The other alternatives available for the state governments for new governance mechanism, as per R. S. Pandey's assessment, are privatization and making government agencies efficient. Based on the three principles of T's: Trusting the community, Train the community members, and Transfer movement assets and power to them. Nagaland state initiated implementation of Communitisation in three sectors: health, education, and power. Studies conducted to assess the success and failures of Communitisation in Nagaland have indicated that it has brought positives changes and people's perspective toward government institutions have transformed. However, the level of success is uneven in all the villages and localities and varied factors such as lack of political connection and awareness have affected the implementation of this policy (Pathak 2014). Communitisation in Nagaland has been characterized as 'empowerment,' 'delegation,' 'decentralization,' and 'privatization,' all at the same time, where the state has taken up the role of 'assister,' 'partner,' 'monitor,' and 'supervisor' in implementing developmental policies (Pandey 2010: 16). The posture adopted by the state government in Nagaland state is indeed a major deviation from authoritarian measures that state agencies in the region had usually followed. Most notably, the transformation in government's policy in Nagaland by giving much emphasis on the role of 'community' in governance has happened five years after Ceasefire Agreement signed between Naga political rebels and Government of India in 1997, which transforms the political situation in Nagaland state. Nonetheless, one question that can be raised here is 'how far can the state go in transferring its authority to the 'community' despite knowing the fully well that by doing so it is undermining its own governing mechanism and power. While the devolution of power from state to local bodies has often been heralded as a major innovation in the field of governance, it also implies the inability of the state machinery in fulfilling its role as the main agency for development in the region.

Community Taking the Role of Agents for Development

In some states of Northeast India, the community has emerged as active agents of development, taking up projects of road constructions and repairs, and various other developmental activities which are usually handled by the state authorities. The engagement of community with developmental activities is not actually new in the context of Northeast India; most of the communities in the Northeast have the tradition of communitarianism as an intrinsic part of their social life. However, what actually set apart the new initiatives taken up by various communities in the remote parts of Northeast India is the nature of work and costs involved in these projects. The Tousem Sub-divisions road construction project taken up by Amstrong Panmei in 2012, an IAS Officer in Manipur state, with active support from villagers in the area involves 100-kilometer long motorable road that will connect two states—Assam and Manipur (Sharma 2012). The Central government had actually sanctioned 101 crores for the said road construction project in 1982, but at the ground level, nothing has happened even after ten years. Perplexed with the situation, the young IAS officer who hails from the same district started generating funds from his friends, peer groups, and donors from all over the country for taking up the road construction work with the active involvement of villagers in this area. The volume of work and fund involves goes much beyond what local communities can afford. Usually, these activities are taken up by the state agencies, while the role of the public has been limited to giving their land for the developmental purpose, for which in return they receive financial compensation. This initiative opens up a question, what the public could do when the situation arises where the state machinery has failed to deliver developmental projects and relinquish its responsibilities. The failure of state agencies in ushering the developmental projects that were promised or initiated by it eventually leave the people with no other choice, but to take up the unfinished task. The initiatives by vested individuals and community have not only happened as they have 'communitarian' values ingrained in their cultural ethos and social life, but the despair of failed promises by the state actor is a major factor for 'people' to come together and initiate collective actions.

In the same district of Manipur state, the denizens of Tamenglong town have also taken up repairing roads on their own in 2016 generating funds from individuals across the country and abroad. Bob Shukla wrote in one of the media campaign note that the citizens of Tamenglong district in Manipur are emerging as 'Ambassadors for change and development... strive ahead through collective efforts with no support whatsoever from the government' (Shukla 2016). The project started with small groups of volunteers taking-up minor repair works, which gradually turn into a mass movement, increasing the volume of work and involvement of a large number of individuals, even those who lived outside the district also extending support. It culminated into forming of an organization, Society for Enhancement of Tamenglong (SET), by people who shared the idea of 'self-determination' and not waiting for 'lethargic government' to bring development. Donations have poured in from various individuals within the community, and includes strangers who have no relation with the people and place. SET has been able to generate Rs. 4 lakhs through crowd-funding, as per their estimation that the required amount for the work project will cost Rs. 20 lakhs, which they seek to receive through the generous donors. As an alternative to state machinery, the process of generating funds through crowd-funding and initiating the projects through voluntary service from the community members have become a norm in society that are 'neglected' or 'forgotten' by the state agencies.

There were numerous individuals across the country and other parts of the world, who have shared the campaign for road construction in a remote corner of Northeast India, by sharing the call for financial donations in social media. The external help that the 'local community' in Tamenglong district of Manipur receives, in terms of the media campaign and financial donations, only serves as an impetus. But the ultimate agency involved in this project has been the local community, who actually sacrificed their labor to implement the project. There was assurance by the state agencies that the project on road construction being sanctioned decade ago would be put into task soon, but such promises, as usual, have not gone beyond press statements. Thus, the community initiatives in Tamenglong have turned the face of development into 'care for the self' as an alternative to the state-sponsored development which fundamentally relies on the principle of 'care from the other.'

Similarly, denizens of Ukhrul Town in Manipur state formed an Ukhrul Town Road Movement (UTRM) in 2016, as road condition of the town had worsened, and district administration has not been able to maintain it properly. The initiative to repair roads began with debates and discussion in social media among the concern individuals from Ukhrul, and they decided to form a committee to implement the project. As part of their first phase of the project, they generated around Rs. 6 lakhs through crowd-funding, mostly contributions from the community members. Work on this project was materialized through voluntary service from interested individuals in Ukhrul town. The Committee members of UTRM have not approached any governmental agencies or NGOs for funding, but they have received massive support from Church leaders and local organizations. One of the reasons that they have not worked or associated with the state agencies is that in the past people have approached various departments and district administrators, but there was no actual implementation of developmental projects on the ground. Thus, the distrust on the state agencies had also made the community not to co-opt with it and managed the projects on their own.

In terms of execution and approach, the development projects initiated by the public in Ukhrul and Tamenglong Districts in Manipur State have followed similar models and patterns: crowd-funding of projects, labor through voluntary service by individuals, and no relations with the state agencies and NGOs. It is likely that the very concept of public funding of road constructions has been inspired by one another as most of the initiatives have been widely publicized through social media and got attention from varied quarters. The initiative being taken up by Armstrong Panmei being one of the most cited stories in national media. What all these movements share is the perennial problems of administrative failure and can consider in terms of what Amartya Sen termed as a failure in 'reach' of development in peripheral areas of the states and administration (Sen 2005). The failure of state machinery has compelled the public to act by themselves; which means that the public has not acted willingly on their own, but they are reacting to the situation where the state agencies are not dispensing their responsibilities. The reasons that have been put forward by individuals engage in this collective action for the development of their localities have distinctively pointed out that failure in 'management of promise' has compelled them to take matters in their own hands. With the change in political party and leadership in Manipur after an election to State Assembly in 2017, the roads in major districts headquarters were repaired by the state agencies, meanwhile the mode of the community taking initiatives for basic infrastructures continues to be taken up by people living interiors villages in the state. Thus, the problems in state's models on development continue to ignite the community to take collective action in Northeast India wherever the 'promises' by the state is not delivered.

Conclusion

The states (whether the central state and federal unit) in Northeast India have always struggled to find a place with the community, where they operate upon and exercise their authority over heterogeneous population. In the midst of violent conflicts in the region, developmental projects were introduced as an alternative to political confrontation. While the Northeast region may have developed much during the post-independence era, the question remains is whether the expectation of the common people is fulfilled by the state or not. On the other hand, it is gradually been asserted in the Northeast India that the 'project of development' is not only in the hands of the state agencies, but needs co-option of other partners in the society. The need for community participation in governance and development is realized by the state agencies; and the community-based organizations have also meddled with the state's policy, thus staking their own role in development. However, what we are witnessing in the region is the community taking the role of agencies for 'development,' which is usually preserved as the role of the state. From being mark as alternatives to political conflict, the project of development in Northeast India today is becoming a contested terrain between states and community. While electoral politics have used development as an agenda, the failure of promises on development has gradually led the common people to resort to political confrontations and violent protest, turning it into an agenda in identity politics. Thus, the mirage of development may have provided temporal respite to the community in the region from violent conflicts, but it has gradually turned its head against the very situation that the state and community attempts to escape. Development has become one of the reasons for people to indulge in violent political confrontations with the state and other communities.

Development in Northeast India has to be seen also from people's point of view, who are living within the 'zones of enclosures,' who are not just subservient to state's authority, but continue to manage their own political space by influencing decisions of the state or by taking direct public action for welfare of society. While the interest of the state and community comes to collide on varied issues every now and then in the region, the democratic systems in the country are used by people to assert their rights and make themselves as stakeholders of public affairs. In this context, development continues to be a political terrain in the region where the state and community come to confront against one another and try to assert its position as the sole authority of public welfare. The nature of the relationship between the state and community oscillates from 'disharmonic' to 'harmonic,' which Roy Burman (1989) considers as two major aspects of community's outlook toward the state in Northeast India.

References

Bhaumik, S. (2009). *Troubled Periphery: Crisis of India's Northeast.* New Delhi: Sage.

Hassan, M. S. (2006). Explaining Manipur's Breakdown and Mizoram's Peace: The State and Identities in Northeast India. *Crisis States Programme*, LSE Working Paper 79, 1–34.

McDuie-Ra, D. (2007). Anti-development or Identity Crisis? Misreading Civil Society in Meghalaya, India. *Asian Ethnicity, 8*(1), 43–59.

Nongbri, T. (2014). *Development, Masculinity, and Christianity: Essays and Verses from India's North East.* Shimla: Indian Institute of Advanced Study.

Pandey, R. S. (2010). *Communitisation: The Third Way of Governance.* New Delhi: Concept Publishing Company.

Pathak, N. (2014). *Communitisation of Public Services in Nagaland: A Step Towards Creating an Alternative Model of Delivering Public Services?.* Pune, Maharashtra: Kalpavriksh.

Patnaik, P. (2010). A Left Approach to Development. *Economic and Political Weekly, 45*(30), 33–37.

Pieterse, J. N. (2000). After Post-development. *Third World Quarterly, 21*(2), 175–191.

Roy Burman, B. K. (1989). Problems and Prospects of Tribal Development in North-East India. *Economic and Political Weekly, 24*(13), 693–697.

Scott, J. C. (2010). *The Art of Not Being Govern: An Anarchist History of Upland Southeast Asia.* New Delhi: Orient Longman.

Sen, A. (2005). The Three R's of Reform. *Economic and Political Weekly, 40*(9), 1971–1974.

Sharma, M. S. (2012, November 4). Naga IAS Officer Builds a 100-km Road in Manipur Without Government Help. *The Times of India*, Retrieved from https://timesofindia.indiatimes.com/.
Shukla, B. (2016). *Repair Needed in Tamenglong (Manipur)!! Not Only of Roads but also of the Government Attitude!!* Retrieved from https://www.change.org.
Verghese, B. G. (1997). *India's Northeast Resurgent: Ethnicity, Insurgency, Governance, Development*. New Delhi: Konark Publishers.

CHAPTER 10

(Re)Producing Class. On Development as Middle Class Mission

Anna Romanowicz

Middle Classes Charmed by Women's Issues and Development

The importance of development in post-independence India is hard to dispute. The first Prime Minister after the colonial rule, Jawaharlal Nehru, announced in his speech delivered to the Constituent Assembly on the eve of independence that: 'The future is not one of ease or resting but of incessant striving so that we may fulfil the pledges we have so often taken and the one we shall take today. The service of India means the service of the millions who suffer. It means ending of poverty and ignorance and disease and inequality of opportunity. The ambition of the greatest man of our generation has been to wipe every tear from every eye. That may be beyond us, but as long as there are tears and suffering, so long our work will not be over' (Nehru 1947).

A. Romanowicz (✉)
Department of Ethnology and Cultural Anthropology,
Jagiellonian University, Krakow, Poland
e-mail: anna.romanowicz@uj.edu.pl

D. N. Pathak and A. K. Das (eds.), *Investigating Developmentalism*,
https://doi.org/10.1007/978-3-030-17443-9_10

In the following sections, I attempt to put some light on people who carry work of 'ending of poverty and ignorance and disease and inequality of opportunity'. It is impossible to certainly determine who Nehru himself had in mind by stating 'our work will not be over' (Nehru 1947). Did he mean all citizens of India? Perhaps. There are, however, some hints that might point at the special role of middle classes in this endeavour. As Pavan K. Verma noticed: 'Unfortunately, the elegance of his [Nehru's] prose and the content of his speech inspired only a minuscule of number of Indians, mostly from the middle classes, who had access to a radio and, more importantly, could understand English. For, to the overwhelming majority of Indians, despite the years of British rule, English and the way of life of which it was both a symbol and an instrument were incomprehensible and alien' (Varma 2007: 2).

It is hard to dispute—or to fully portray on the following pages—that India's strive for development has been arduous and persistent to the extent (as the editors of this book suggest) that it is nowadays an obvious statement that India is a 'developmental society'. Not only development as such, but also its successes and failures have been a vivid topics for both popular and academic debate and practice. For almost a year in 2011 and 2012, I participated in (dis)enchantment with development—I volunteered with Shakti and the Women's Foundation, organizations fighting prostitution and sex-trafficking in one of Indian metropolises. I combined work in the NGOs with ethnographic participant observation. As such, I cooperated[1] with activists whose goal was to end sex-trafficking and/or prostitution.[2] As agreed by them, members of transnational middle classes, the latter was one of the most tenacious problems of contemporary India. Following, in their opinion, the problem persists among the poor (so-called beneficiaries of the organizations)—as such, it is inscribed in development programmes. The lack of adequate statistics might be caused by delicacy and illegality of the investigated matter, nevertheless the nightmare of sex slavery affects millions of people (not only in India, but all over the globe). Perhaps it is not numbers, but the nightmare itself, that should bring our attention to find a solution to the problem defined in such way. Paraphrasing the words of Nehru—the work is not over.

I argue that for the participants of my research, the members of transnational middle classes employed in development sector, the perception of (forced) prostitution as a nightmare is not the only motivation for fighting it. Overlooked in the existing literature on the subject is another motivation—that is (re)production of class status of the employees of the organizations. In other words, the enchantment of progress and development of Indian society is caused not only by the needs of the poorest sections of society, but also to answer our (middle classes) needs of social status reproduction. In other words, this chapter takes as a fact that the enchantment with development among members of transnational middle class engaged in development work in India exists. More importantly, however, it discusses the rationale for this enchantment. I focus on the means, motivations and interests of the actors fighting sex-trafficking and prostitution, with whom I conducted my fieldwork.[3] Departing from the question on what development is (Ferguson 1990; Escobar 1995), I shift the attention to the ways development is being practised (Sharma 2008). However, I am not inclined to a mere description. My aim is to discuss why development is practised in a particular way. I believe that answering the latter question, we must ask about the actors who shape the scope of contemporary development programmes. In doing so, I draw from actor-oriented perspective in post-development studies (Long and Long 1992; Long 2001). Development is not an anonymous, faceless discourse. People engaged in its projects, actively shape the scope and outcomes of development programmes; the respondents whom I met during my fieldwork (and myself)—as a part of non-governmental organizations—were brokers and translators between various developmental institutions and local communities (Lewis and Mosse 2006: 13; Escobar 1995: 110).

Before I proceed further, I will provide a historical context for involvement of middle classes in development projects since the independence in 1947 and even—briefly—in colonial times. Although my description is necessarily sketchy, it proves that this involvement in contemporary times is far from coincidental. As Nehru words quoted above suggest members of middle classes seemed to be charmed by the idea of 'helping the poor'. Leela Fernandez noticed, English education, introduced by colonialists, became a distinction between 'new' middle class and lower and landed classes (Fernandes 2006: 2–5). It is important to note that the former was an avant-garde of Indian women's organizations. At first, these organizations were dominated by men, but spatial mobility and availability of printed materials, as well as increased knowledge of English (Forbes 2008; Sarkar and Sarkar 2007), enabled women from Indian new middle classes to join their ranks. In nationalist discourse, women were pictured as guardians of home in its cultural and spiritual sense. They were to defend India from Western traditions, considered to be detrimental. On this basis, the idea of 'modern woman' emerged (Chatterjee 1989). As Partha Chatterjee puts it:

> The new patriarchy was also sharply distinguished from the immediate social and cultural condition in which the majority of people lived, for the "new" woman was quite the reverse of the "common" woman, who was coarse, vulgar, loud, quarrelsome, devoid of superior moral sense, sexually promiscuous, subjected to brutal physical oppression by males. Alongside the parody of Westernized woman, this other construct is repeatedly emphasized in the literature of the 19th century through a host of lower-class female characters who make their appearance in the social milieu of the new middle class – maidservants, washing woman, barbers, peddlers, procuresses, *prostitutes.* (Chatterjee 1989: 627, emphasis mine).

'Prostitutes' were seen as a counterexample of a 'new woman'. Women subjectivities were shaped in reference not only to colonialists, but also to upper/middle classes notions of morality. In other words, the image of 'new woman' was based on the experiences and perceptions of middle and upper classes. Following this reasoning, since 1870s sex and entertainment workers were being seen as immoral. As unsuitable to the image of 'proper woman' created by upper and middle classes, prostitutes were to be saved from their fate and 'brought back' to the ranks of 'normal', respectful society. To achieve this goal, middle- and upper-class members established special associations and rescue homes (Forbes 2008: 181–188).

In late colonial period, the drive for women's emancipation gained on significance, which was reflected in growing numbers of associations of social reformers, devoted to make the idea of 'new woman' a reality. This drive, importantly, was accompanied with the growing number of middle classes who recreated Indian traditions in opposition to the colonial state. However, in the same time, 'the specifities of the colonial rule both shaped and intensified the significance of the educated middle classes' (Fernandes 2011: 63). Both social reformers and members of women's associations belonged to the middle classes. As a telling example, we might take a fact that the leadership of three major women's rights organizations[4] after the First World War consisted of members of urban middle and upper classes (Desai 2008: 24; Forbes 2008: 72; Rai 2008: 28). The social composition of women's organization bore certain consequences. First, the goal of these organizations was predominantly defined on a basis of upper- and middle-class experiences and perceptions. Second, and consequently, working-class issues tended to be ignored. Third, as the constitution of the independent Indian nation was committed to resolve most of middle- and upper-class concerns, their members seemed to agree that there is no need to continue their struggle for women's emancipation. Not surprisingly, this assumption was one of the major reasons for a decline of women's movement in independent India (Desai 2008).

This relative satisfaction with the situation of women in India ended in the 1970s. Not only international feminist criticized the state of women's development all over the world (Boserup 1970), but also—following a general disappointment with government policies—the activists decided to examine whether the Indian state kept its promises to uplift women in areas of working conditions, health and political participation. The results of this examination were far from satisfactory (Desai 2008: 26; Sharma 2008: 35; Forbes 2008: 243) and created a strong impulse to change the situation (Menon 1999: 19). Since 1975, as a part of so-called second wave feminism in India, various organizations were established to join their efforts against issues such as rape, dowry deaths or discrimination of Indian women (Omvedt 2011). The question of prostitution was undertaken within *devadasi* abolition movement, but it received more support from Dalit than women's organizations (Tambe 2008: 89–90). Significantly, however: '[...] there has so far been no sustained movement or campaign organized on issues such as equal wages and work for women agriculturers and urban toiling women, even though many left organizations have made these a theoretical priority' (Omvedt 2011: 180).

The new wave of Indian feminism, led by members of middle classes, was unable to bring up and unify the women's movement around the problems that did not touch upon their closest social circles. Was the situation to change in the following years? Economic liberalization, being introduced since the late 1980s, led to the boom of non-governmental organizations (cf. Alvarez 1999). This brought two important consequences. First, members of (growing) middle classes were provided with new job opportunities—the pool of government jobs was supplemented by non-governmental sector. Second, the meaning of the role of middle classes development project changed. In the pre-liberalization era, the task of middle classes was understood to be a support of austerity and self-restraint. In a shared goal of development of the nation, middle classes were to help the poor by being noble themselves, by contributing to the joint mission of development (Deshpande 1997). As Harsh Mander recollects:

> I was born eight years after India won her freedom – a time when the country was much poorer, much hungrier, in much worse health and more hopelessly trapped in historical bondages of caste and gender than it is today. But I remember my childhood as a period defined by a culture of egalitarian and secular idealism. There was an ethos of relative restraint among people of privilege. The excesses of erstwhile maharajas and landlords were rejected as decadent. Conspicuous consumption was considered vulgar in the face of massive deprivation among the vast majority of our fellow citizens. Young people born in wealthy and middle-class homes were taught to live modestly. Children were instructed not to waste food, as there were 'hungry children outside'. I recall getting my first set of new clothes only when I was eight years old. (Mander 2015)

However, since economic liberalization, personal success is measured by consumption capability. The poor are not to be uplifted by common efforts, but by the voluntary support of those who economically succeed in life (Baviskar and Ray 2011: 6; Fernandes 2006: 37–39; Deshpande 1997: 297–298; Upadhya 2011). There has been a decline of public discourse about development understood as government's responsibility (Deshpande 1997: 303). The project of development changed its attire as implementing of structural adjustment policies required the state to delegate its welfare role to third-sector organizations (Edwards and Hulme 1996: 4; Sharma 2008). In the following sections, I will closely examine the role of middle classes in this new development project.

Wanted: Middle Class

As I mentioned in the beginning of this chapter, my study is based on ethnographic fieldwork which I conducted in two organizations fighting prostitution and sex-trafficking in one of Indian metropolises: Shakti and the Women's Foundation. But how to understand non-governmental organization? Siddartha Sen claims that 'In India, NGOs can be defined as organizations that are generally formed by professionals or quasi-professionals from the middle- or lower-middle class, either to serve or work with the poor […]. The NGOs are generally non-membership organizations and have salaried employees' (Sen 1999: 332). In other words, he assumes that non-governmental organizations hire middle-class professionals. Far from being a 'natural' process, I argue that the mechanisms that lead to this particular social composition of non-governmental organizations in India should be examined. However, in the existing literature on development, the issue of class is overlooked. One of the most important anthropologists working on the subject associates class analysis with Marxist tradition and dismisses it as shallow and reductionist, based on the assumptions of imperialism instead of carefully examining a dynamic processes of domination and resistance (Ferguson 1990: 12–13). His claims are based on purely economic understanding of class as he implies that Marxist notion of the latter is derived from social and cultural dimensions. His understanding of Marx might be debated, however it remains a fact that he claims that: 'In place of class interest, then, I prefer to use the broader concept of "category interest", where a "category" occupies a certain specified structural position in society and possesses certain interests corresponding to that position' (Ferguson 1990: 130, italics original). Similar views are presented by Jean-Pierre Olivier de Sardan who states that category of social class is 'rigid, mechanical, economic', thus he chooses to employ the category of a 'strategic group' (Olivier de Sardan 2005: 191).[5] I am far from denouncing Marxist category of class as purely economistic. However, in order to simplify the analysis, in this chapter I rest on the definition of class as understood within Bourdiesian tradition (Liechty 2003; Saavala 2010; Lardinois and Thapan 2006). Hereby, of a special importance is the notion of cultural capital, that is 'cultural signals (e.g. widely shared [...] attitudes, preferences, formal knowledge, behaviours, goods and credentials) used for social and cultural exclusion' (Lamont and Lareau 1988: 156). However, cultural capital also consists of identities, such as 'caste, community, or region' (Deshpande 2003: 140–141). Based on my fieldwork, I argue that categories of race, gender, religion, nationality and caste should be considered identities of which the class status of NGO employees is comprised. They are not, as it is suggested within intersectional perspective, equivalents or alternatives to class. In other words, it is not a question of—for example—class *or* race. Race is hereby seen as a part of class status. The employees of the Women's Foundation belonged to different (no) castes, religions, nationalities and represented different gender and race identities; thus, there is no indication that these factors either implicated higher rank or prevented them from being hired in the organization.

I believe that *shared* middle-class self-identification of my respondents (and myself) cannot be ignored. However, other than self-identification, what are the indicators of middle classness? In the following part, I look at two issues. First, if being a professional worker is understood as possessing certain skills, are the latter related to the middle-class status? Second, to what extent and in which ways does possessing these skills enable people to fill professional job positions in the NGO? I argue that to obtain a job in the Women's Foundation, one had to fulfil the criteria consistent with particular middle-class competences and identities. Suitable candidates had to present a relevant education and fluency in English. Not without significance was also an economic status of themselves and their families. Adequate financial resources were required to obtain a 'proper' education—necessary for getting a job in the NGO. In this way, social class was being reproduced. Additionally, foreigner interns[6] were able to spend significant period of time to live in India without remuneration for their work. For example, Rychele, an American citizen, worked in anti-sex-trafficking organizations for almost two years thanks to money raised through private sponsors and government organizations, in addition to the financial support from her parents. Therefore, an appropriate social position in 'developed' countries provided the interns with an access to appropriate funds along with a proper education and knowledge of English. Elisabeth, 27, was a US citizen. She narrates:

> He [the brother] travels a lot, nationally, a little bit of business and technology creative side... My mother is a property manager, so my family and some other investors own condominiums and some other properties and my mother does the macro management for them and my father used to own a music store and now he is doing like a management of the events for a mall. [...] He has a marketing university degree, mother has a history degree, she was a history teacher. My brother has an engineering degree, I graduated university in business, human resource management degree, in 2006. Starting in high school, like, I've always loved travel, I've always been very, very curious and so, I've always known that I wanted to join Peace Corp [...], it just seemed like a really cool way to learn a language and to, just to be plunge in everything that was unknown and then it, like, made me really curious, so last year of university I applied and I went to North Africa, Morocco as a small business volunteer and basically I was like a liaison between the ministry, government ministry of [...] Morocco, and a women's cooperative. They made [...] and embroideries and things and I worked with them to improve, or create, like accounting, computer classes, marketing, basic packaging, basic target market, target development, just different things and I taught English, I worked at kids camps so I did environment, just whatever came up.

Similar stories were shared by employees of Indian citizenship. Preeti, a Brahmin from Bengal, was raised in Calcutta. Her mother worked at the higher managerial position for the United Nations, and her father was recognized in the international banking sector. With a monthly personal income of 37,000 INR, she perceived herself as middle-middle class. Her parents, she stated, were upper-middle class—earning as much as 9 and more lakhs a month. Preeti obtained her B.A. degree in psychology, and an MBA in media management, but was very devoted to social work. Despite the age of 24, she has already possessed an extensive experience in the development sector:

> from childhood I interned with a lot of organizations, from the age of 15 to the age of 23 I've done lots of internships in education [...] in organizations who work in education and I've been a teacher for underprivileged children as well as developmentally handicapped.

Fluent knowledge of English and its corporate jargon were required not only to keep the job, but also to get it. Vacancies were posted on the organization's website in English, as well as spread via personal networks. The latter reinforces the significance of belonging to 'appropriate' social networks. Without them, at least Internet access (in addition to English skills mentioned above) was required. It has to be noticed that technical language of job announcements could be a challenge itself. Those who could not find themselves in this particular reality were simply left out—beyond the development sector or in lower positions, where their influence on the process of decision-making was less significant. A telling example is that of the office boy who—even if his English was very limited—submitted his resume in this language, using a 'proper' jargon. He described his career objective as follows: 'To work in a computer dynamic and global environment, provides scope for challenges and opportunities'.

In addition to particular skills, a mindset in support of the Women's Foundation mission and vision was a requirement to obtain a position in the organization. During my stay at the organization, only one person—and only in private—admitted not to believe in the Women's Foundation stand on prostitution and sex-trafficking. Interns were required to sign the statement by which one obligated him/herself to read international documents on these issues: the UNICEF code of conduct with regard to child protection and child rights, the UN Convention of the Rights of the Child (CRC) and the UN Convention on the Elimination of All Forms of Discrimination Against Women (CEDAW) and to follow the principles in their work. In case of permanent employees, the strong commitment to the Women's Foundation cause seemed a must as well. Sevita, who participated in job interviews in search for a new member of the organization, confessed her outrage about one of the candidates to Dina, another employee of the organization. The interviewed person claimed to be in favour of legalizing sex work as a method of STD prevention. The assertion was opposite to the Women's Foundation stand on the matter; thus, both women discussed it passionately.

Enchanted Middle Classes

Following the neoliberal policies of decentralization of governmental responsibility, and the ineffectiveness of development programmes, participatory development was invented as a remedy (Sinha 2007; Van Ardenne 2004; Sillitoe et al. 2002; Korten 1987). In short, participatory approach entails that programmes aimed at development and empowerment will be based on specific needs as defined and articulated by the community in question; what is more, these programmes should be—ideally—implemented by the community or with assurance of a maximum participation of the community members. In this context, NGOs' employees ought to act as facilitators rather than appliers from above. The shift towards participatory development was massive, thus:

> Early interest in participation was often based within the NGO community, but perhaps the most significant shift over the 1990s has been that participatory discourse rapidly became part of the official aims and objectives of governments and international development agencies. (Williams 2004: 557)

For example, in Nepal—as argued by Lauren G. Leve—the development industry landmarks are empowerment and participation (Leve 2001: 108), but also in other contexts, participatory empowerment became a synonym of sustainable development (Fisher 1997: 455). In theory, participatory development seems just effective and very much needed. One might say that contemporary development apparatus would be unthinkable without beneficiaries' participation—the voice of the unprivileged should be heard and listened to. Therefore, such a noble cause quickly became a necessary ingredient (and even a foundation) of majority of development activities all over the world. In the same time, however, including participatory dimension in NGOs programmes assures their legitimization to the public and the donors (Williams 2004: 553; Rahnema 1992: 129–131). I argued elsewhere (Romanowicz 2017) that an approach which appears to be noble and just, in practice—due to the donors and public pressure of accountability—becomes a buzz word with no substance. To be accountable, NGOs must show results which are measured with bureaucratic tools. These practices, paradoxically, significantly curb the participatory dimensions of NGOs activities through 'shifting agency into the hands of professional intermediaries' (Batiwala 2010: 119; cf. Chambers 1995). Maia Green shows how in Tanzania bureaucratic participatory practices:

> construct the target communities of development interventions as passive agents awaiting the emancipatory intervention of development organizations. Despite the claims of the empowerment rhetoric, poor people lacking the capacity to bring about social transformation by themselves can only participate in development through development agency institutional structures for participation. (Green 2000: 68)

The most startling example from my own fieldwork is the conversation which I had with the president of Shakti, Neha and two potential donors. After informal conversation, Neha asked for financial support for our organization-to-be.[7] The women insisted to know more about the community we worked with, and thus they asked me about my role in Shakti. I specified that my main role was to conduct research in order to assess the community's needs and adjust the NGOs programmes accordingly. I was surprised to find Neha correcting me abruptly: 'I can tell you what the needs of these people are right away. Education, empowerment and development. This is needed to lead them out of prostitution'. Perhaps there is no need to mention that at that time I have not even started a 'proper' fieldwork in the community.[8]

Not only this episode, but also other similar situation in both Shakti and the Women's Foundation, left me puzzled about the motivations of the NGOs' employees, my co-workers. On one hand, I have already been aquatinted with some criticism of participatory approach. Thus, I was not entirely surprised that declarations differ from reality. On the other hand, I kept asking myself about the reasons of such dissonance. In other words, a mere critique of participatory approaches to development does not answer the questions about the reasons for this state of affairs. It is not only a question of whether participatory development delivers its promises. It is also a question of why—as in case of organizations I cooperated with—it does not work. As I argued in the beginning of this chapter, I believe that looking at the actors engaged in spreading the idea of participatory development. I focus on process of empowerment first and only secondary of its outcomes (Jakimow and Kilby 2006: 2). My co-workers understood the need of participatory development and empowerment. In fact, in our many conversations, they enthusiastically supported it. Nevertheless, in practice the empowerment, they *delivered* to the community of beneficiaries was far from participatory (Romanowicz 2017). Were their intentions mischievous? Were they cynical? I cannot answer in positive to any of these questions. Rather, as Pierre Bourdieu notes:

> It is not easy to speak of practice other than negatively – especially those aspects of practice that are seemingly most mechanical, most opposed to the logic of thought and discourse. All the automatic reflexes of "thinking in couples" tend to exclude the idea that the pursuit of conscious goals, in whatever area, can presuppose a permanent dialectic between an organizing consciousness and automatic behaviours. The usual obligatory choice between the language of consciousness and the language of the mechanical model would perhaps be less compelling if it did not correspond to a fundamental division in the dominant world-view. (Bourdieu 1990: 80)

In context of state politics,[9] Akhil Gupta claims that even sincere intentions of fighting poverty are deterred by soulless bureaucratic procedures: 'that no matter how noble the intentions of programs, and no matter how sincere the officials in charge of them, the overt goal of helping the poor is subverted by the very procedures of the bureaucracy' (Gupta 2012: 23). He further claims that it is uncaring modality of the state, and not the bureaucrats whom should be blamed for false promises of development or even a structural violence against the poor (Gupta 2012: 23). I think, however, that it is not so much the issue of guilt that should be discussed here. In pointing at NGOs' employees at complicit in the process, I do not mean to accuse us. My aim is to explain the ways in which the system in which their work is carried leaves very little (if at all) space to follow one's declarations of a need for participatory development, not matter how much one is enchanted with the idea itself.

I believe that even if the analogies to Akhil Gupta's argument about the uncaring modality of the non-governmental bureaucracies can be drawn, there is also an important difference. As a result of recruitment process and requirements posed for candidates for a position in NGO sector (presented in the section above), as well as a result of a lack of affirmative action in this sector, non-governmental organizations tend to be middle-class enterprises. This specific social composition influences the scope of programmes implemented by these organizations. In short, just as it was a case of pre-independent women's associations and post-independent women's movement, the interests of middle classes—and not working-class supposed-to-be beneficiaries—come to the fore. Work in the NGO sector is of a special attractiveness for the members of middle classes as it enables them to define and act upon morality of lower classes. Social actors engage in various social practices, 'including pro-social practices such as giving donation, attending courses on green technologies or organizing charity dinners' (van Aaken et al. 2013: 355), and social work in non-governmental organizations, and their goal is to acquire and increase the economic and cultural capitals (van Aaken et al. 2013: 355). Members of middle class believe to be educated, well informed, competent and even destined to interfere and change people's lives. Even if the intention is genuine, the outcome must be restricted by the system they operate in. In neoliberal setting, systemic causes of poverty and discrimination are not fought against. Instead, they are concealed by false narrative of possibility of changing one's fate with a mere wish and motivation to do so. My co-workers devoted their skills and time with an aim to eradicate poverty and uproot something that they perceived as violence against women. Their actions were based on a virtue of altruism. What is more, their actions were possible because of the vacuum left by the state. One of my Indian co-workers, Preeti, stated that:

> [...] my need as an individual to contribute to this change is very hard.. which is why I work in the developmental sector. [...] It might sound a little pretentious or stupid, but I feel that India needs people like me (...) I'm not an expert.. Someone who wants to bring change should go and bring change.

Although it is difficult to question her intentions, one has to notice that they were embedded in difference between her as a professional development agent and 'the poor'—people from the community she is determined to help. Elisabeth, the American intern, presents a similar attitude:

> Now that I have a knowledge, I think I cannot stop. Unfortunately I think it is difficult to secure a career in this field, I'm not sure – if it is possible – yes, if it is not possible then I will have to work in other jobs while still working in this area, because it is something that absolutely enrages me and I just, I cannot not do anything at this point. And after that [stay in Morocco]

> I realized like it's not, I just don't wanna have, because are exposed to so much change, out of your comfort zones through that two years, going back to normal office job seemed horrible to me.

The self-perception of being knowledgeable, well-versed in contemporary problems, of being able to take a stand, to see injustice seems to be common among middle-class members. In other words, they see and fix the wrongs by doing rights. They are destined to solve the problems of the poor and to lead them. This mindset is in consistence with introduction on neoliberal policies:

> With economic liberalization bringing the middle class to centre stage, it is argued that this group can educate the rest of the society about civic and democratic virtues, collectively creating a civil society that will reform the state and politics at large. (Baviskar and Ray 2011: 4)

As I mentioned, there has been an important shift in (self)perception of Indian middle class in post-liberalization period. Whilst previously they were committed to the idea of self-restraint, introduction of neoliberalism was marked with consumption capability as defining feature. This led to changes in perception of ways to eradicate poverty: government's responsibility has been heavily supported by the voluntary support of private individuals and organizations (Upadhya 2011: 170; Radhakrishnan 2011: 202).

What is interesting, not only third sector was affected by these changes. As Carol Upadhya and Smitha Radhakrishnan report, IT industry—a symbol of Indian economic progress since 1990s—is believed to be embodiment of fairness. In other words, it is believed that entry into IT sector is secured by merit only, while caste, class and gender play minimum (if at all) role. However, the authors argue that such an image is purely a myth. Jobs in the IT sector are secured mainly by the members of the 'old' middle classes who are able to engage their economic and cultural capitals in obtaining and securing employment in this sector[10] (Upadhya 2011: 167–192; Radhakrishnan 2011: 193–219). Moreover, IT industry became a site for cultural representation of middle classes and their virtues. The owner of one of the biggest companies, Infosys, describes himself as middle class. Even if it is difficult to agree with this self-perception (he should be considered rather upper class), it important to see what virtues he advertises as middle-class virtues.

> The Murthy [Infosys owner] icon also embodies the collapsing of the nation into the new middle class: his constant refrain is that capitalism and the accumulation of wealth, rather than socialism, are ones that will eradicate poverty and make India a global power, this being the justification for his entrepreneurial activities as well as his support for liberalization. He does not hesitate to draw parallel between his devotion to Infosys and the sacrifice of the nationalist leaders [...]. In a recent interview, responding to a question about balancing work with family, he said: I don't strike a balance. Infosys comes first. If India has to fully redeem on her promise, a few generations of leaders have to put the interests of the country ahead of their personal interest... [...] Leaders must be ready to sacrifice their personal lives and the family must be ready to undergo that hardship. (Upadhya 2011: 182)

Murthy represents middle classes values; middle classes who—by their personal involvement—are considered to be destined to change people's lives and to uplift them from poverty. As we have seen, a very similar mindset is present in the NGO sector.

However, this altruism is based on and embedded in differentiating practices.[11] NGOs' employees, both foreign and Indian, create a class distinction between 'knowledgeable Us' and 'ignorant Them'. Their enchantment with development has very practical reasons and bears a consequence of reproducing their cultural hegemony. Similar consequence is caused by my academic enchantment with development. Despite the declared wish for participatory development, limiting the scope of the community involvement serves NGOs' employees as a mechanism facilitating class distinction. Bureaucratic empowerment pictures beneficiaries as submissive and inert addressees and predicts their engagement in developmental programmes at absolutely minimum level. In contrast, the NGOs' professionals are depicted as active agents for change and thus policy makers and controllers. Bureaucratic empowerment does not only serve the interest of donors and demands of the wider public, but it is actually *attractive* to middle classes as it reinforces and legitimizes their social status. In other words, participatory development and empowerment serve as a tool for reproducing cultural capital and it is in a deep interest—along with neoliberal policies which introduced this perception of development—of transnational middle classes. In the era neoliberalism—the era of restoration of class power (Harvey 1990)—development is inscribed in middle-class politics of (re)producing hegemony (cf. Lawson 2011).

Notes

1. It is important to note that I—due to my political views—did not support organizations' cause. Nevertheless, supporting organizations' work in order to conduct my fieldwork, as well as gaining additional cultural capital by research that led me to obtaining Ph.D. degree, (re)produced my middle-class status.
2. Both issues are often confused (Gangoli 2008: 27; Romanowicz 2017: 91–92).
3. The chapter focuses on this fraction of middle classes who believes that sex-trafficking and prostitution are social evils. I do not deny the importance of activities of organizations and movements which consider prostitution to be a sex work, however—in a manner of anthropological investigation—I focus on the material which I gathered during my fieldwork. In other words, regardless of my personal opinion, I use the term 'prostitution' which reflects beliefs of my respondents.
4. The Women's Indian Association, the National Council of Women in India and the All India Women's Conference.
5. The intersectional analysis highlighting the axis of race, class, gender, caste or/and nationality is prevalently employed in the post-development studies (i.e. Escobar 1995). Barbara Heron describes how gender, race and bourgeoisie identities are constructed by Canadian development professionals through their overseas experiences (Heron 1999). Most notably in the Indian context, the class aspect is brought by Sangeeta Kamat in her study about NGOs working among the indigenous population in Kerala (Kamat 2002). What is more, Celayne Heaton Shrestha mentions how middle-class identity of development workers is negotiated in the interactions with the community of beneficiaries in Nepal (Heaton Shrestha 2006).
6. The group of interns consisted of both Indian and foreign nationals, including Americans of Indian descent.
7. That time Shakti was not registered.
8. Which—due to misunderstandings with Neha and eventually my abandonment of her organization—I have never completed.
9. The chapter does not allow the space to fully develop the issues of state politics towards NGOs. For further details see, Sen (1999) and Romanowicz (2017).
10. Even if social mobility for lower-middle classes is possible for and within the industry, it is relatively limited.
11. See also Susan Brin Hyatt on a similar argument about volunteers in the USA (Hyatt 2001: 206).

References

Alvarez, S. (1999). Advocating Feminism: The Latin American Feminist NGO 'Boom'. *International Feminist Journal of Politics, 1*(2), 181–209.

Batiwala, S. (2010). Taking the Power Out of Empowerment—An Experiential Account. In A. Cornwall & D. Eade (Eds.), *Deconstructing Development Discourse: Buzzwords and Fuzzwords.* Rugby, UK: Practical Action.

Baviskar, A., & Ray, R. (Eds.). (2011). *Elite and Everyman: The Cultural Politics of the Indian Middle Classes.* Routledge: New Delhi.

Boserup, E. (1970). *Woman's Role in Economic Development.* New York: St. Martin's Press.

Bourdieu, P. (1990). *The Logic of Practice.* Stanford, CA: Stanford University Press.

Chambers, R. (1995). *NGOs and Development: The Primacy of The Personal.* Brighton, UK: Institute of Development Studies.

Chatterjee, P. (1989). Colonialism, Nationalism, and Colonialized Women: The Contest in India. *American Ethnologist, 16*(4), 622–633.

Desai, N. (2008). From Accommodation to Articulation: Women's Movement in India. In L. Dube, E. Leacock, & S. Ardener (Eds.). (1986). *Visibility and Power: Essays on Women in Society and Development.* Oxford: Oxford University Press; In M. E. John (Ed.), *Women's Studies in India: A Reader.* New Delhi: Penguin Books.

Deshpande, S. (1997). From Development to Adjustment: Economic Ideologies, the Middle Class and 50 Years of Independence. *Review of Development and Change, 2*(2), 294–318.

Deshpande, S. (2003). *Contemporary India: A Sociological View.* Viking: New Delhi.

Edwards, M., & Hulme, D. (1996). *Non-governmental Organizations Performance and Accountability: Beyond the Magic Bullet.* London: Earthscan.

Escobar, A. (1995). *Encountering Development: The Making and Unmaking of the Third World.* Princeton, NJ: Princeton University Press.

Ferguson, J. (1990). *The Anti-Politics Machine: "Development," Depoliticization, and Bureaucratic Power in Lesotho.* Minneapolis: University of Minnesota Press.

Fernandes, L. (2006). *India's New Middle Class Democratic Politics in An Era of Economic Reform.* Minneapolis: University of Minnesota Press.

Fernandes, L. (2011). Hegemony and Inequality: Theoretical Reflections on India's 'New' Middle Class. In A. Baviskar & R. Ray (Eds.), *Elite and Everyman: The Cultural Politics of the Indian Middle Classes.* New Delhi: Routledge.

Fisher, W. F. (1997). Doing Good? The Politics and Antipolitics of NGO Practices. *Annual Review of Anthropology, 26*(1), 439–464.

Forbes, G. H. (2008). *Women in Modern India.* Cambridge, UK: Cambridge University Press.

Gangoli, G. (2008). Immorality, Hurt and Choice: Indian Feminists and Prostitution. In R. Sahni, V. K. Shankar, & H. Apte (Eds.), *Prostitution and Beyond: An Analysis of Sex Workers in India*. Los Angeles, CA: Sage.
Green, M. (2000). Participatory Development and the Appropriation of Agency in Southern Tanzania. *Critique of Anthropology, 20*(1), 67–89.
Gupta, A. (2012). *Red Tape: Bureaucracy, Structural Violence, and Poverty in India*. Durham: Duke University Press.
Harvey, D. (1990). *The Condition of Postmodernity: An Enquiry into the Orgins of Cultural Change*. Oxford and Cambridge, MA: Blackwell.
Heaton Shrestha, C. (2006). "They Can't Mix Like We Can": Bracketing Differences and the Professionalization of NGOs in Nepal. In D. Lewis & D. Mosse (Eds.), *Development Brokers and Translators: The Ethnography of Aid and Agencies*. Bloomfield, CT: Kumarian Press.
Heron, B. A. (1999). *Desire for Development: The Education of White Women as Development Workers* (PhD thesis). University of Toronto.
Hyatt, S. B. (2001). From Citizen to Volunteer: Neoliberal Governance and the Erasure of Poverty. In J. Goode & J. Maskovsky (Eds.), *New Poverty Studies: The Ethnography of Power, Politics, and Impoverished People in the United States*. New York: New York University Press.
Jakimow, T., & Kilby, P. (2006). Empowering Women: A Critique of the Blueprint for Self-Help Groups in India. *Indian Journal of Gender Studies, 13*(3), 375–400.
Kamat, S. (2002). *Development Hegemony: NGOs and The State in India*. Delhi: Oxford University Press.
Korten, D. (1987). Third Generation NGO strategies: A Key to People-Centered Development. *World Development, 15*(1), 145–159.
Lamont, M., & Lareau, A. (1988). Cultural Capital: Allusions, Gaps and Glissandos in Recent Theoretical Developments. *Sociological Theory, 6*(2), 153–168.
Lardinois, R., & Thapan, M. (2006). *Reading Pierre Bourdieu in a Dual Context: Essays from India and France*. London: Routledge.
Lawson, V. (2011). Decentring Poverty Studies: Middle Class Alliances and The Social Construction of Poverty. *Singapore Journal of Tropical Geography, 33*(11), 1–19.
Leve, L. G. (2001). Between Jesse Helms and Ram Bahadur: Participation and Empowerment in Women's Literacy Programming in Nepal. *PoLAR: Political Legal Anthropology Review, 24*(1), 108–128.
Lewis, D., & Mosse, D. (Eds.). (2006). *Development Brokers and Translators: The Ethnography of Aid and Agencies*. Bloomfield, CT: Kumarian Press.
Liechty, M. (2003). *Suitably Modern: Making Middle-Class Culture in a New Consumer Society*. Princeton, NJ: Princeton University Press.
Long, N. (2001). *Development Sociology: Actor Perspectives*. London: Routledge.

Long, N., & Long, A. (1992). *Battlefields of Knowledge: The Interlocking of Theory and Practice in Social Research and Development*. London: Routledge.
Mander, H. (2015). *Looking Away. Inequality, Prejudice and Indifference in New India*. New Delhi: Speaking Tiger.
Menon, N. (1999). *Gender and Politics in India*. New Delhi: Oxford University Press.
Nehru, J. (1947/2007). A Tryst With Destiny. *Guardian*. https://www.theguardian.com/theguardian/2007/may/01/greatspeeches. Accessed on January 2018.
Olivier de Sardan, J.-P. (2005). *Anthropology and Development: Understanding Contemporary Social Change*. London and New York: Zed Books.
Omvedt, G. (2011). Women's Movement: Some Ideological Debates. In M. Chaudhuri (Ed.), *Feminism in India*. London: Zed.
Radhakrishnan, S. (2011). Gender, the IT Revolution and Making of a Middle-Class India. In A. Baviskar & R. Ray (Eds.), *Elite and Everyman: The Cultural Politics of the Indian Middle Classes*. New Delhi: Routledge.
Rahnema, M. (1992). Participation. In W. Sachs (Ed.), *The Development Dictionary: A Guide to Knowledge as Power*. London: Zed Books.
Rai, S. (2008). *The Gender Politics of Development Essays in Hope and Despair*. New Delhi: Zubaan.
Romanowicz, A. (2017). *Unintended Revolution: Middle Class, Development and Non-governmental Organizations*. Kraków: Jagiellonian University Press.
Saavala, M. (2010). *Middle-Class Moralities: Everyday Struggle Over Belonging and Prestige in India*. New Delhi: Orient Blackswan.
Sarkar, S., & Sarkar, T. (2007). *Women and Social Reform in Modern India: A Reader*. Ranikhet: Permanent Black.
Sen, S. (1999). Some Aspects of State–NGO Relationships in India in the Post-Independence Era. *Development and Change, 30*(2), 327–355.
Sharma, A. (2008). *Logics of Empowerment Development, Gender, and Governance in Neoliberal India*. Minneapolis: University of Minnesota Press.
Sillitoe, P., Bicker, A., & Pottier, J. (2002). *Participating in Development: Approaches to Indigenous Knowledge*. London: Routledge.
Sinha, N. (2007). *Empowerment of Women Through Political Participation*. Delhi: Kalpaz Publications.
Tambe, A. (2008). Different Issues/Different Voices: Organization of Women in Prostitution in India. In R. Sahni, V. K. Shankar, & Apte, H (Eds.), *Prostitution and Beyond an Analysis of Sex Workers in India*. Los Angeles, CA: Sage.
Upadhya, C. (2011). Software and the 'New' Middle Class in the 'New India'. In A. Baviskar & R. Ray (Eds.), *Elite and Everyman: The Cultural Politics of the Indian Middle Classes*. New Delhi: Routledge.

van Aaken, D., Splitter, V., & Seidl, D. (2013). Why Do Corporate Actors Engage in Pro-social Behaviour? *A Bourdieusian Perspective on Corporate Social Responsibility Organization, 20,* 349–371.

Van Ardenne, A. (2004). From Exclusive to Inclusive Development. In M. Spoor (Ed.), *Globalisation, Poverty and Conflict: A Critical "Development" Reader.* Dordrecht: Kluwer Academic.

Varma, P. K. (2007). *The Great Indian Middle Class.* Delhi: Penguin Books.

Williams, G. (2004). Evaluating Participatory Development: Tyranny, Power and (Re)Politicisation. *Third World Quarterly, 25*(3), 557–578.

CHAPTER 11

Frictions in Resistance: Imagining Post-neoliberal Developmental Possibilities

Tathagatan Ravindran

Introduction

The crisis of global neoliberal hegemony is no longer in question. The triumphalist euphoria in the neoliberal camp that characterized the 1990s, which ranged from discussions on a possible end to business cycles (Weber 1997) to pronouncements such as 'the end of history' following the final victory of neoliberal capitalism (Fukuyama 1992), is clearly a thing of the past. A decade after the eruption of the ongoing financial crisis, despite continuing to be the policy framework many governments all over the world adhere to, neoliberalism rests on shaky grounds.

Critics have pointed out how neoliberalism increases inequalities (Stiglitz 2002, 2012; Picketty 2014), drives down real wages throughout the world caused by a 'race to the bottom' (Collins and Mayer 2010; Tonelson 2002) and a greater threat to the environment (Parr 2014), all of which amounts to a restoration of the class power of the capitalist economic elites which was challenged during the era marked by the Keynesian consensus.

T. Ravindran (✉)
Departamento de Estudios Sociales, Universidad Icesi, Cali, Colombia

D. N. Pathak and A. K. Das (eds.), *Investigating Developmentalism*,
https://doi.org/10.1007/978-3-030-17443-9_11

Ever since the eruption of protests during the WTO ministerial conference in 1999, neoliberal globalization has encountered globalized resistance. Similar protests were organized during meetings and summits of the World Economic Forum, Group of Eight (G8) and the International Monetary Fund in the subsequent years. Alternatives such as the World Social Forum emerged that visibilized the globalized character of resistance to neoliberalism. Leftist political formations, both moderate and relatively radical, formed governments in most Latin American countries, which in turn, led to a deviation from neoliberal orthodoxy and the implementation of economic policies that brought back the state as a major if not the most important economic actor. These governments also frustrated the attempts of successive governments of the USA to convert the entire hemisphere into a free trade zone. The unquestioned dominance of the USA in the Latin American economy was also interrupted by the new economic and political partnerships the leftist governments forged with China and Russia.

In contrast to Latin America, Indian economic policies have continued to stick to neoliberal orthodoxy. Though some governments have pursued them more aggressively, the neoliberal doctrine has remained the economic commonsense of successive governments that came to power since 1991.

In the sphere of mainstream parliamentary politics, the left parties have been the only forces that have consistently opposed these policies. On the other hand, the country has also witnessed the emergence of several social movements that questioned the development paradigm. The issues over which they mobilized were heterogeneous and included displacement by dams and industrial development projects and defense of common natural resources. Some of them are localized while the others operate on a larger scale, the best example of the latter being the Narmada Bachao Andolan. These movements retained their autonomy, but there have been attempts to build alliances at the national level, the most significant being the formation of the National Alliance of People's Movements (NAPM).

Resistances to neoliberalism in India have been dispersed and fragmented in both ideological and organizational terms. However, such tendencies and processes are not unique to India, which calls for an analysis of the Indian experiences in relation to similar cases in the Global South. This chapter begins with an analysis of the collective resistance mounted against neoliberalism by diverse political sectors in India and broadly maps out the ideological currents that inform these processes. It then examines the roots of the frictions and conflicts between the diverse forces that are engaged in resistance to neoliberal development policies. The following section relates

Indian experiences to that of Latin American countries that have been in the forefront of resistance to neoliberalism, analyses the frictions between multiple political actors in those countries and their similarities with the Indian case and also elaborates on the lessons the Latin American experiences can offer to Indian political sectors involved in resistance to neoliberalism.

Frictions in Indian Resistance to Neoliberalism

Despite some similarities in their agendas, there are also significant differences between the political vision and program of the left parties and the social movements. Both are highly critical of neoliberal developmental agendas and call for an end to corporate loot of the country's natural resources. Both uphold the right to work as a fundamental right. However, there are major divergences in their visions of an alternative society.

The Communist parties lay great emphasis on the development of productive forces and the necessity of public ownership of the commanding heights of the economy to achieve the same. The political program of the Communist Party of India (Marxist), for instance, calls for the rapid growth of productive forces, and the modernization and democratization the public sector industries, freeing them from bureaucratic controls and corruption, and making them competitive so that they can occupy a commanding position in the economy. The political program of the Communist Party of India, in a similar vein, calls for removing the shackles which restrict the rapid growth of productive forces and making the public sector cost-effective and competitive. Marxist economists associated with the Communist parties criticize neoliberal economic policies, among other things of having failed to generate sustained economic growth (Chandrasekhar and Ghosh 2004) and argue that an economic policy based on a progressive redistribution of wealth not only reduces poverty and improves human development indicators, but also fuels more rapid and more sustained growth by creating more demand and expanding the domestic market (Patnaik 2016).

The social movements that are part of the NAPM, on the other hand, hold on to a perspective that problematizes the idea of the inevitability of achieving higher economic growth. Rather, they maintain that the goal of development should be to achieve peace, fulfillment and happiness, and not 'prosperity in terms of material acquisition' (Bakshi 1996: 256). The principles outlined by the NAPM as the basis for 'people's development' include upholding values of austerity and simplicity as opposed to focusing on economic growth. Though the left parties also lay significant emphasis on political and economic decentralization, the NAPM takes the idea to a different level, advocating self-reliance of both urban and rural communities for their basic needs with less dependence on external markets. For organizations like the Azadi Bachao Andolan that are part of the NAPM, heavy industries should be a last resort. Ecological sustainability is a central concern as they stress the need to look for alternatives to overexploited resources like metals and petrol and rely on renewable energy and consider the conservation of soil, water and forests to be a high priority in their political agenda (Bakshi 1996).

The relationship between the left parties and the kind of social movements that were part of the NAPM alliance has been tense. Initially, the former entertained no sympathies for these movements. Bidwai (2015) observes that the left parties saw movements that opposed dams, river diversion schemes, mining ventures, polluting industries and coal-fired power stations as enemies of development and as Luddites opposing progress. For instance, during the 1970s and 1980s, they entered into confrontations with movements that agitated against the Silent Valley hydroelectric project in Kerala, Sardar Sarovar project in Madhya Pradesh and Maharashtra, the Tehri dam in the Himalayas and nuclear power plants in various states.

The scenario began to change gradually. From 1998, the Communist parties have taken ecological issues into consideration and such discussions started appearing in political resolutions of its congresses (Bidwai 2015). Eventually, they officially declared their support to the Narmada Bachao Andolan. The idea to form a united alliance with social movements against neoliberalism was also being given serious consideration in the left parties. However, the relations between the left parties and social movement activists like Medha Patkar severely deteriorated when the latter participated in protests against the industrialization strategies of the left front government in West Bengal that triggered fierce resistance from peasants in Singur and Nandigram who refused to give up their agricultural lands in exchange for a compensation.

Various organizations representing diverse political currents protested against the displacement of peasants in Singur and Nandigram, ranging from the opportunistic Trinamool Congress to radical left groups like the SUCI and the Maoists. However, it is the position held by Medha Patkar and the specific ideological factors that motivated her participation in the protests that are crucial to the discussion here. Medha Patkar and many of the social movements that are part of the NAPM, if not all, take inspiration from the environmental ethic of Mahatma Gandhi. Martinez Alier and Guha observe that Gandhi's 'heavy polemic' against industrialization converted him into the ′patron saint′ of the Indian environmental movement (1997: 154). Environmentalists believe that Gandhi foresaw the impending ecological crisis of modern industrial society, hence his insistence on voluntary frugality, simplicity and minimization of wants as an alternative to industrial society. His disciple J. C. Kumarappa, who tried to systematize and advance the implications of Gandhian praxis, further developed Gandhi's ideas on the economy and the environment. His critique of industrial society is vehement. To quote Martinez Alier and Guha (1997),

> 'There can be no industrialization without predation', he wrote, whereas agriculture is and ought to be 'the greatest among occupations', in which man attempts to control nature and his own environment in such a way as to produce the best results. (p. 159)

In this context, the idea of industrialization along with modern capitalism is resisted by many activists who believe in alternative forms of development keeping the nature and environment at forefront. In India, many environmental activists have been influenced by Gandhian model of development. Even now, critics argue against the large scale development and urge the state to support sustainable agriculture.

Frictions in International Perspective

A political discourse that holds the minimization of wants, frugality and a critique of limitless growth is not unique to India. In the west, the degrowth paradigm questioned the reigning doxa that associated well-being with economic growth. The origins of the paradigm can be traced to the Club of Rome Report published in 1972 that makes the case for degrowth based on the argument that there are ecological limits to current rates of economic and population growth. The degrowth argument went on to influence various new discourses on development, most notably 'alternative development' (Hettne 1995; Rahman 1993; Max-Neef 1982) and 'post-development' (Escobar 1992; Sachs 1997; Rahnema and Bawtree 1997) discourses. All these intellectual currents represented the disenchantment with the promises of the mainstream development discourse.

In Latin America, similar perspectives emerged from the indigenous and later some Afrodescendant movements. It began with attempts to revalorize indigenous cultures that the dominant society not only devalued but also blamed for the backwardness of Latin American nations. The Mexican anthropologist Bonfil Batalla (1982), for instance, who emerged as one of the most ardent proponents of indigenous liberation in the continent, argues that Western civilization is characterized by egoism, betrayal, insatiable appetite for material goods and greed while indigenous civilization is characterized by solidarity, respect, austerity and love. Positing a strong opposition between what he calls indigenous community life and modern/western urban life, he argues that indigenous forms of organization of production and indigenous technologies are superior to the western when evaluated according to their own ethical and civilizational frameworks. He calls for a recuperation of traditional indigenous knowledge systems and a transition toward ethnodevelopment based on the cultural particularities of indigenous groups (Bonfil Batalla 1995).

Recently, the critique of the development paradigm in Latin America has been expressed through the concept of *buen vivir* or *vivir bien*, which can be roughly translated as living well or collective well-being (Walsh 2010; Farah and Vasapollo 2011). The former itself is a translation of terms in indigenous languages, *sumaq qamaña* in Aymara and *sumaq kawsay* in Quechua. Villalba (2013) observes that in contrast to the dualist modern ontology that creates a division between nature and society, the relational ontology of the indigenous peoples blurs that distinction. She also argues that the concept of development is incompatible with indigenous cosmovision and their non-linear conception of time. To quote her, 'Moreover, the break with Western development also comes because these Andean worldviews do not conceive a beginning or end in time. Therefore, there can be no "development" insofar as there is no preliminary situation of underdevelopment' (p. 1430). The concept of living well is contrasted to that of living better that characterizes the spirit of capitalism. Harmony, complementarity, solidarity and reciprocity are seen as characteristics of the former as opposed to consumerism, competition, opulence and profiteering that define the latter (Villalba 2013).

For Acosta (2013), *buen vivir* is a concept that goes beyond the understanding of progress in a productivist sense. Gudynas (2013) asserts that it is a philosophy that understands quality of life not just in terms of material well-being, but also spiritual well-being and constitutes a radical break from the linear notion of history that urges the rest of the world to imitate the Western way of life. However, he also insists that rather than a return to the past, the political project of *buen vivir* calls for interactions between multiple knowledge systems.

According to Lang and Mokrani (2013), *buen vivir* is a vision that can address the contemporary 'crisis of civilisation' as it is an alternative to the hegemonic concept of development formulated not only by neoliberalism but also any version of progressivism. It critiques the dominant understanding of the relationship between nature and peoples/societies and proposes a different conception of the same based on alternative civilizational frameworks such as indigenous worldviews, ecological perspectives, eco-communitarian views, eco-feminist positions, anti-colonial positions and the approaches by eco-territorial movements (Lang and Mokrani 2013: 130).

Despite being fiercely critical of neoliberalism, the traditional left and the perspective of *buen vivir* differ significantly when it comes to the question of how they imagine post-neoliberal or even post-capitalist futures. Referring to the debate between the traditional left paradigms of socialist economic growth and that of *buen vivir*, Immanuel Wallerstein (2010) observes:

> There is a more fundamental issue at stake. It is the nature of the 'other world that is possible' – to use the slogan of the World Social Forum. Is it one based on constant economic growth, even if this is 'socialist' and would raise the real income of people in the global South? Or is it what some are calling a change in civilizational values.....This will not be an easy debate to resolve. It is currently a debate among the Latin American left forces. But analogous situations underlie much of the internal strains in Asia, Africa, and even Europe. It may turn out to be the great debate of the twenty-first century.

As Wallerstein notes, this debate has actually played out in the most concrete terms in Latin America. The following section examines contemporary conflicts in two Latin American countries over development policy and identifies the lessons these experiences could offer to Indian scholars and activists engaged in imagining and constructing alternatives to neoliberalism. The countries chosen are Bolivia and Ecuador, both of which interrupted the majestic march of neoliberalism in the continent. Despite taking bold decisions to break with a policy framework that seemed unquestionable all over the globe, these two states are also emblematic cases of tensions between two distinct forms of imagining post-neoliberal futures discussed above.

Latin American Experiments

Widely seen as a backyard of the USA, Latin America had been the laboratory of neoliberal policies and the Andean region was no exception. The neoliberal economic policies implemented in Bolivia and Ecuador included the privatization of state enterprises, increasing foreign investment, firing of public workers, lowering of protections and tariffs, ending of state subsidies for locally produced agricultural products and reduction of social welfare spending. Neoliberal reforms reduced real wages and increased inequality significantly (Kohl and Farthing 2006; Sawyer 2004).

At the beginning of the new century, both the countries were rocked by protests against neoliberal policies. After a 'lost decade' of neoliberal hegemony in Bolivia from 1985 to 1999, diverse social movements emerged that contested the same policies that eventually culminated in the election of leftist indigenous candidate Evo Morales in 2005. In Ecuador too, similar political processes unfolded that eventually led to the victory of left-wing economist Rafael Correa in the 2006 presidential elections.

The new left governments gradually started reversing the neoliberal policies of previous governments. Right from the beginning of his Presidency, Evo Morales declared his intentions of not only doing away with neoliberalism but transcending capitalism. Gas was nationalized through a decree in 2006. However, it was a partial nationalization that only involved an increase in the royalties the gas companies pay for the state. Nevertheless, it increased state revenues to be spent on social welfare programs. The government gained up to 70% of the revenue generated from hydrocarbons (Farthing and Kohl 2014). Subsequently, similar kinds of nationalizations were implemented in electricity, telecommunications and mines, enabling an increase in public investment. As a consequence of these policies, an estimated million people (nearly 10% of the country's total population) have escaped poverty and the middle class increased by 10% of the population (Farthing and Kohl 2014).

Initial attempts to diversify the economy and add value to natural gas, iron ore and lithium through industrialization have also started. Policies of the Morales government like obligatory wage hikes, increase in public investment, nationalizations, increase in taxes for companies involved in the extraction of hydrocarbons and rejection of free trade pacts stand in contrast to the neoliberal economic program that prescribes the reverse: wage deregulation, reduction in public investment, privatizations, tax cuts for corporations to attract more investment and free trade pacts. Though the pace of these transformations has been slow, the fact that there has been a turn in these policies away from the neoliberal model cannot be ignored.

The Ecuadorian leftist president Rafael Correa too implemented policies that marked a major departure from neoliberal orthodoxy. When Correa began his presidency, 38% of the government revenue went toward the external debt. Correa decided to restructure the external debt, reducing it by 75%, arguing that it was contracted illegitimately by the earlier corrupt governments to benefit economic elites (Becker 2010). He redirected those funds toward the social sector. He doubled a monthly payment to poor families to $30 a month and gave $100 million in housing subsidies. Public investment increased from 4% of GDP in 2006 to 14.8% in 2013 and government revenue increased from 27% of GDP in 2007 to 44% in 2012 (Weisbrot et al. 2017). As a consequence of progressive redistribution policies and an increase in social spending, the poverty rate declined by 38% and extreme poverty by 47%.

Correa also took an openly confrontational stance with the International Monetary Fund and the World Bank. For instance, he once threatened to expel the World Bank's representative in Ecuador if they continue with their pressurizing tactics and refused to let the International Monetary Fund monitor the government's economic policy. Correa also shut down a US military base, which was one of the major demands of the social movements.

Ecuador's achievements have also captured the interest of Indian Marxist economists. Jayati Ghosh, for instance, considers Ecuador as 'one of the most exciting places on Earth right now' that shows 'how much can be achieved with political will, even in uncertain economic times' (Ghosh 2012). In an article publishes in *The Guardian*, she explains how Ecuador made a transition from being a banana republic plagued by inequality, instability and a poorly performing economy to a state that initiated a new experiment in alternative development from which the rest of the world can learn.

Despite these tremendous achievements, the new left regimes have also faced severe criticisms from many progressive intellectuals, as antagonisms surfaced between them and communities that opposed their extractivist development projects. Most of the progressive redistributive initiatives of these governments that helped reduce poverty and inequality were financed through the additional resources generated by increasing the share of the state in revenues from extractive activities. In both Bolivia and Ecuador, indigenous and in some cases, non-indigenous groups organized against these projects as oil and gas fields were predominantly located in their ancestral territories.

In Bolivia, consequently, cracks began to surface in the broad coalition of indigenous organizations that had signed a pact to support the government of Evo Morales. Indigenous people residing in territories identified for hydrocarbon exploration in the departments of Tarija, Santa Cruz and La Paz protested against the lack of mechanisms through which they would be consulted prior to the initiation of a project (Bebbington and Bebbington 2011). Indigenous organizations like the *Consejo Nacional de Ayllus y Markas de Qollasuyu* (CONAMAQ) argued that the indigenous communities should have the right to veto decisions to begin extractive ventures in their ancestral territories (Fontana and Grugel 2016). The government rejected the demand arguing that such a move can deprive the government of the resources to fund development projects and social welfare schemes.

In Ecuador, similar tensions erupted between indigenous social movements and the Correa administration over plans to start new extractive industrial ventures in indigenous territories. The former opposed Correa's decision to open more oil fields for exploration and start new mining projects. Correa, however, argued that extractivist ventures are inevitable to create resources to fund social welfare programs. While Correa affirmed that Ecuador cannot afford to be 'a beggar sitting atop a sack of gold,' indigenous leader Ankush responded in an interview with Alexander Zaitchik, 'The forest has always given us everything we need, and we are planning to defend it, as our ancestors would, with the strength of the spear. To get the gold, they will have to kill every one of us first' (Zaitchik 2013). The day the mining bill was passed, protests broke out in different parts of the country. The government responded by dubbing the protestors 'extortionists,' 'infantile leftists,' 'romantic ecologists' and even 'terrorists.' Some protestors were arrested on charges of terrorism.

Adhering to the concept of *buen vivir*, indigenous communities opposing extractivist projects saw the pursuit of economic growth in itself as the problem with mainstream development discourse. Some anthropologists have explained the resistance to extractivist projects through discussions on ontology. For instance, Marisol de la Cadena (2015), in her pathbreaking ethnography of Quechua indigenous people in Peru, points out that the *ayllu*, which has been considered the basic form of social organization of the indigenous people in the Andes is composed of both human and non-human entities such as plants, animals, mountains and rivers, and all of them are inherently connected. Moreover, there is a kinship type bond between the people and the territory, and the people and place are bounded intimately into a single unit. For de la Cadena, it is this relationship that motivates these communities to oppose extractivist projects such as mining and save their mountains from destruction. The people opposing the mining projects do not see the mountain as environment or resource, but as entities that are intimately connected to them as in a family. Escobar (2010) argues that such a worldview is the product of 'relational ontologies' that reject divisions between nature and culture, and individual and community.

Strikingly similar views on mountains and ancestral territory can be heard in India too. Padel and Das (2010) reveal that identical discourses are held by indigenous communities in Orissa opposing mining ventures, who consider the mountains to be sacred and where there is a taboo on cutting trees on its topmost part. When Adivasis from the Kondh community in Orissa protesting bauxite mining at the Niyamgiri hills say 'they even destroyed our Gods' (Padel and Das 2010: 336) and when Adivasis from the Vasava community in the Narmada Valley resisting the Sardar Sarovar Project make statements like 'Our gods are here, in the forest, the river, the land. We can't move them from one place to another like a transistor radio,' (McGirk 1992) they express an understanding of the world rooted in relational ontology. Ontological explanations of these worldviews depart from the understanding that rather than there being one reality or world out there and multiple cultural representations of it, there are multiple realities or worlds (Blaser 2014).

Does the opposition mounted by some indigenous organizations mean that the policies of the new left governments in Ecuador and Bolivia have not benefited the indigenous-popular sectors? Does the persistence of extractivist policies mean that, for the indigenous people, the left governments and the previous neoliberal regimes two sides of the same coin? Though the dominant narrative constructed by scholars in Latin America has been that of indigenous people resisting extractivist development policies (Escobar 2010; Zibechi 2010; Turner 1995; Acuña 2015) all over the continent, my own ethnographic research in Andean Bolivia destabilizes it. In Bolivia, for instance, large indigenous sectors support the development strategies of the leftist government of Evo Morales. While some lowland indigenous groups oppose the government's extractivist developmentalist projects as they trample upon their collective rights to territory and are also ecologically destructive, highland indigenous peasant organizations like the CSUTCB and the Bartolina Sisa and most urban indigenous people in cities like El Alto, considered the largest indigenous city in the Americas, support the same policies as revenue from these projects have financed direct cash transfers and public works on a large scale. Whenever indigenous organizations opposing the development paradigm of the government organized protest marches, other indigenous sectors held counter protests in defense of the government. In other words, the same policies that lead to enchantment in certain marginalized sections of the populations create disenchantment in others. This process that pits certain historically marginalized indigenous groups against the others has turned out to be one of the major dilemmas of progressive governments in Latin America.

In contrast to the widespread idea of indigenous people believing in a life based on frugality and limited consumption, many indigenous sectors, especially those who live in these cities are shrewd business strategists who have mastered new techniques of capital accumulation. In Andean Bolivia, a new class of rich traders from the indigenous-popular sectors has been replacing the traditional bourgeoisie from various spheres of the economy, especially external commerce. In the Bolivian administrative capital La Paz, they control 90% of the commerce. The major reason for the success of the popular sector traders is the creation of their own parallel institutional structures which also enabled the control of various commercial routes and spaces. Their economic logics are the product of an articulation between modern logics of capital accumulation and indigenous economic practices based on reciprocity. Very often, the latter is used for the fulfillment of goals like capital accumulation.

Similarly, indigenous people of Quichua descent in the Ecuadorian town of Otavalo are engaged in a highly successful international trade of colorful textiles. In Ecuador too, there is a proliferation of discourses similar to those in Bolivia such as the neglect of indigenous interests by the left government of Rafael Correa and the threat to the environment and ancestral indigenous territories from extractivist developmental policies of the government (Jameson 2011; Radcliffe 2012; Martínez Novo 2014). Though indigenous organizations such as the CONAIE now vehemently oppose the government, Correa continues to enjoy popularity among large sections of the country's indigenous population as evidenced by the support he has won in successive elections. Candidates supported by the CONAIE have been able to garner very little electoral support. Alberto Acosta, a former minister of Energy and Mines in Correa's cabinet, contested the presidential elections of 2013 on an anti-extractivist platform, but only managed to win 3.26% of the total votes, finishing far behind not only Correa who got reelected but also the candidates representing the right-wing oligarchy. Though electoral behavior cannot be seen as the ultimate index of political orientation, the possibility of the popularity of Correa among indigenous sectors being due to his redistributive developmentalist policies cannot be overruled.

Besides reducing poverty and inequality through direct cash transfers and other social welfare schemes, redistributive extractive policies have also financed megaprojects such as an extensive car cable system that connects the cities of La Paz and El Alto in Bolivia. The spectacular display of these megaprojects generates a collective sense of triumphalism that the country is marching forward into progress. It is this mindset that characterizes the affective dimensions of developmentalism. Jamali (2013) in his work on Baloch fishermen in Pakistan shows how this developmentalist mindset creates geographies of anticipation and desire.

In both the countries, there are some indigenous sectors that support the development agenda of the government and some others who oppose, each one of them adhering to a different vision of indigenous political liberation and well-being. While the government ignores the voices of dissent against extractivist ventures in some indigenous territories, the social movements opposing extractivism and their intellectual allies do not take into account the demands of large sections of other indigenous-popular sectors who benefit from the progressive redistribution of wealth the same extractive industries enable. The only way out of this highly polarized conflict is to strike a balance between contradictory demands and interests of different social sectors. To put it more concretely, on the one hand, the governments have to carry on with the redistributive policies that have led to the reduction of poverty and inequality, and improved education, health and public infrastructure. It is precisely these initiatives that have helped these governments enjoy great popular support and indigenous-popular sectors continue to mobilize to demand more public investment in development projects. On the other hand, they also need to take into account the tensions these same policies have generated with certain indigenous groups whose collective territorial rights have been trampled upon due to the fact that extractive industries drive the government's development model. So far, the tendency of these governments has been to demonize the movements that struggle for collective territorial rights against extractivist ventures, in their efforts to increase extractive ventures that facilitate greater redistributive public investment. In doing so, the new left governments in Ecuador and Bolivia do not consider possibilities for compromise and consensual solutions. Though it is not an easy task, the first step toward striking a balance between these two demands is to recognize the legitimacy of both sides and then begin a long-term dialogue. The problem is that currently, all those possibilities are foreclosed.

Lessons for India

The Communist parties in India have been keenly following the left turn in Latin American politics. In the run-up to the 20th Congress of the Party, there were debates on whether to pursue a Chinese model or a Latin American model. Eventually, the party refrained from choosing one of them, but the political resolution adopted at the 20th Congress hails contemporary political transformations in Latin America. To quote from the resolution,

> Venezuela and Bolivia have been in the forefront in implementing policies which have reversed privatization, established state control over oil and gas resources, implemented extensive land reforms, promoted collective enterprises and ushered in democratization of the political system. Along with the governments in Ecuador and Nicaragua, they have focused on improving health care and education, and redistribution of wealth to reduce income inequalities..... The existence of Left governments is a result of the prolonged struggles of the working people and the popular movements against neo-liberalism and privatization. (Communist Party of India [Marxist] 2012)

Left leaders have considered the Latin American experience as something which the Indian government can learn from. For instance, the then Secretary of the CPI (M) Prakash Karat chose to speak on Latin American resistance to neoliberalism at a talk delivered at the University of Delhi during campaigns of protests during the visit of the American president George Bush to India in 2006. During the lecture, he repeatedly spoke on what Manmohan Singh can learn from the progressive initiatives of Latin American left governments. Latin American experiments definitely provide important insights into imagining alternatives to the neoliberal economic development model that the current Indian government vigorously adheres to. The achievements of the new left regimes in challenging imperialism implementing economic policies that go against the economic orthodoxy of the times and reducing economic and social disparities through them have undoubtedly been impressive. Nevertheless, the lessons Latin American experiences can offer are more far-ranging. The challenges faced by these movements and the complex new antagonisms these experiments have created also impart valuable lessons for any progressive political project.

Will the left parties ally with Adivasis protesting against projects of mining and also take seriously their worldviews rooted in relational ontologies? Will they be willing to enter into long-term political dialogues with a wide and hugely diverse range of social movements who not only have a common interest in resisting the neoliberal development paradigm but also hold different perspectives on various political questions? Similar questions that have created dilemmas for the Latin American left are also crucial concerns that could affect the possibility of building a united resistance to neoliberalism in India. It has been proved repeatedly that the Left's efforts to create a Third Front of non-BJP and non-Congress parties with regional and so-called socialist political parties are only bound to fail, given that opportunism rather than any consistent ideological commitment guides the decisions of the latter. In that context, the only alternative is to build alliances with popular movements from various corners of the country who are in resistance to neoliberal policies.

Born out of several mass mobilizations against neoliberalism, Latin American progressive governments implemented alternative economic policies that challenged neoliberal orthodoxy. However, the same policies simultaneously enchanted certain historically marginalized social sectors who saw in them a major break with the earlier era and disenchanted others who saw continuities between the two eras. Such tensions and frictions between diverse marginalized sectors are part and parcel of any political process that seeks radical alternatives to neoliberal orthodoxy. Though such tensions played out in Latin America in the context of the formation of leftist governments, in the Indian case, they can also hamper possibilities of successfully developing alternative political formations that can challenge the neoliberal establishment both through sustained grassroots mobilizations as well as electoral politics.

The following questions emerge in this context: What are the implications of these frictions for the process of building a radical political alternative? Are alliances between politically diverse sectors based on common opposition to something effective and more importantly, durable?

The durability of any political alliance requires that it goes beyond mere strategic issue-based unity. In Gramscian terms, it results in the construction of a new collective will, which is the product of all sectors in the alliance exerting mutual influence on each other and transforming each other's identities, without completely erasing each other's particularity (Laclau and Mouffe 1985). Gramsci's insights can thus serve the Indian left reorient their struggles and strategies. In these times characterized by an articulation between aggressive right-wing communal Fascism and neoliberalism, the urgency of forging a united front of popular resistance is ever greater. Constructing such alliances and engaging the multiple frictions that may emerge from them is to traverse a messy and thorny terrain, but that is the need of the hour.

References

Acosta, A. (2013). *El Buen Vivir: Sumak Kawsay, una oportunidad para imaginar otros mundos*. Barcelona: Icaria.

Acuña, R. M. (2015). The Politics of Extractive Governance: Indigenous Peoples and Socio-Environmental Conflicts. *The Extractive Industries and Society, 2*(1), 85–92.

Bakshi, R. (1996). 'Development, Not Destruction': Alternative Politics in the Making. *Economic and Political Weekly, 31*(5), 255–257.

Bebbington, A., & Humphreys Bebbington, D. (2011). An Andean Avatar: Post-Neoliberal and Neoliberal Strategies for Securing the Unobtainable. *New Political Economy, 16*(1), 131–145.

Becker, M. (2010). *Pachakutik: Indigenous Movements and Electoral Politics in Ecuador*. Lanham, MD: Rowman & Littlefield.

Bidwai, P. (2015). *The Phoenix Moment: Challenges Confronting the Indian Left*. Noida: Harper Collins.

Blaser, M. (2014). Ontology and Indigeneity: On the Political Ontology of Heterogeneous Assemblages. *Cultural Geographies, 21*(1), 49–58.

Bonfil Batalla, G. (1982). El etnodesarrollo: sus premisas jurídicas, políticas y de organización. In *América Latina: Etnodesarrollo y Etnocidio*. Mexico: Ediciones FLACSO, Colección, 25.

Bonfil Batalla, G. (1995). Obras Escogidas de Guillermo Bonfil. Mexico city: Instituto Nacional.

Chandrasekhar, C. P., & Ghosh, J. (2004). *The Market That Failed: Neoliberal Economic Reforms in India*. Delhi: Leftword.

Collins, J. L., & Mayer, V. (2010). *Both Hands Tied: Welfare Reform and the Race to the Bottom in the Low-Wage Labor Market*. Chicago, IL: University of Chicago Press.

Communist Party of India (Marxist). (2012). Draft Political Resolution for the 20th Congress. Available at https://cpim.org/sites/default/files/documents/2012-20Cong-Draft-Pol-Res.pdf.

De la Cadena, M. (2015). *Earth Beings: Ecologies of Practice Across Andean Worlds.* Durham: Duke University Press.

Escobar, A. (1992). *Imagining a Post-Development Era? Critical Thought, Development and Social Movements. Social Text,* (31/32), 20–56.

Escobar, A. (2010). Latin America at a Crossroads: Alternative Modernizations, Post-liberalism, or Post-development? *Cultural Studies, 24*(1), 1–65.

Farah, I., & Vasapollo, L. (2011). *Vivir bien: ¿Paradigma no capitalista?* La Paz: CIDES-UMSA.

Farthing, L. C., & Kohl, B. H. (2014). *Evo's Bolivia: Continuity and Change.* Austin: University of Texas Press.

Fontana, L. B., & Grugel, J. (2016). The Politics of Indigenous Participation Through "Free Prior Informed Consent": Reflections from the Bolivian Case. *World Development, 77,* 249–261.

Fukuyama, F. (1992). *The End of History.* New York: Free Press.

Ghosh, J. (2012, Jan 9). Could Ecuador Be the Most Radical and Exciting Place on Earth? *Economist.*

Gudynas, E. (2013). Extracciones, extractivismos y extrahecciones. Un marco conceptual sobre la apropiación de recursos naturales. *Observatorio del desarrollo, 18,* 1–17.

Hettne, B. (1995). *Development Theory and the Three Worlds: Towards an International Political Economy of Development.* New York: Longman Scientific and Technical.

Jamali, H. A. (2013). *The Anxiety of Development: Megaprojects and the Politics of Place in Gwadar, Pakistan* (Crossroads Asia Working Paper Series, No. 6). Crossroads Asia, Bonn.

Jameson, K. P. (2011). The indigenous movement in Ecuador: The struggle for a plurinational state. *Latin American Perspectives, 38*(1), 63–73.

Kohl, B., & Farthing, L. C. (2006). *Impasse in Bolivia: Neoliberal Hegemony and Popular Resistance.* London: Zed Books.

Laclau, E., & Mouffe, C. (1985). *Hegemony and Socialist Strategy: Towards a Radical Democratic Politics.* London: Verso.

Lang, M., & Mokrani, D. (2013). *Beyond Development: Alternative Visions from Latin America.* Amsterdam: Rosa Luxemburg Foundation and Transnational Institute.

Martinez-Alier, J., & Guha, R. (1997). *Varieties of Environmentalism: Essays North and South.* London: Earthscan.

Max-Neef, M. A. (1982). *From the Outside Looking In: Experiences in "Barefoot Economics".* Uppsala: Dag Hammarskjöld Foundation.

McGirk, T. (1992, September). Dam-Builders vs River Goddess: Tim McGirk in India's Narmada Valley Sees 'Developers' Clash with Tribal People. *Independent.* Retrieved from http://www.independent.co.uk/news/world/dam-builders-vs-river-goddess-tim-mcgirk-in-indias-narmada-valley-sees-developers-clash-with-tribal-1549873.html.

Novo, C. M. (2014). Managing Diversity in Postneoliberal Ecuador. *The Journal of Latin American and Caribbean Anthropology, 19*(1), 103–125.

Padel, F., & Das, S. (2010). Cultural Genocide and the Rhetoric of Sustainable Mining in East India. *Contemporary South Asia, 18*(3), 333–341.

Parr, A. (2014). *The Wrath of Capital: Neoliberalism and Climate Change Politics*. New York: Columbia University Press.

Patnaik, P. (2016, January). *Growth Through Redistribution*. Retrieved from http://www.macroscan.org/cur/jan16/pdf/Redistribution.pdf.

Picketty, T. (2014). *Capital in the Twenty First Century*. Boston: Harvard University Press.

Radcliffe, S. A. (2012). Development For a Postneoliberal Era? Sumak Kawsay, Living Well and the Limits to Decolonisation in Ecuador. *Geoforum, 43*(2), 240–249.

Rahman, M. A. (1993). *People's Self-development: Perspectives on Participatory Action Research*, 315–335.

Rahnema, M., & Bawtree, V. (1997). *The Post-Development Reader*. London: Zed Books.

Sachs, W. (Ed.). (1997). *The Development Dictionary: A Guide to Knowledge As Power*. New Delhi: Orient Blackswan.

Sawyer, S. (2004). *Crude Chronicles: Indigenous Politics, Multinational Oil, and Neoliberalism in Ecuador*. Durham, NC: Duke University Press.

Stiglitz, J. E. (2002). *Globalization and its Discontents*. New York: Norton.

Stiglitz, J. E. (2012). *The Price of Inequality: How Today's Divided Society Endangers our Future*. W. W. Norton & Company.

Tonelson, A. (2002). *The Race to the Bottom: Why a Worldwide Worker Surplus and Uncontrolled Free Trade are Sinking American Living Standards*. New York: Basic Books.

Turner, T. (1995). An Indigenous People's Struggle for Socially Equitable and Ecologically Sustainable Production: The Kayapo Revolt Against Extractivism. *Journal of Latin American Anthropology, 1*(1), 98–121.

Villalba, U. (2013). Buen Vivir vs Development: A Paradigm Shift in the Andes? *Third World Quarterly, 34*(8), 1427–1442.

Wallerstein, I. (2010, August 25). *Contradictions in the Latin American Left*. Retrieved from http://www.cadtm.org/Contradictions-in-the-Latin.

Walsh, C. (2010). Development as Buen Vivir: Institutional Arrangements and (de) colonial Entanglements. *Development, 53*(1), 15–21.

Weber, S. (1997). The End of the Business Cycle? *Foreign Affairs, 76*(4), 65–82.

Weisbrot, M., Johnston, J., & Merling, L. (2017). Una década de reformas: políticas macroeconómicas y cambios institucionales en Ecuador y sus resultados. Washington, DC, Estados Unidos: Center for Economic Policy Research.

Zaitchik, A. (2013, February 10). *To Get the Gold, They Will Have to Kill Everyone of Us.* Retrieved from https://www.salon.com/2013/02/10/to_get_the_gold_they_will_have_to_kill_every_one_of_us/.
Zibechi, R. (2010, July 19). *Bolivia and Ecuador: The State Against the Indigenous People.* Retrieved from http://amazonwatch.org/news/2010/0719-bolivia-and-ecuador-the-state-against-the-indigenous-people.

Index

D. N. Pathak and A. K. Das (eds.), *Investigating Developmentalism*,
https://doi.org/10.1007/978-3-030-17443-9

FSC
www.fsc.org
MIX
Papier | Fördert
gute Waldnutzung
FSC® C083411

Kolibri 360 GmbH
Ferdinand-Jühlke-Straße 7
99095 Erfurt, Deutschland
produktsicherheit@kolibri360.de